EXPERIENCES IN
PERSONALITY

RESEARCH, ASSESSMENT, AND CHANGE

D1249834

MATTHEW R. MERRENS
State University of New York–Plattsburgh

GARY G. BRANNIGAN
State University of New York–Plattsburgh

JOHN WILEY & SONS, INC.

New York • Chichester • Weinheim • Brisbane • Singapore • Toronto

To Jenn and Matt

MRM

To my wife, Linda, and sons, Marc and Michael

GGB

EXECUTIVE EDITOR	Christopher J. Rogers
MARKETING MANAGER	Kimberly Manzi
SENIOR PRODUCTION EDITOR	Jeanie Berke
TEXT DESIGNER	Silver Editions
COVER DESIGNER	Laura Boucher
COVER PHOTO	Diana Ong
AUTHOR PHOTOS	Robin Brown

This book was set in 11/13 Garamond Book Condensed by Silver Editions and printed and bound by Port City Press, Inc. The cover was printed by Lehigh Press.

Recognizing the importance of preserving what has been written, it is a policy of John Wiley & Sons, Inc. to have books of enduring value published in the United States printed on acid-free paper, and we exert our best efforts to that end.

The paper in this book was manufactured by a mill whose forest management programs included sustained yield harvesting of its timberlands. Sustained yield harvesting principles ensure that the number of trees cut each year does not exceed the amount of new growth.

Library of Congress Cataloging-In-Publication Data
Merrens, Matthew R.
 Experiences in personality : research, assessment, and change /
Matthew R. Merrens, Gary G. Brannigan.
   p.   cm.
 Includes bibliographical references.
 ISBN 0-471-13937-8 (pbk. : alk. paper)
 1. Personality. I. Brannigan, Gary G. II. Title.
 BF698.M416 1998   97-15015
 155.2—dc21   CIP

Printed in the United States of America

10 9 8 7 6 5 4 3

About the Authors

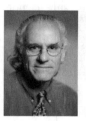 **Matthew R. Merrens** (Ph.D., University of Montana) is Professor of Psychology at SUNY–Plattsburgh. His research has focused on personality assessment, behavior modification, and teaching technology. He is the coeditor of *The Undaunted Psychologist: Adventures in Research*, *The Social Psychologists: Research Adventures*, and *The Developmental Psychologists: Research Adventures across the Life Span*. Dr. Merrens received the SUNY Chancellor's Award for Excellence in Teaching. He is a consulting clinical psychologist. His interests focus on family and outdoor activities.

 **Gary G. Brannigan** (Ph.D., University of Delaware) is a Professor of Psychology at SUNY–Plattsburgh and a fellow of the Society for Personality Assessment. He also served as Director of the Psychological Services Clinic at SUNY–Plattsburgh and was a consultant to several local agencies. His research focuses primarily on psychological assessment and therapy with children. He is currently serving on the editorial boards of two journals. In addition to coediting *The Undaunted Psychologist: Adventures in Research*, *The Social Psychologists: Research Adventures*, and *The Developmental Psychologists: Research Adventures across the Life Span* and editing *The Enlightened Educator: Research Adventures in the Schools*, he has published numerous articles, chapters, books, and tests, including (with A. Tolor) *Research and Clinical Applications of the Bender-Gestalt Test* and (with N. Brunner) *The Modified Version of the Bender-Gestalt Test* (now in its second edition). His interests include sports, art, music, and fine dining.

Introduction

Experiences in Personality: Research, Assessment, and Change is designed to be used as a supplement to traditional personality texts. This book is arranged to cover the standard topics in personality and to provide you with readings and active learning exercises. We feel strongly that this approach will enable you to involve yourself more significantly in the topics you are studying and ultimately to gain insight, understanding, and an appreciation of the field. All too often traditional texts present materials in a dry, static manner. It is our belief that this book will provide a more favorable learning climate that will enable you to engage with the topics more successfully.

There are three types of articles and activities in this book: Readings, Spotlights, and Active Learning Exercises. Readings and Spotlights have been selected and adapted to complement and extend your textbook. Although they are varied and diverse, they seek to give you a closer look at the theories, research, and applications in exploring personality.

Active Learning Exercises are significant components of this book. You will be asked to gather data on yourself and others. You will participate in assessment, behavior recording, and behavior change projects and learn about personality through active engagement as an investigator, a subject, an observer, and a writer. You will get to think about and participate in many of the topics you study. This will make the process of learning more dynamic and interesting, and will give you a better understanding of how you function and see yourself.

Collecting data on yourself and others is a useful way to explore a concept and to gain insight into significant dimensions of personality. None of the Active Learning Exercises attempts to assess or focus on abnormality or deviance. The objective is to explore normal personality features. Low or high scores are found in the typical college sample. However, if you feel uncomfortable completing any exercise, you should stop and not feel coerced into doing so. If you are collecting data on other people, you may need to receive permission from a special campus committee established for the protection of human subjects. We do not view any of the projects in this book as intrusive or upsetting, but we feel it is important to let you know what's ahead.

ACKNOWLEDGMENTS

We are deeply indebted to Chris Rogers, Executive Editor at John Wiley & Sons. We have worked with Chris on several books, and his keen insights and encouragement have always served to enhance our books. Chris was instrumental in shaping this project, especially in the early stages. His ongoing support and confidence are greatly appreciated. We also appreciate the excellent counsel of Barbara Bredenko, Assistant Editor and Karen Dubno, former Editor. Barbara worked with us throughout the length of the project. Her editorial analysis, gentle prodding, and advice helped bring this book to fruition. The reviewers of this book also provided many suggestions for clarifying and improving the chapters. We thank Susan E. Allen, Baylor University, Jerrold L. Downey, University of South Alabama, James J. Johnson, Illinois State University, Gary Leak, Creighton University, Joseph Lowman, University of North Carolina, Chapel Hill, and Lawrence E. Murphy, University of San Francisco.

We are grateful to the State University of New York-Plattsburgh for providing the supportive environment that enabled us to pursue this project. The advice and help of our colleagues, especially Bill Tooke and Drew Westen, was invaluable. In addition, the assistance of Melynda Kraft and Kim Cline, who critiqued the chapters, and the many students who field tested the Active Learning Exercises, was very important to the final outcome. Their suggestions made this book more reader-focused and accessible.

Our secretary and friend, Judy Dashnaw, deserves the highest commendation. Her superior skills in editing and word processing, as well as her patience and dedication to quality, served to make this a successful project.

Finally, we would like to thank our wives, Roberta Merrens and Linda Brannigan, for their efforts in reading and proofing the chapters in this book. Their comments, thoughts, and ongoing support contributed greatly to the quality of this volume.

Matthew R. Merrens

Gary G. Brannigan

CONTENTS

CHAPTER 4: TRAIT, MOTIVE, AND NEED PERSPECTIVES

CHAPTER 5: GENETIC AND EVOLUTIONARY PERSPECTIVES

CHAPTER 6: BEHAVIORAL PERSPECTIVES

CHAPTER 7: HUMANISTIC PERSPECTIVE

CHAPTER 8: COGNITIVE PERSPECTIVES

CHAPTER
1

Studying
Personality

Introduction

Personality is a common term that we all use to describe features and characteristics of human behavior. People describe others as "having a good personality," "having a lousy personality," or sometimes even "having no personality." People actively seek information about their own personality in astrology/horoscope columns in the newspaper, in fortune cookies at Chinese restaurants, from tarot card readers and fortune tellers, and through the use of folk wisdom and proverbs that our culture endorses. People are constantly looking for explanations and information about their personality to help plan their lives and make decisions. Several years ago it was revealed that former First Lady Nancy Reagan consulted a psychic for guidance to help the President make decisions. These pseudoscientific sources remain popular and enjoy widespread usage despite a lack of evidence supporting their credibility.

In this chapter you will look at a number of nonscientific approaches to the understanding of personality. You will also get the chance to examine your beliefs about proverbs, write your own personality interpretation based on the strategies employed by fortune tellers, and explore the operation of generalized personality interpretations.

NAME _____

DATE _____

ACTIVE LEARNING EXERCISE 1.1
THE POWER OF FOLK WISDOM*

To explore the impact of proverbs and folk wisdom on your beliefs about personality, answer True or False to the following popular sayings:

1. _____ Look before you leap

2. _____ If at first you don't succeed, try, try again.

3. _____ You can't teach an old dog new tricks.

4. _____ Where there's a will, there's a way.

5. _____ Out of sight, out of mind.

6. _____ Two heads are better than one.

7. _____ Never look a gift horse in the mouth.

8. _____ Many hands make light work.

9. _____ Better safe than sorry.

10. _____ Opposites attract.

11. _____ People who hesitate are lost.

12. _____ Once bitten, twice shy.

13. _____ It's never too late to learn.

14. _____ Time and tide wait for no one.

15. _____ Absence makes the heart grow fonder.

16. _____ If you want something done right, do it yourself.

17. _____ All that glitters is not gold.

18. _____ Too many cooks spoil the broth.

19. _____ Nothing ventured, nothing gained.

20. _____ Birds of a feather flock together.

*Adapted from Stanovich, K. E. (1992). *How to think straight about psychology* (3rd ed.). New York: HarperCollins. Reprinted by permission of Addison-Wesley Educational Publishers, Inc.

Once you have completed this questionnaire, notice that items 1 through 10 are exactly the opposite of items 11 through 20. For example, item 20, "Birds of a feather flock together," is opposite to item 10, "Opposites attract."

1. How many times do you endorse or reject a proverb in items 1–10 and its opposite in items 11–20?

2. How do you reconcile any contradictions?

READING

YOU KNOW WHAT THEY SAY . . .*

Alfie Kohn

Editors' Note:

We frequently hear and use proverbs, often as a way of understanding and gaining insight into behavior. In this article, Alfie Kohn selects a number of common sayings, some of which you rated in Active Learning Exercise 1.1, and reviews the psychological research literature to determine what is scientifically known about their validity.

Proverbs are heirlooms, treasured and passed on from generation to generation. These pithy, unforgettable phrases seem to sum up timeless wisdom about human nature. But are the truisms really true? Stacked up against the results of psychological research, they're pretty hit-and-miss: Some home-grown adages hit; some maxims miss.

. . . Cry and you cry alone. Misery may love company (depressed people are more likely to seek emotional support than are people who are not depressed), but company clearly does not love misery. In 1976, psychologist James C. Coyne, while at Miami University, asked 45 female college students to talk on the phone for 20 minutes with other women, some of whom were depressed—although the students weren't told that. Later, the students indicated they had much less interest in spending time with the depressed women than with the others. Such reactions are part of a vicious circle that is all too common among unhappy people: Their behavior drives away the very people whose support and acceptance they need, thereby worsening their depression and intensifying their need for support. These findings are also important because they suggest that when depressed people say others view them negatively, they may well be right.

. . . Spare the rod and spoil the child. Few proverbs have been so thoroughly disproved—or have caused so much harm—as this one. Nearly 40 years of research have shown conclusively that the "rod" produces children who are more aggressive than their peers. "Physical punishment teaches that the way to solve problems is to beat up others," says Leonard Eron, a research psychologist at the University of Illinois at Chicago. He and others explain that having children focus on what they did wrong and why it was wrong encourages them to internalize control of their own actions. But physical punishment, while suppressing misbehavior in the short run, ultimately promotes nothing more than a determination to avoid getting caught. In 1960 Eron and his colleagues studied 870 8-year-olds in rural New York and found a clear-cut relationship between the severity of the physical punishment they received—ranging from none at all to slaps and spankings—and how aggressive other children

judged them to be. Twenty-two years later, the researchers tracked down some of these same people and found that the aggressive kids were now aggressive adults. And those adults now had aggressive children of their own.

. . . The squeaky wheel gets the grease. Obviously we don't get everything we ask for, but many people get more than others just by demanding it. Salaries are a case in point. Psychologist Brenda Major and her colleagues at the State University of New York at Buffalo asked management students, most of whom had real-world work experience under their belts, to play the role of a personnel supervisor at a department store. Folders from mock applicants indicated what salary levels were expected—some of them below, some at and some above the range advertised. The result? Pay expectations didn't affect who was offered a job. But of the applicants who were hired, those who squeaked louder got more grease—in their palms. "Although applicants did not receive exactly what they asked for," the researchers say, "the more pay an applicant requested, the more pay he or she was offered."

. . . Actions speak louder than words. Common sense suggests that our impressions of people are shaped more by how they act than by what they say about themselves. But Brandeis University psychologist Teresa M. Amabile and her student Loren G. Kabat tested this idea by videotaping women while they deliberately acted either introverted or extroverted in conversations and while they described themselves as having one or the other personality trait. Then, 160 students watched the videotapes and evaluated how "outgoing," "friendly," "shy" or "withdrawn" the women were. When the women's self-descriptions and actual behavior conflicted, the students usually gave more credence to behavior. In general, the students' judgments were influenced about 20 times more strongly by what the women did than by what they said about themselves. Actions speak louder than words not only when we judge the character of adults but when we try to shape the character of children. Adults who want to encourage children to be generous should practice what they preach, according to psychologists James H. Bryan and Nancy Hodges Walbek of Northwestern University. These researchers awarded gift certificates to fourth-graders for playing a miniature bowling game and offered them a chance to put some of their winnings in a box "for the poor children" if they chose. The children had previously seen adults who either donated or didn't and who preached either generosity or selfishness. When the adults' actions didn't match their advice, the researchers found, the children were more likely to pay attention to the deeds than to the words.

... Beauty is only skin deep. Psychologists Karen Dion, Ellen Berscheid and Elaine Hatfield found in 1972 that when people are good-looking, we assume many other good things about them. These researchers asked 60 students to describe people's character solely on the basis of their photographs. The more attractive people were rated as more socially desirable and likely to have more prestigious jobs and happier marriages than those who were less attractive. This study, entitled "What Is Beautiful Is Good," unleashed a torrent of social psychological studies on attractiveness. Scores of researchers since then have uncovered a major self-fulfilling prophecy: Because attractive people are treated as if they have more to offer, they live up to our positive expectations. Sadly, those less pleasing to look at live down to our negative expectations. In studies looking at the relationship between attractiveness and personality, good-looking people turn out to have higher self-esteem and to be happier, less neurotic and more resistant to peer pressure than those who are less attractive. The list goes on. Those blessed with good looks also have more influence on others, get higher salaries, receive more lenient decisions in court, are thought by their students to be superior teachers and are more valued as friends, colleagues and lovers. The general pattern is true of both men and women. One of the most distressing findings is that attractiveness is related to the perception—and perhaps even the reality—of serious mental disorders. Psychologist Warren H. Jones and his colleagues at the University of Tulsa found that it was assumed that ugly people were more likely to be psychologically disturbed than were good-looking ones. Even when Jones and his co-workers made a point of telling people to disregard attractiveness, they still rated the unattractive people as more troubled. When Kevin O'Grady, a psychologist at the University of New Mexico, stopped people on the street and asked them to fill out a questionnaire assessing their chances of ever developing psychological disorders, he found that the better looking people were, the more remote seemed their chances of becoming mentally ill. The trouble is, these predictions may be right. A study by psychologist Amerigo Farina and colleagues at the University of Connecticut showed that female psychiatric patients were relatively unattractive compared with other women—and not simply because their troubles had spoiled their looks. A study of a similar group of female patients showed that, judging by yearbook photographs, they were less attractive than their peers even back in high school, before they were hospitalized. "The way we treat attractive versus unattractive people shapes the way they think about themselves," says University of

Hawaii psychologist Hatfield, "and, as a consequence, the kind of people they become." Beauty in our culture is clearly more than a superficial matter.

... Beauty is as beauty does. The central finding of the research on attractiveness is that what is beautiful is indeed good. But psychologist Alan E. Gross and colleague Christine Crofton of the University of Missouri at St. Louis wondered whether the reverse is also true: Is what is good beautiful? In other words, do our judgments of people's attractiveness rest partly on how we view their character? Gross and Crofton sorted photos of women by their attractiveness and attached them to invented personality descriptions. Some were presented as good students, friendly, energetic and so on; others as average; and a third group as losers. People were asked to evaluate how attractive they found these people. It turned out that the more favorably described they were, the better-looking they were judged to be, regardless of how physically attractive they really were. (Other researchers have found that character descriptions affect how women's attractiveness is judged but not men's.)

... Marry in haste, repent at leisure. Any way you look at it, this proverb is true. If "marrying in haste" means marrying young, then many studies support the adage. People who wed as teenagers are twice as likely to get divorced as those who wed in their 20s. If "haste" means a whirlwind romance before marriage—at whatever age—that, too, can lead to marital problems. A large-scale British study from the 1970s revealed that 20 percent of those who were divorced—as opposed to only 8 percent of those still married—had known their partner for less than a year before tying the knot.

... Familiarity breeds contempt. Yes, intimate knowledge can lead to passionate hatred, but familiarity is usually more likely to breed liking than contempt. In a classic series of studies, psychologist Robert Zajonc of the University of Michigan showed people a set of seven-letter Turkish words. They didn't know what the words meant, but the more often people saw certain words, the more likely they were to say they meant something good. Likewise, after being shown yearbook photographs of men they didn't know, people said they liked the men whose photos they had seen more often. If you already have reason to dislike something or someone strongly, greater exposure probably won't change your feelings. But most of us seem to find things and people more likable as we get used to them—at least up to a point. David J. Hargreaves, a psychologist at the University of Leicester, in England, believes that after enough exposure to a piece of music, say, or a work of art, a person will find it less pleasant. Too much familiarity, Hargreaves contends, can leave us wanting less.

... He who lives by the sword dies by the sword. If the contemporary "sword" is a handgun, then this maxim seems to be true. A study of more than 700 gunshot deaths in the Seattle area from 1978 to 1983 showed that most of them had occurred in homes where a gun was kept. Moreover, the guns were far more likely to kill a resident than an intruder. In only two cases was a stranger killed; the rest were accidental deaths, suicides or homicides in which the victim was either a friend of the gun owner or a member of the family.

Many proverbs, like muscles and expert witnesses, come in opposing pairs. For every adage counseling caution, such as "Look before you leap," there is one exhorting us to throw caution to the winds, such as, "He who hesitates is lost." We are told that "Too many cooks spoil the broth" but also advised that "Many hands make light work." People tell us that "Variety is the spice of life," but they also say that "Old shoes are easiest."

Intrigued by the way we react to such conflicting advice, psychologist Karl Halvor Teigen of the University of Bergen, Norway, devised a clever experiment in 1986. He transformed 24 proverbs into their opposites. Thus, for example, "Fear is stronger than love" became "Love is stronger than fear," and "Truth needs no colors" became "Truth needs colors."

Teigen gave his students lists that contained some authentic sayings and some that he had just reversed, asking them to rate how original and true the proverbs were. The result: no significant difference between the wisdom of the ages and Teigen's newly minted counterfeits.

When proverbs conflict, which ones should we believe? You can pick the one that suits the moment, or you can lean on the psychological experts. Here's how three pairs of proverbs stack up against the research:

. . . You're never too old to learn vs. You can't teach an old dog new tricks. People learn new things their whole lives through, but aging does make the process somewhat harder. As a rule, older adults have more difficulties with intellectual functioning than do younger adults. For example, some studies suggest that beyond age 60, people find it more difficult to remember texts they read or hear and have trouble distinguishing between more- and less-important ideas in the text. But since there is considerable variation among people of any given age, there are a good number of elderly exceptions to the rule. Psychologists Warner Schaie and Christopher Hertzog of Pennsylvania State University have been testing a group of 162 people at seven-year intervals since 1956 to see how their intelligence changes. A number of measures have shown a decline in ability that becomes evident after age 60. But Schaie and other researchers have found that, up to a point, older people can be taught skills that will compensate for or reverse this decline. Many types of training seem to help in the short run, although the effects don't always last. Psychologist Paul Baltes and his colleagues at the Max Planck Institute in Berlin, for example, put more than 200 older people through a training program that helped them to identify rules and concepts useful in solving problems on intelligence tests. The people's scores did improve. Although they had begun to fall back after six months, they were still ahead of where they were before the training began. In a study conducted by Schaie and psychologist Sherry L. Willis, a

group of people whose average age was over 72 were given five one-hour training sessions similar to those used by Baltes, then tested and compared with their own levels of cognitive ability of 14 years earlier. The training brought 40 percent back to their previous mark and helped many others to a less dramatic extent. A "substantial proportion" of older people, Schaie and Willis conclude, were victims of the "use it or lose it" rule: Their intellectual abilities probably declined due to disuse. But those abilities are not really lost, they say. They can be regained, at least in part, through "relatively simple and inexpensive educational training techniques."

. . . Absence makes the heart grow fonder vs. Out of sight, out of mind. The effect of absence depends on how you felt to begin with. If a lover is absent (assuming you aren't distracted by someone new), separation is likely to intensify whatever you felt before you were torn apart. If you felt positively, absence will allow you to cling to an idealized version of your beloved that can't be contradicted by real-life imperfections. That's the conclusion of Abraham Tesser, a psychologist at the University of Georgia, based on more than a decade of work with attitudes toward everything from people to paintings. "Absence has the potential for making the heart grow fonder," he says, but if your feelings start out negative, "absence will make the heart grow colder." Psychologist Phillip Shaver and his colleagues at the University of Denver came up with a similar conclusion. They asked 400 college freshmen what they felt about the people they left back home. It turned out that their relationships with family members had improved, but high school romances tended to disintegrate with distance. High school loves weren't necessarily forgotten; they just weren't remembered as being all that great after all.

. . . Birds of a feather flock together vs. Opposites attract. People are more like birds than magnets. After lots of research, the idea that opposites attract still has gained little experimental support, according to psychologist Richard W. Lewak of Del Mar Psychiatric Clinic and his co-workers in California. Many studies have shown that people who share the same racial, religious and economic backgrounds usually flock together, as do those with similar political views. And when it comes to attraction powerful enough to draw people into wedlock, "Marriage partners tend to be more alike than different," the researchers say. Lewak's own work shows that we tend to marry people whose IQ's are more or less similar to our own. And, as psychologist Bernard Murstein of Connecticut College and other researchers have found, despite our fantasies of marrying the most magnificent-looking person possible, we're likely to wind up with someone about as attractive as we are. According to University of Michigan psychologist David M. Buss, the principle that people are attracted to those similar to themselves is "one of the most well established replicable findings in the psychology and biology of human mating."

READING
FORTUNE - TELLERS NEVER STARVE*
William Lindsay Gresham

Editors' Note:

Former First Lady Nancy Reagan consulted a psychic to help determine President Reagan's schedule. Current First Lady Hillary Rodham Clinton consulted a New Age spiritualist to help her gain self-understanding. We are constantly inundated with "psychic readers" on TV who claim to bring insight, understanding, wealth, and relationships to those who call the 900 number. This article by William Gresham helps us understand the process of fortune telling.

A young woman in a beauty parlor was babbling to a friend. "My dear," she said, "you *must* consult him—I just *know* he can help you. Why, he saved my marriage. You remember when that woman—well, I did just what *he* said, and everything was all right. It's the most wonderful experience. He looks right into your *heart*, and you come away feeling so much better!"

"What's his address?" asked the friend, fishing for a pencil. As she jotted the address down, the beautician, leaning over her shoulder, made a mental note of it; beauticians have their troubles, too.

"If I didn't have him to turn to, I couldn't get along," said the first woman. "He's the most wonderful man!"

Her pastor? Unfortunately, no. Her psychiatrist? She couldn't have spelled the word. No, the lady was talking about her fortune-teller.

No one knows exactly how much money the American public spends yearly on swamis, astrologers, tea-leaf readers, crystal gazers, "character analysts," and "mental-science counselors"— most of them as much fortune-tellers as the old gypsy in her caravan. Fifteen years ago, the "fees" of these people were estimated at $125,000,000, and [they] may easily have doubled by now [this estimate of "fees" was made in 1934 and is likely to be dramatically higher today—Eds.].

There was a time when people in trouble automatically turned to the minister. The materialism of our age has cut off this source of aid and comfort from multitudes. There will be a time, no doubt, when the worried automatically turn to a psychiatrist. But that time is not yet. Psychiatry, despite its rapid growth since the war ["World War II"], is still scarce, costly, and a little terrifying to most people. Meanwhile, there is no one to give comfort and advice to millions of our people except the fortune-teller. For every psychiatrist treating the mind, there are scores of "psychists" reading the mind; for every patient on an analyst's couch, there are a hundred gazing into a swami's crystal ball.

It is usual, but inaccurate, to dismiss the occult worker as a mere swindler, a spiritual confidence man. Some seers, it is true, are out-and-out crooks. But the majority of them depend on "repeat trade," and to bring a customer back again and again you must give him *something* for his money. By trial and error, by shrewd observation of men, many fortune-tellers have worked out long since many of the great truths that official psychology has only just discovered. Before Freud, the soothsayers knew that little boys are often jealous of their fathers; before Adler, they recognized that a brash manner usually conceals a sense of inferiority. As the alchemist preceded the chemist, the herb doctor the druggist, and the midwife the obstetrician, so the average "mind reader" anticipates in technique and knowledge the psychiatrist. He is, in fact, the psychiatrist of the poor; and when he is clever enough he sometimes becomes the psychiatrist of the rich as well.

Bouvier's Law Dictionary defines a fortune-teller as "one who pretends to be able to reveal future events; one who pretends to knowledge of futurity." And this sort of prediction, when done for money, is illegal in many localities. The law, however, leaves room for a multitude of evasions. Even in states where the law cracks down, those throngs who crave "knowledge of the future" find it easy to get.

The most legal method of fortune-telling is also the most efficient. A crystal ball may be seized and produced in court as evidence; the ghost of your grandmother, giving you sage advice in a dark room, may be grasped in the hand [and] revealed as phosphorescent cheesecloth. But the "cold reader," as he is called in the trade, has no gimmicks except his knowledge of men and his colossal nerve. He reads your mind "cold"—when you walk in, he has never seen you before and knows nothing about you. He looks you over, proceeds to pluck out of your mind your past, your troubles, your hopes, and your fears. As long as he remembers to add "Of course, I do not claim any occult knowledge of the future!" he is usually pretty safe legally.

The cold reader may have started with an M.D. or Ph.D. before he discovered the rich rewards of occultism. I know of a girl trained as a psychiatric social worker now reading palms in a carnival "mitt camp." She is making so much money that she is hardly likely to go back to pounding tenement stairs and bearding (to confront boldly) drunken husbands in their dens. Her professional knowledge paid very little before she learned to give it an occult disguise.

One "reader" ruefully tells an ironic story on himself. [With a] thirst for more legality, more dignity, he once sought out a struggling young doctor in a small eastern city and made him a proposition. The "mentalist" had many customers, chiefly women in middle life, whose main worry was their health. Could he send them to the doctor—for, of course, a certain percentage of the fee? The young medico thought of his professional ethics; but he also thought of his empty pockets. He accepted and for some time both doctor and reader did well.

But the doctor was still worried about the ethics of fee-splitting. Then he had an inspiration—why split them? He had a legal right to be a psychological counselor himself! Eventually his medical knowledge made him so successful as a reader that the poor fortune-teller, hopelessly outclassed, had to leave town and try his luck elsewhere.

Few secrets are harder to uncover than the "secret knowledge" of the cold reader. Stage magicians, sworn foes of the occult racketeer, speak with contempt of the spirit medium whose tricks they can unmask: but they speak of the cold reader with uneasy wonder. "Just a little applied psychology!" they tell you hastily, and turn the talk to the latest thing in card manipulations. Yet some of them, who began by trying to expose the mind reader, have been fascinated and drawn into this trade. More than one able magician got additional fame by doing mind-reading shows over the radio. A friend of mine, for many years a successful tax consultant, became a mind reader just for the fun of it. He had learned about human nature from the woes of his tax clients.

A successful magician turned mentalist told me, "The first season I went out, working hotels as an entertainer and giving private readings on the side, I took a whole trunkful of gimmicks along. After six weeks I shipped them all back home. I carried on with nothing but the cold reading. I'm telling you, Bill, a lad who can work the cold reading will never starve."

Very little has ever been written about the technique of cold reading. Those who know it have a stake in keeping it unknown by others. But in the catalogue of an occult supply house—dealing in crystals, *ectoplasm*, and brain waves helped out by hidden telephone wires—I found listed a few manuscripts, the "confessions" of old "office mediums" who had, supposedly, "packed the racket in." Half-illiterate, rambling, wretchedly mimeographed, these confessions form the only known textbook of this strange calling. They combine two things: a medium's eye view of human nature and a set of instructions for manipulating it. Using their formulas as a basis, I have been able to read minds for hours on end at charity parties without disappointing a single customer.

Very much compressed, the old manuscripts give the reader's breakdown of human problems somewhat like this:

I. YOUNG GIRL

A. Wild type
1. I can't catch, or hold, my man.
2. My conscience is bothering me.
3. I'm in trouble.

B. Home girl
1. I'm afraid of men.
2. I'm afraid of life and responsibility.
3. I'm afraid of Mom.

C. Career girl (usually jealous of a brother)
1. Under twenty-five: I'm ambitious. I hate and despise men and marriage!
2. Over twenty-five: I'm panicky. Maybe no one will marry me!

II. MATURE WOMAN (30–50)

A. Still wild
1. Why isn't it as much fun anymore? I'm lonely.
2. I'm afraid of getting my face scarred, or burning to death in a fire. (This never misses.)
3. I've got to believe in something—the occult, a new religion that doesn't include morals, or you, Mr. Fortune-teller!

B. Wife and mother
1. Is my husband seeing another woman?
2. When will he make more money?
3. I'm worried about the children . . .

III. SPINSTER

A. Still presentable
1. When will I meet him?

B. Given up hope
1. My best friend has done me dirt.
2. I'm crushed—a gigolo has got my savings!

IV. YOUNG MAN

A. Wild-oats farmer
1. Is there a system for beating the races?
2. What do you do when you get a girl in trouble?
   a. Is she playing me for a sucker?

B. Good boy
1. Will I be a success?
2. How can I improve my education?
3. Is my girl two-timing me?
   a. She's mixed up with Type A.
4. I'm afraid of Mom!

V. MATURE MAN

A. Wolf, married or single
  1. Girl trouble
    a. I can't get her!
    b. I can't get rid of her!
    c. Her male relatives are after me!
    d. Does my wife know?
B. Businessman
  1. Where's the money going to come from?
  2. Will this deal work out?
  3. Did I do right in that deal?
  4. What does my wife do all day?

VI. ELDERLY PEOPLE

A. Woman
  1. Will my daughter get a good husband?
  2. Will That Creature be a good wife to my son?
  3. Will the children (or grandchildren) be all right?
B. Man
  1. Will I ever have enough money to retire on?
  2. I'm afraid to die.
C. Both
  1. Am I going to need an operation?

VII. WISE GUY

A. Toughie
  1. Make one false move, fortune-teller, and I bust ya one! (Ease him out quick.)
B. Defensive bravado
  1. I'm smarter than most people; I see through you. (Flatter him; he'll end by eating out of your hand.)

This, needless to say, is not all there is to human nature; but it is all most people bring with them to the fortune-teller. The cynicism of this analysis is for many a cold reader's private benefit. What he *tells* the client is full of the milk of human kindness.

The manuscripts follow this up with a set of formula readings designed to cover the basic problems of each type. There is an exploratory opening, followed by a character analysis; then it passes to the main subject of human interest. Love and money, health and loss, friends and enemies, dangers and dreams. A dash of mystery, a solemn warning, a piece of good advice. Then the close, designed to convince the "mark" of your supernal wisdom and bring him back next week.

Memorizing these formulas may serve an amateur well. I was once asked to help a friend out by reading palms at her party. I memorized a stock spiel for young women and took on about twenty of the girls. They all looked alike to me—so I told them all exactly the same thing. Later I hid in the pantry to overhear

them comparing notes in the kitchen, expecting laughter as they saw the joke. They never caught on! Instead, there was a chorus of, "Isn't he wonderful! I just sat there and never opened my mouth, and the things that he told me—my dear, I've never confided them to a soul! The man's psychic!"

In that pantry I learned an important rule of fortune-telling: the human mind is a sieve. It holds what interests it and lets all the rest go. My fortune-teller's rapid twenty-minute spiel gave clients more than they could remember, and they remembered only the "hits."

For those professional readers who are only interested in having the client back, a memorized spiel is only a springboard. He may fall back on it to cover an awkward mistake or to deal with a tough client whose face tells him nothing. Usually, however, he relies on his ability to read faces and to lead the client into unconscious admissions. Both skills take long practice to develop, and a man who has them isn't entirely a fraud—he will know more about you in ten minutes than your husband or wife has been able to figure out in ten years.

Of the skilled cold readers I know, I have found only one who was willing to talk freely—a smooth-tongued old gentleman with a benevolent eye and nerves of cast iron, whom I shall call John Doe, "Doctor of Mental Science."

"Go ahead, son—print anything you like. You'll have a hundred chumps writing in to know where they can get in touch with the wonderful Power. My boy, you can't knock a lop-eared mark!"

This traditional phrase of the con man—it means that a natural-born sucker cannot be undeceived—is no exaggeration. Human gullibility is infinite. There was once in New York City a "materializing medium" who got his hooks into a prosperous investment broker. This hardheaded businessman had a passion for the ballet and had in his youth adored the great Pavlova.

A show girl I know met the medium on the street one afternoon. "I've got a chump upstairs," he told her. "Come on up for laughs."

As the girl tells the story, she and the broker sat side by side on a couch. The medium darkened the room somewhat, but everything remained clearly visible; then he retired into the next room to go into his "trance."

"I *know* Pavlova's going to appear today!" said the mark, trembling with excitement.

Suddenly, his pants rolled up to show his hairy legs, a scarf draped about him, the medium cavorted into the room. He did a pirouette and a few clumsy kicks, then went out.

"Wasn't she wonderful!" breathed the broker. "Pavlova to the life, just as I remember her!"

No, he wasn't nearsighted; but you can't knock a lop-eared mark. Dr. John Doe's clients, whom I watched all one afternoon from behind double doors he left ajar for me, never knew how often they nodded, gasped, or stammered half-finished sentences of information. They left swearing they'd never opened their mouths.

When I couldn't see how he did his stuff, the Doctor would explain, "Now that little woman with the run-down heels, for instance . . ."

She crossed the floor toward the Doctor of Mental Science, clutching her pocketbook. On her ring finger there was a telltale mark—she had removed her wedding ring, with a muddled idea of fooling the fortune-teller. By the time she sat down he had her classified.

Wife, probably at least two small children—she had the hunted look. Age, about thirty-five; looks beginning to go; clothes good last year, but this year made over inexpertly (that meant less money this year than last). No servants—the hands gave him that. Conservative, unimaginative, timid—the uninspired get-up and the timorous mouth and eyes gave him that. Strain in the eyes, anxiety and self-pity in the mouth. Probably husband trouble.

"My dear lady," he began, speaking quickly and almost inaudibly. The client, concentrating all her attention to hear him, forgot to be wary. "My dear lady, I am glad you have taken this opportunity to consult me, for I feel I can be of help . . . you understand, of course, I make no claim to occult powers and do not predict the future in any way . . ."

That was in case she was a policewoman, though she wasn't the type. Policewomen are easy to spot; they are almost the only women in the world with poker faces.

"Now I see that your *husband* is giving you some anxiety, isn't that so?" Right: the lady's eyes widened, sure sign of a hit. The Doctor fished. "There is another person, a woman . . ."

Wrong: the eyes narrowed. Try money. Ah, warmer—

". . . and this sum of money which must be paid . . . I see that this is not the main difficulty; there is some anxiety concerning your husband, a lack of will power—the eyes have widened again—"to stand up for himself to his boss . . . or is it that he lacks will power in his leisure hours"—aha!—"when his weakness for a few drinks . . . or gambling . . . I seem to see cards on a table . . ."

Whoa! The brows have knitted!

"No, his weakness for these things is not sufficient, as I said, to cause you alarm, but on the other hand there is one temptation which he cannot resist, which takes the money you need, not for yourself—for I can see you are not vain and greedy like so many women"—

Nothing like a little flattery to soften 'em up.

"—but for your young children. And I seem to see crowds, bright colors, . . . horses, that's it! Madame, your husband is addicted to betting on the races, isn't he?"

The eyes filled with tears. While the lady used her handkerchief, the Doctor continued:

"Now there is no way I could have known this, isn't that right, and you did not speak a word . . . you see, I just plucked it out of your mind . . ."

You're in, Doctor, you're in. Treat her kindly now, and she'll tell you her whole life story. When she runs out of breath, you can tell it right back to her, and she'll go away swearing she never opened her mouth.

That is the sort of opening my cold reader friend dreams of, and he gets it more often than a layman would suspect. Most of his clients are women, most of the women have worries, and the more worried a woman is the more she wants a chance to tell somebody about it. Many readings, after the opening has opened up the client, become listenings. At the end my fortune-teller friend comes in with a little common-sense advice, a little sympathy, and a reminder of how great his powers are. The client goes home almost dizzy with relief; next week, when the load is back on her mind, she can always come back to him. The arrangement is ideal for both.

With less-worried clients, a reader may pass from his opening to his character analysis, combining formula material and what he sees in the sucker's face. Of course, what he sees and what he says are two differing things!

A spiteful woman has a telltale line at the corner of her mouth. "You have suffered a great deal," says Dr. Doe, "from the machinations of malicious and ill-natured people around you. You tend to be too trusting and generous . . ." That's the way she sees herself.

A bad-tempered man betrays himself in nostrils and lips. "You are naturally passionate and impetuous, easily stirred by unfairness, but the world's lack of understanding has caused you to keep yourself under rigid control . . ." That's what *he* thinks: his wife thinks otherwise.

The self-righteous of both sexes wear a curious cold smirk. "The baseness of the world was once a great shock to you; you have a fine and sensitive nature; you have had to learn to keep yourself aloof . . ." The thicker you slice it, the better they like it.

The cold reader, in short, may learn to describe people as they see themselves. He never forgets that every man thinks he's unique, that every woman *knows* she is. The more commonplace the client, the longer it is possible for a fortune-teller to dwell on, "Now I couldn't tell this to every woman, but I can see that you are an unusually sensitive type."

A reader like Dr. Doe does not forget that every wife, sometime or other, muses on the great career she might have had if she hadn't married. If she's intelligent, it was the arts; if she's stupid, it was the screen; and if she's neurotic, it was probably the theatre. The fortune-teller's most lucrative clients are not necessarily women, however. Financial and political leaders often are the most rewarding. With them, the gambit is money, and there are many prosperous soothsayers peddling market advice in the nation's capital. A story is current about one of them who specialized entirely in financial predictions.

He got his information from one of the hush-hush Washington newsletters, now defunct. He trusted it implicitly; he would read it every week, embroider its bald facts with occult trimmings, add a few scraps picked up here and there, and dish it out to his distinguished clients. They, on their part, trusted *him*; one of them went so far as to take down every word he said in shorthand.

One day the good prophet happened to learn of a financial scandal about to break. No one else knew of it, and he could not resist the temptation to pass it along to his note-taking sucker. When he next picked up his newsletter, there it was, and in his own words!

A little research established the fact that his client with the shorthand was a trusted informant of the newsletter who passed the story on!

"You can't trust anybody nowadays," the fortune-teller complained bitterly. "*Now*, what am I gonna do for my market tips?"

Other significant topics are friends and enemies. To describe a woman's friend, you describe her physical opposite; but for her enemy, you describe the woman herself, and she will identify someone she loathes. Loss is a very important subject, for everyone has lost something—and everyone will react to the word.

Sometimes the reaction is dangerous. Most people, missing a valuable object, think at first that it is mislaid; only later do they suspect theft. Accordingly, when one old-time mind reader who had worked in theatres got the usual "Was my diamond ring lost or stolen?" she answered, "Your first supposition was correct." Her questioner, unfortunately, had begun by suspecting her maid; she walked out of the theatre and had the girl arrested.

The maid was innocent. She was also young, sensitive, and piously brought up; and she felt the disgrace of her arrest so keenly that she hanged herself in her cell. The medium retired from public performances for a few years.

Dr. Doe usually concludes by inviting questions, thus starting the most suspicious sucker talking; and whatever the client says, the reader cuts in with, "Ah, you remember I read that in your mind." His purpose now is to establish something very like what psychoanalysts call a *transference*. The client must be brought to depend on the reader absolutely, to defer all decisions until he can be consulted, to leave all responsibilities in his hands. A qualified psychoanalyst eventually builds up his patient's power of independent action and sets him free; but the technique of Dr. Doe is to try to keep him dependent forever—or until his money gives out. Thus, it is undeniable that fortune-telling often does serious harm. In addition to those suckers who are simply swin-

dled out of large sums, many others are bled slowly, and the psychological damage may be serious. Dr. Doe frankly admits that, as a cold reader, he encourages his victims, with his talk of occult power, in ignorance and confused thinking and superstition. Thus, even where he does no actual mental harm, the temporary relief he gives may keep a sick mind from treatment until it is too late.

To refute this, it may be pointed out that only an amateur reader will fool around with the psychotic and the seriously neurotic, and even he won't do it after one lesson. An amateur reader, who shall be nameless because she is my wife, learned this at a party. A career woman present was making herself offensive, particularly to a young man too shy to defend himself. With some idea of shutting her up, the amateur suggested a reading, which was eagerly accepted. But the reading never got past one whispered sentence.

Result: pandemonium. Shrieks, hysterics, infinitely embarrassing personal confessions, all accompanied by a desperate clinging to the "inspired psychic." The author of this article looked at his watch, announced that there was just time to make the last train, tucked the frightened cold reader under his arm, and ran. Once safe in Grand Central, he asked, "What on earth did you tell her?"

"Goodness," gasped the psychic, "all I said was that when she was a baby her mother didn't want her!"

Too true, in this instance, for a neurotic to take without fireworks. No skilled professional would have told the lady that. He wants no hysterics for the clients in the waiting room to hear. When he gets a "disturbed" individual, he dishes out soothing syrup and suggests a visit to the family doctor.

And most people who consult the fortune-teller are, after all, in no great need of psychiatry. They may think they want to know the future. If that is the case, they will often get what they deserve—a lie; there is perhaps no human desire at once so arrogant and so cowardly, so dishonest and so foolish, as the wish to know what's in store—to be God, instead of trusting Him. But most of the reader's clients actually need only a little common-sense advice, a little sympathy, a listening ear, and a few kind words. These such readers as Dr. Doe have in great plenty, and they will go on providing them until properly trained psychological counselors are as common as blackberries. Until then, the fortune-teller is the only impersonal adviser millions of people have, and though he is far from the best imaginable, he is usually better than nothing. His clients, however muddled in their heads when they leave him, are at least lighter in their hearts and better able to shoulder the burden that waits for them at home.

In his own cynical and mercenary way, even Dr. Doe often helps to make the world a cheerier place; for he has learned too well that "you'll never get rich peddling gloom!"

NAME _____

DATE _____

ACTIVE LEARNING EXERCISE 1.2

PERSONALITY INTERPRETATION OF A COLLEGE STUDENT

Now that you've read about fortune-tellers and how they operate, try your hand at writing a personality interpretation of a typical college student. Because you are a college student, you can simply report normative, typical events and concerns that you and your peers are experiencing, and it is likely to be a very good interpretation that will be highly rated and praised by others. It is important for you to see that providing interpretations that say nothing more than everyone already knows is often seen as amazing and unbelievable.

1. My personality description of a typical college student.

2. Compare your personality description to those of your classmates. What issues, problems, concerns, crises, goals, and lifestyle behaviors do they have in common?

SPOTLIGHT
THE BARNUM EFFECT

In a classic study of student acceptance of generalized personality interpretations, Ulrich, Stachnik, and Stainton (1963)* observed how subjects rated interpretations that they believed were derived from actual personality instruments. Students were administered the Bell Adjustment Inventory (a standard self-report instrument) and the House-Tree-Person test (a freehand drawing projective test) and given an interpretation 1 week later. All participants were given the same generalized interpretation (similar to the one used in Active Learning Exercise 1.3). Subjects' ratings of the interpretation, as well as written qualitative comments, were extremely favorable. Interpretations were typically considered "Excellent" or "Good" even when subjects believed other students (rather than experienced psychologists) were interpreting their evaluations. Student comments included the following:

> On the nose! Very good. I wish you had said more, but what you did mention was all true without a doubt.

> I believe this interpretation applies to me individually, as there are too many facets which fit me too well to be a generalization.

> I feel the interpretation does apply to me individually. For the first time things that I have been vaguely aware of have been put into concise and constructive statements which I would like to use as a plan for improving myself.

The main finding in this study was that the vast majority of people are likely to accept personality interpretations that are stated in very general terms as accurate descriptions of their own personality, without the slightest glimmer of awareness that the same interpretation could apply to anyone.

*Based on material in Ulrich, R. D., Stachnik, T. J., & Stainton, R. N. (1963). Student acceptance of generalized personality interpretations. *Psychological Reports, 13*, 831–834.

NAME _____

DATE _____

ACTIVE LEARNING EXERCISE 1.3
THE BARNUM EFFECT

P. T. Barnum, the famous circus entrepreneur, stated, "There's a sucker born every minute." One aspect of being a "sucker" is gullibility, the willingness to accept something without much scrutiny. The Barnum effect in personality refers to the willingness of people to accept vague, generalized statements as personalized, meaningful, and significant comments on their personality. For example, being told that you prefer change and variety, or that you have had doubts about decisions you have made, are circumstances that pertain to almost everyone. Therefore, interpretations of your personality that contain statements of this type should not be evaluated too highly since your personality is quite unique and these statements are so general as to characterize just about anybody. If you went for an annual medical checkup and your physician provided a report that stated that you have two eyes, hair, bones, and so on, you might question his or her competence and would certainly feel that you have not learned any useful information from the examination. Indeed, what the physician told you might be true for most people. However, when it comes to personality interpretations, most people will accept very vague statements quite easily and without doubting the professional competence of the psychologist. In fact, psychologists aren't the only ones who obtain enthusiastic responses from people by giving them generalized personality statements. The popularity of astrology, palmistry, numerology, and other pseudosciences illustrates the fact that people quite readily accept generalized statements as fact. During the past 25 years, a large amount of research has confirmed that the Barnum effect is a reliable phenomenon. To explore this effect personally, follow the directions in the following section. You can gain some firsthand experience in understanding why P. T. Barnum said that "there's a sucker born every minute" and why research is so important in the investigation of personality.

To perform this exercise, you will need to select a person who is unfamiliar with personality research, definitely someone who has not taken this course. The person you select becomes your research subject. Tell the subject that you are enrolled in a class in personality, and are learning about personality tests and would like to practice your skills. Tell the subject to make two different drawings for you, one of a person (no stick figures; artistic ability is not important) and another of a tree. Tell the subject that you will review the drawings and present an interpretation in 1 week. One week later, do so. The personality interpretation you will provide, given below, is a generalized, vague series of statements used in many experiments. Be sure to use this interpretation. Be sure to copy it in your own handwriting, with the subject's name written at the top. After the subject has read the personality interpretation, give him or her the following Rating Scales and Barnum Personality Interpretation and ask for an evaluation of the interpretation. Encourage the subject to provide some written comments in addition to the basic rating. After the ratings are completed, it is *very important* to reveal the actual nature of the experiment to the subject. As part of this "debriefing," you should answer all questions, explain the purpose of the exercise, and furnish references for further reading. In addition, your subject should be encouraged to share his or her personal reactions to the study.

THE "BARNUM PERSONALITY INTERPRETATION"*

You prefer a certain amount of change and variety and become dissatisfied when hemmed in by restrictions and limitations. You pride yourself on being an independent thinker and do not accept others' opinions without satisfactory proof. You have found it unwise to be too frank in revealing yourself to others. At times you are extroverted, affable, and sociable, while at other times you are introverted, wary, and reserved. Some of your aspirations tend to be pretty unrealistic. You have a strong need for other people to like you and for them to admire you.

You have a tendency to be critical of yourself. You have a great deal of unused capacity which you have not turned to your advantage. While you have some personality weaknesses, you are generally able to compensate for them. Your sexual adjustment has presented some problems for you. Disciplined and controlled on the outside, you tend to be worrisome and insecure inside. At times you have serious doubts as to whether you have made the right decision or done the right thing.

*Adapted from Forer, B. R. (1949). The fallacy of personal validation: A classroom demonstration of gullibility. *Journal of Abnormal and Social Psychology, 44,* 118–123.

RATING SCALES

A. Please rate the interpretation of your personality according to the following scale:

I feel that the interpretation was:

EXCELLENT	GOOD	AVERAGE	POOR	VERY POOR

B. Please make any additional comments about the test interpretation that you feel would be appropriate.

BARNUM ANALYSIS

If you are doing this as a class project, tabulate the class data for comparison with research findings. From Merrens and Richards (1970),* the following table presents subjects' ratings of the statement: "I feel the interpretation of my personality was":

EXCELLENT	GOOD	AVERAGE	POOR	VERY POOR
40%	38%	18%	4%	0%

1. Compare your class findings to these results, which are typical of the vast majority of studies in the area.

*Merrens, M. R., & Richards, W. S. (1970). Acceptance of generalized vs. bona fide personality interpretations. *Psychological Reports, 27,* 691–694.

2. If your findings were different (e.g., the subject rated the "Barnum" interpretation poorly), why do you think this was the case?

3. Clinicians (i.e., psychiatrists, clinical psychologists, and social workers) are often asked to assess clients and write reports that describe their clients' personalities. How do you think the Barnum effect applies to these evaluations?

4. Do you think it matters who the subjects believe will actually perform the interpretation? For example, do you think that if you told subjects that an experienced psychologist will interpret the assessment tests you use, their interpretations would be altered? If so, how?

5. What impact, if any, did this experience have on you and your view of psychological evaluations?

NAME _____

DATE _____

ACTIVE LEARNING EXERCISE 1.4

A PERSONAL PERSONALITY THEORY*

Instructions: For each of the following statements, circle the number that corresponds most closely to your point of view.

1. Human behavior results primarily from *heredity*, what has been genetically transmitted by parents, or from *environment*, the external circumstances and experiences that shape a person after conception has occurred.

	1	2	3	4	5	6	7	
heredity								environment

2. An important part of every person is a *self*, some central aspect of personality referred to as "I" or "me," or there really is *no self* in personality.

	1	2	3	4	5	6	7	
self								no self

3. Personality is relatively *unchanging*, with each person showing the same behavior throughout a lifetime, or personality is relatively *changing*, with each person showing different behavior throughout a lifetime.

	1	2	3	4	5	6	7	
unchanging								changing

4. The most important influences on behavior are *past* events, what has previously occurred to a person, or *future* events, what a person seeks to bring about by striving to meet certain goals.

	1	2	3	4	5	6	7	
past								future

5. The most important characteristics about people are *general* ones, those commonly shared by many people, or *unique* ones, those that make each person different from every other person.

	1	2	3	4	5	6	7	
general								unique

*Potkay, C. R., & Allen, B. P. (1986). *Personality: Theory, research, and applications.* Monterey, CA: Brooks/Cole. Reprinted by permission of Charles R. Potkay.

6. People are motivated to cooperate with others mainly because they are self-centered, expecting to receive some personal gain, or mainly because they are altruistic, seeking to work with others only for the benefit of doing things with and for others.

	2	3	4	5	6	7

self-centered _____ altruistic

7. People learn best when they are motivated by *reward*, involving pleasure, or by *punishment*, involving pain.

	2	3	4	5	6	7

reward _____ punishment

8. The main reason you behave as you do (for example, attend college) is because of conscious *personal* decisions to do so or because *social* factors outside your control leave you little real choice in the matter.

	2	3	4	5	6	7

personal _____ social

9. Human nature is essentially *constructive*, with people showing positive, personal growth and a desire to help others fulfill their potentials, or *destructive*, with people showing behavior that is ultimately self-defeating and a desire to keep others from improving themselves.

	2	3	4	5	6	7

constructive _____ destructive

10. Human beings have *no purpose* or reason for their existence other than what they experience on a day-to-day basis, or human beings have some *purpose* for living that is outside themselves.

	2	3	4	5	6	7

no purpose _____ purpose

The questionnaire you have just completed was developed by Potkay and Allen (1986)* to illustrate that we all have theories of personality. It is a good idea to review your own conceptions prior to investigating the field in depth. You can compare your responses to the ideas of major personality theorists, as organized by Potkay and Allen.

THEORISTS' ASSUMPTIONS ABOUT PERSONALITY

1.

	1	2	3	4	5	6	7	
heredity								environment

Eysenck, Cattell, Sheldon, Freud, Jung   Skinner, Watson, Rotter, Bandura, Rogers

2.

	1	2	3	4	5	6	7	
self								no self

Rogers, Maslow, Erikson, Horney, Jung   Watson, Skinner, Rotter, Mischel

3.

	1	2	3	4	5	6	7	
unchanging								changing

Freud, Eysenck, Cattell   Rogers, Mischel,

4.

	1	2	3	4	5	6	7	
past								future

Freud, Jung, Fromm   Adler, Rogers, Maslow, Rotter

5.

	1	2	3	4	5	6	7	
general								unique

Watson, Skinner, Eysenck Fromm   Adler, Rogers, Bandura, Rotter

*Potkay, C. R., & Allen, B. P. (1986). *Personality: Theory, research, and applications.* Monterey, CA: Brooks/Cole. Reprinted by permission of Charles R. Potkay.

6.

	1	2	3	4	5	6	7	
self-centered								altruistic

Freud, Jung   Adler, Fromm, Maslow, Rogers, Bandura

7.

	1	2	3	4	5	6	7	
reward								punishment

Skinner, Bandura, Freud, Maslow   Watson

8.

	1	2	3	4	5	6	7	
personal								social

Rogers, Maslow, Fromm   Skinner, Bandura, Mischel

9.

	1	2	3	4	5	6	7	
constructive								destructive

Adler, Rogers, Maslow   Freud

10.

	1	2	3	4	5	6	7	
no purpose								purpose

Skinner, Watson, Bandura, Mischel   Adler, Fromm, Horney Rogers, Maslow, Jung

SPOTLIGHT
PERSONALITY ASSESSMENT

Monday's child is fair of face,

Tuesday's child is full of grace,

Wednesday's child is full of woe,

Thursday's child has far to go,

Friday's child is loving and giving,

Saturday's child works for its living,

And a child that's born on the Sabbath day
is fair and wise and good and gay

This poem of unknown authorship, like astrology, proposes that we can determine personality characteristics by knowing the day on which a person was born.

NAME _____

DATE _____

ACTIVE LEARNING EXERCISE 1.5

SELF-RATINGS*

_____

Instructions: Compared with other college students of the same class level and sex as yourself, how would you rate yourself on the following characteristics? Use the following scale in marking your responses.

1 = considerably well below average
2 = well below average
3 = below average
4 = slightly below average
5 = average
6 = slightly above average
7 = above average
8 = well above average
9 = considerably well above average

_____ 1. leadership ability

_____ 2. athletic ability

_____ 3. ability to get along with others

_____ 4. tolerance

_____ 5. energy level

_____ 6. helpfulness

_____ 7. responsibility

_____ 8. creativeness

_____ 9. patience

_____ 10. trustworthiness

_____ 11. sincerity

_____ 12. thoughtfulness

_____ 13. cooperativeness

_____ 14. reasonableness

_____ 15. intelligence

SEE NEXT PAGE FOR INTERPRETATION

After completing the Self-Rating questionnaire, calculate your mean score by adding up all 15 items and dividing by 15. Previous demonstrations by the authors indicate that almost all students will have mean ratings above the average of 5.0. This self-serving bias, termed the better than average phenomenon, suggests that almost all of us see ourselves as better than average. Myers (1993) suggests the following explanations for this self-serving bias: (**1**) we like to present a good image to others and ourselves; (**2**) we assume more responsibility for our successes than our failures and tend to blame occasional failures on circumstances rather than on ourselves; (**3**) we are strongly motivated to maintain, enhance, and preserve ourselves.

Score =

REFERENCE

MYERS, D. G. (1993). *Social psychology* (4th Ed.). New York: McGraw-Hill.

CHAPTER
2

Classical Psychoanalytical Perspective

Introduction

Sigmund Freud ranks among the greatest thinkers in the history of humankind. His contributions to psychology rival those of Galileo, Newton, Einstein, and Darwin in the natural sciences.

The impact of his psychoanalytic theory on all facets of life continues to be felt today. In the last 5 years alone, there have been over 1500 references to Freud in scholarly articles, chapters, and books. His influence does not stop there, though; we frequently encounter references to psychoanalysis and psychoanalytic concepts in art, literature, and film.

In this chapter you will have the opportunity to explore the psychoanalytical approach in depth. For this purpose, we have assembled a variety of readings and exercises to enhance your understanding of Freud's impact on your day-to-day behavior, as well as his contributions to psychology in such areas as personality constructs, defense mechanisms, and dreaming.

NAME _____

DATE _____

ACTIVE LEARNING EXERCISE 2.1
BELIEFS ABOUT FREUDIAN PRINCIPLES*

The following exercise is designed to assess people's beliefs about their everyday behaviors. Before reading further, complete the following questionnaire.

Respond to each statement by circling one of the following responses: strongly disagree [**SD**], disagree [**D**], neutral [**N**], agree [**A**], or strongly agree [**SA**].

1. Events that occurred during childhood have no effect on one's personality in adulthood.   **SD**   **D**   **N**   **A**   **SA**

2. Sexual adjustment is easy for most people.   **SD**   **D**   **N**   **A**   **SA**

3. Culture and society have evolved as ways to curb human beings' natural aggressiveness.   **SD**   **D**   **N**   **A**   **SA**

4. Little boys should not become too attached to their mothers.   **SD**   **D**   **N**   **A**   **SA**

5. It is possible to deliberately "forget" something too painful to remember.   **SD**   **D**   **N**   **A**   **SA**

6. People who chronically smoke, eat, or chew gum have some deep psychological problems.   **SD**   **D**   **N**   **A**   **SA**

7. Competitive people are no more aggressive than noncompetitive people.   **SD**   **D**   **N**   **A**   **SA**

8. Fathers should remain somewhat aloof to their daughters.   **SD**   **D**   **N**   **A**   **SA**

9. Toilet training is natural and not traumatic for most children.   **SD**   **D**   **N**   **A**   **SA**

10. The phallus is a symbol of power.   **SD**   **D**   **N**   **A**   **SA**

11. A man who dates a woman old enough to be his mother has problems.   **SD**   **D**   **N**   **A**   **SA**

12. There are some women who are best described as being "castrating bitches."   **SD**   **D**   **N**   **A**   **SA**

13. Dreams merely replay events that occurred during the day and have no deep meaning.   **SD**   **D**   **N**   **A**   **SA**

14. There is something wrong with a woman who dates a man old enough to be her father.   **SD**   **D**   **N**   **A**   **SA**

15. A student who wants to postpone an exam by saying, "My grandmother lied . . . er, I mean died," should probably be allowed the postponement.   **SD**   **D**   **N**   **A**   **SA**

*Adapted from Miserandino, M. (1994). Freudian principles in everyday life. *Teaching of Psychology, 21* (2), 93–95. Scale reprinted with permission.

SCORING

Each response receives a score of 1 through 5. Items 3, 4, 5, 6, 8, 10, 11, 12, and 14 are scored as follows: strongly disagree = 1, disagree = 2, neutral = 3, agree = 4, and strongly agree = 5. Items 1, 2, 7, 9, 13, and 15 are scored in the reverse direction (e.g., strongly disagree = 5, strongly agree = 1).

1. Total your scores across the 15 items. High scores (maximum score = 75) indicate agreement with the Freudian position, and low scores (minimum score = 15) indicate disagreement with this position.

Score =

2. Calculate a mean and standard deviation for the class.

Mean =

SD =

3. How would you interpret the overall agreement/disagreement with Freud's position?

4. Next, calculate means and standard deviations for each of the 15 items separately:

MEAN	SD	MEAN	SD
1.		9.	
2.		10.	
3.		11.	
4.		12.	
5.		13.	
6.		14.	
7.		15.	
8.			

5. Which *items* seem to elicit the most agreement? Disagreement? Why?

READING

THE ORIGIN AND DEVELOPMENT OF PSYCHOANALYSIS*

Sigmund Freud

FIRST LECTURE

Editors' Note:

Although most people have heard of Sigmund Freud and his theories, very few have actually read his work. In this article, Freud relates in a highly personal manner the origin and development of psychoanalysis. Through his intricate description of a case, we see his ideas evolve.

. . . It is a new and somewhat embarrassing experience for me to appear as lecturer before students of the New World. I assume that I owe this honor to the association of my name with the theme of psychoanalysis, and consequently it is of psychoanalysis that I shall aim to speak. I shall attempt to give you in very brief form an historical survey of the origin and further development of this new method of research and cure.

Granted that it is a merit to have created psychoanalysis, it is not my merit. I was a student, busy with the passing of my last examinations, when another physician of Vienna, Dr. Joseph Breuer, made the first application of this method to the case of an hysterical girl (1880–82). We must now examine the history of this case and its treatment, which can be found in detail in *Studies on Hysteria* . . . published by Dr. Breuer and myself.

But first one word. I have noticed, with considerable satisfaction, that the majority of my hearers do not belong to the medical profession. Now do not fear that a medical education is necessary to follow what I shall have to say. We shall now accompany the doctors a little way, but soon we shall take leave of them and follow Dr. Breuer on a way which is quite his own.

Dr. Breuer's patient was a girl of twenty-one, of a high degree of intelligence. She had developed in the course of her two years' illness a series of physical and mental disturbances which well deserved to be taken seriously. She had a severe paralysis of both right extremities, with anesthesia, and at times the same affection of the members of the left side of the body; disturbance of eye-movements, and much impairment of vision; difficulty in maintaining the position of the head, an intense nervous cough, nausea when she attempted to take nourishment, and at one time for several weeks loss of the power to drink, in spite of tormenting thirst. Her power of speech was also diminished, and this progressed so far that she could neither speak nor understand her mother tongue; and, finally, she was subject to states of "absence," of confusion, delirium, alteration of her whole personality. These states will later claim our attention.

When one hears of such a case, one does not need to be a physician to incline to the opinion that we are concerned here with a serious injury, probably of the brain, for which there is little hope of cure and which will probably lead to the early death of the patient. The doctors will tell us, however, that in one type of case with just as unfavorable symptoms, another, far more favorable, opinion is justified. When one finds such a series of symptoms in the case of a young girl, whose vital organs (heart, kidneys) are shown . . . by objective tests to be normal, but who has suffered from strong emotional disturbances, and when the symptoms differ in certain finer characteristics from what one might logically expect, in a case like this the doctors are not too much disturbed. They consider that there is present no organic lesion of the brain, but that enigmatical state, known since the time of the Greek physicians as hysteria, which can simulate a whole series of symptoms of various diseases. They consider in such a case that the life of the patient is not in danger and that a restoration to health will probably come about of itself. The differentiation of such an hysteria from a severe organic lesion is not always very easy. But we do not need to know how a differential diagnosis of this kind is made; you may be sure that the case of Breuer's patient was such that no skillful physician could fail to diagnose an hysteria. We may also add a word here from the history of the case. The illness first appeared while the patient was caring for her father, whom she tenderly loved, during the severe illness which led to his death, a task which she was compelled to abandon because she herself fell ill.

So far it has seemed best to go with the doctors, but we shall soon part company with them. You must not think that the outlook of a patient with regard to medical aid is essentially bettered when the diagnosis points to hysteria rather than to organic disease of the brain. Against the serious brain diseases

*Freud, S. (1910). The origin and development of psychoanalysis. *The American Journal of Psychology, 21,* 181–218.

medical skill is in most cases powerless, but also in the case of hysterical affections the doctor can do nothing. He must leave it to benign nature, when and how his hopeful prognosis will be realized. Accordingly, with the recognition of the disease as hysteria, little is changed in the situation of the patient, but there is a great change in the attitude of the doctor. We can observe that he acts quite differently toward hystericals than toward patients suffering from organic diseases. He will not bring the same interest to the former as to the latter, since their suffering is much less serious and yet seems to set up the claim to be valued just as seriously.

But there is another motive in this action. The physician, who through his studies has learned so much that is hidden from the laity, can realize in his thought the causes and alterations of the brain disorders in patients suffering from apoplexy or dementia, a representation which must be right up to a certain point, for by it he is enabled to understand the nature of each symptom. But before the details of hysterical symptoms, all his knowledge, his anatomical-physiological and pathological education, desert him. He cannot understand hysteria. He is in the same position before it as the layman. And that is not agreeable to anyone who is in the habit of setting such a high valuation upon his knowledge. Hystericals, accordingly, tend to lose his sympathy; he considers them persons who overstep the laws of his science, as the orthodox regard heretics; he ascribes to them all possible evils, blames them for exaggeration and intentional deceit, "simulation," and he punishes them by withdrawing his interest.

Now Dr. Breuer did not deserve this reproach in this case; he gave his patient sympathy and interest, although at first he did not understand how to help her. Probably this was easier for him on account of those superior qualities of the patient's mind and character, to which he bears witness in his account of the case.

His sympathetic observation soon found the means which made the first help possible. It had been noticed that the patient, in her states of "absence," of psychic alteration, usually mumbled over several words to herself. These seemed to spring from associations with which her thoughts were busy. The doctor, who was able to get these words, put her in a sort of hypnosis and repeated them to her over and over, in order to bring up any associations that they might have. The patient yielded to his suggestion and reproduced for him those psychic creations which controlled her thoughts during her "absences," and which betrayed themselves in these single spoken words. These were fancies, deeply sad, often poetically beautiful, day dreams, we might call them, which commonly took as their starting point the situation of a girl beside the sick-bed of her father. Whenever she had related a number of such fancies, she was, as it were, freed and restored to her normal mental life. This state of health would last for several hours, and then give place on the next day to a new "absence," which was removed in the same way by relating the newly created fancies. It was impossible not to get the impression that the psychic alteration which was expressed in the "absence," was a consequence of the excitations originating from these intensely emotional fancy-images. The patient herself, who at this time of her illness strangely enough understood and spoke only English, gave this new kind of treatment the name "talking cure," or jokingly designated it as "chimney sweeping."

The doctor soon hit upon the fact that through such cleansing of the soul more could be accomplished than a temporary removal of the constantly recurring mental "clouds." Symptoms of the disease would disappear when in hypnosis the patient could be made to remember the situation and the associative connections under which they first appeared, provided free vent was given to the emotions which they aroused. "There was in the summer a time of intense heat, and the patient had suffered very much from thirst; for, without any apparent reason, she had suddenly become unable to drink. She would take a glass of water in her hand, but as soon as it touched her lips she would push it away as though suffering from hydrophobia. Obviously for these few seconds she was in her absent state. She ate only fruit, melons and the like, in order to relieve this tormenting thirst. When this had been going on about six weeks, she was talking one day in hypnosis about her English governess, whom she disliked, and finally told, with every sign of disgust, how she had come into the room of the governess, and how that lady's little dog, that she abhorred, had drunk out of a glass. Out of respect for the conventions the patient had remained silent. Now, after she had given energetic expression to her restrained anger, she asked for a drink, drank a large quantity of water without trouble, and woke from hypnosis with a glass at her lips. The symptom thereupon vanished permanently."

Permit me to dwell for a moment on this experience. No one had ever cured an hysterical symptom by such means before, or had come so near understanding its cause. This would be a pregnant discovery if the expectation could be confirmed that still other, perhaps the majority of symptoms, originated in this way and could be removed by the same method. Breuer spared no pains to convince himself of this and investigated the pathogenesis of the other more serious symptoms in a more orderly way. Such was indeed the case; almost all the symptoms originated in exactly this way, as remnants, as precipitates, if you like, of affectively-toned experiences, which for that reason we later called "psychic traumata." The nature of the symptoms became clear through their relation to the scene which caused them. They were, to use the technical term, "determined" by the scene whose memory traces they embodied, and so could no longer be described as arbitrary or enigmatical functions of the neurosis.

Only one variation from what might be expected must be mentioned. It was not always a single experience which occasioned the symptom, but usually several, perhaps many similar, repeated traumata co-operated in this effect. It was necessary to repeat the whole series of pathogenic memories in chronological sequence, and of course in reverse order, the last first and the first last. It was quite impossible to reach the first and often most essential trauma directly, without first clearing away those coming later.

You will of course want to hear me speak of other examples of the causation of hysterical symptoms beside this of inability to drink on account of the disgust caused by the dog drinking from the glass. I must, however, if I hold to my programme, limit myself to very few examples. Breuer relates, for instance, that his patient's visual disturbances could be traced back to external causes, in the following way. "The patient, with tears in her eyes, was sitting by the sick-bed when her father suddenly asked her what time it was. She could not see distinctly, strained her eyes to see, brought the watch near her eyes so that the dial seemed very large, or else she tried hard to suppress her tears, so that the sick man might not see them."

All the pathogenic impressions sprang from the time when she shared in the care of her sick father. "Once she was watching at night in the greatest anxiety for the patient, who was in a high fever, and in suspense, for a surgeon was expected from Vienna, to operate on the patient. Her mother had gone out for a little while, and Anna sat by the sick-bed, her right arm hanging over the back of her chair. She fell into a revery and saw a black snake emerge, as it were, from the wall and approach the sick man as though to bite him. (It is very probable that several snakes had actually been seen in the meadow behind the house, that she had already been frightened by them, and that these former experiences furnished the material for the hallucination.) She tried to drive off the creature, but was as though paralyzed. Her right arm, which was hanging over the back of the chair, had 'gone to sleep,' become anesthetic and paretic, and as she was looking at it, the fingers changed into little snakes with death-heads. (The nails.) Probably she attempted to drive away the snake with her paralyzed right hand, and so the anesthesia and paralysis of this member formed associations with the snake hallucination. When this had vanished, she tried in her anguish to speak, but could not. She could not express herself in any language, until finally she thought of the words of an English nursery song, and thereafter she could think and speak only in this language." When the memory of this scene was revived in hypnosis the paralysis of the right arm, which had existed since the beginning of the illness, was cured and the treatment ended.

When, a number of years later, I began to use Breuer's researches and treatment on my own patients, my experiences completely coincided with his. In the case of a woman of about forty, there was a tic, a peculiar smacking noise which manifested itself whenever she was laboring under any excitement, without any obvious cause. It had its origin in two experiences which had this common element, that she attempted to make no noise, but that by a sort of counter-will this noise broke the stillness. On the first occasion, she had finally after much trouble put her sick child to sleep, and she tried to be very quiet so as not to awaken it. On the second occasion, during a ride with both her children in a thunderstorm the horses took fright, and she carefully avoided any noise for fear of frightening them still more. I give this example instead of many others which are cited in the *Studies on Hysteria*.

Ladies and gentlemen, if you will permit me to generalize, as is indispensable in so brief a presentation, we may express our results up to this point in the formula: *Our hysterical patients suffer from reminiscences*. Their symptoms are the remnants and the memory symbols of certain (traumatic) experiences.

A comparison with other memory symbols from other sources will perhaps enable us better to understand this symbolism. The memorials and monuments with which we adorn our great cities, are also such memory symbols. If you walk through London you will find before one of the greatest railway stations of the city a richly decorated Gothic pillar— "Charing Cross." One of the old Plantagenet kings, in the thirteenth century, caused the body of his beloved queen Eleanor to be borne to Westminster, and had Gothic crosses erected at each of the stations where the coffin was set down. Charing Cross is the last of these monuments, which preserve the memory of this sad journey. In another part of the city, you will see a high pillar of more modern construction, which is merely called "the monument." This is in memory of the great fire which broke out in the neighborhood in the year 1666, and destroyed a great part of the city. These monuments are memory symbols like the hysterical symptoms; so far the comparison seems justified. But what would you say to a Londoner who today stood sadly before the monument to the funeral of Queen Eleanor, instead of going about his business with the haste engendered by modern industrial conditions, or rejoicing with the young queen of his own heart? Or to another, who before the "Monument" bemoaned the burning of his loved native city, which long since has arisen again so much more splendid than before?

Now hystericals and all neurotics behave like these two unpractical Londoners, not only in that they remember the painful experiences of the distant past, but because they are still strongly affected by them. They cannot escape from the past and neglect present reality in its favor. This fixation of the mental life on the pathogenic traumata is an essential, and practically a most significant characteristic of the neurosis. I will willingly concede the objection which you are probably formulating, as you think over the history of Breuer's patient. All her traumata originated at the time when she was caring for her sick father, and her symptoms could only be regarded as memory symbols of his sickness and death. They corresponded to mourning, and a fixation on thoughts of the dead so short a time after death is certainly not pathological, but rather corresponds to normal emotional behavior. I concede this: there is nothing abnormal in the fixation of feeling on the trauma shown by Breuer's patient. But in other cases, like that of the tic that I have mentioned, the occasions for which lay ten and fifteen years back, the characteristic of this abnormal clinging to the past is very clear, and Breuer's patient would probably have developed it, if she had not come under the "cathartic treatment" such a short time after the traumatic experiences and the beginning of the disease.

We have so far only explained the relation of the hysterical symptoms to the life history of the patient; now by considering two further moments which Breuer observed, we may get a hint as to the processes of the beginning of the illness and those of the cure. With regard to the first, it is especially to be noted that Breuer's patient in almost all pathogenic situations had to suppress a strong excitement, instead of giving vent to it by appropriate words and deeds. In the little experience with her governess' dog, she suppressed, through regard for the conventions, all manifestations of her very intense disgust. While she was seated by her father's sick-bed, she was careful to betray nothing of her anxiety and her painful depression to the patient. When, later, she reproduced the same scene before the physician, the emotion which she had suppressed on the occurrence of the scene burst out with especial strength, as though it had been pent up all along. The symptom which had been caused by that scene reached its greatest intensity while the doctor was striving to revive the memory of the scene, and vanished after it had been fully laid bare. On the other hand, experience shows that if the patient is reproducing the traumatic scene to the physician, the process has no curative effect if, by some peculiar chance, there is no development of emotion. It is apparently these emotional processes upon which the illness of the patient and the restoration to health are dependent. We feel justified in regarding "emotion" as a quantity which may become increased, derived and displaced. So we are forced to the conclusion that the patient fell ill because the emotion developed in the pathogenic situation was prevented from escaping normally, and that the essence of the sickness lies in the fact that these "imprisoned" emotions undergo a series of abnormal changes. In part they are preserved as a lasting charge and as a source of constant disturbance in psychical life; in part they undergo a change into unusual bodily innervations and inhibitions, which present themselves as the physical symptoms of the case. We have coined the name "hysterical conversion" for the latter process. Part of our mental energy is, under normal conditions, conducted off by way of physical innervation and gives what we call "the expression of emotions." Hysterical conversion exaggerates this part of the course of a mental process which is emotionally colored; it corresponds to a far more intense emotional expression, which finds outlet by new paths. If a stream flows in two channels, an overflow of one will take place as soon as the current in the other meets with an obstacle.

You see that we are in a fair way to arrive at a purely psychological theory of hysteria, in which we assign the first rank to the affective processes. A second observation of Breuer compels us to ascribe to the altered condition of consciousness a great part in determining the characteristics of the disease. His patient showed many sorts of mental states, conditions of "absence," confusion and alteration of character, besides her normal state. In her normal state she was entirely ignorant of the pathogenic scenes and of their connection with her symptoms. She had forgotten those scenes, or at any rate had dissociated them from their pathogenic connection. When the patient was hypnotized, it was possible, after considerable difficulty, to recall those scenes to her memory, and by this means of recall the symptoms were removed. It would have been extremely perplexing to know how to interpret this fact, if hypnotic practice and experiments had not pointed out the way. Through the study of hypnotic phenomena, the conception, strange though it was at first, has become familiar, that in one and the same individual several mental groupings are possible, which may remain relatively independent of each other, "know nothing" of each other, and which may cause a splitting of consciousness along lines which they lay down. Cases of such a sort, known as "double personality," occasionally appear spontaneously. If in such a division of personality consciousnesss remains constantly bound up with one of the two states, this is called the *conscious* mental state, and the other the *unconscious*. In the well-known phenomena of so-called post hypnotic suggestion, in which a command given in hypnosis is later executed in the normal state as though by an imperative suggestion, we have an excellent basis for understanding how the unconscious state can influence the conscious, although the latter is ignorant of the existence of the former. In the same way it is quite possible to explain the facts in hysterical cases. Breuer came to the conclusion that the hysterical symptoms originated in such peculiar mental states, which he called "hypnoidal states." Experiences of an emotional nature, which occur during such hypnoidal states easily become pathogenic, since such states do not present the conditions for a normal draining off of the emotion of the exciting processes. And as a result there arises a peculiar product of this exciting process, that is, the symptom, and this is projected like a foreign body into the normal state. The latter has, then, no conception of the significance of the hypnoidal pathogenic situation. Where a symptom arises, we also find an amnesia, a memory gap, and the filling of this gap includes the removal of the conditions under which the symptom originated.

I am afraid that this portion of my treatment will not seem very clear, but you must remember that we are dealing here with new and difficult views, which perhaps could not be made much clearer. This all goes to show that our knowledge in this field is not very far advanced. Breuer's idea of the hypnoidal states has, moreover, been shown to be superfluous and a hindrance to further investigation, and has been dropped from present conceptions of psychoanalysis. Later I shall at least suggest what other influences and processes have been disclosed besides that of the hypnoidal states, to which Breuer limited the causal moment.

You have probably also felt, and rightly, that Breuer's investigations gave you only a very incomplete theory and insufficient explanation of the phenomena which we have observed. But complete theories do not fall from Heaven, and you would have had still greater reason to be distrustful, had any one offered you at the beginning of his observations a well-rounded theory, without any gaps; such a theory could only be the child of his speculations and not the fruit of an unprejudiced investigation of the facts.

SPOTLIGHT
COPING WITH DISASTER*

How do people cope with an impending disaster whose occurrence is highly likely, but whose timing is uncertain? "Date with an Earthquake," a research study by Darrin Lehman and Shelley Taylor, dealt with this issue.

Following a 1983 safety report on the vulnerability of the UCLA campus in the event of a major earthquake (1,500 to 2,000 fatalities, 3,000–4,000 serious injuries, and substantial property damage was estimated), Lehman and Taylor interviewed students who lived in campus housing. Even though housing assignments were made by a modified lottery system, students were generally well aware of the safety status of the various living situations.

They selected students who lived in housing with seismic ratings of either "good" or "very poor" (likely to suffer severe structural damage or collapse). Among other tasks, the subjects were asked to respond to a brief questionnaire indicating the extent to which they agreed (on a 4-point scale ranging from "not at all" to "very true") with each of 10 earthquake-related coping statements.

In analyzing the results, the researchers found that those students living in more dangerous conditions were more likely to endorse items that questioned the seriousness of the earthquake situation and cast doubt on estimates by seismology experts. Specifically, the items they tended to agree with were:

1. There may be an earthquake, but it won't be that bad.

2. The center of the earthquake will be far away from here and have little impact on us.

3. The likelihood that a major earthquake will occur here has been greatly exaggerated.

4. Los Angeles was fine in the 1971 earthquake and it will be fine in the next one too.

How might Freud have interpreted these behaviors?

*Based on material in Lehman, D. P., & Taylor, S. E. (1988). Date with an earthquake: Coping with a probable, unpredictable disaster. *Personality and Social Psychology Bulletin, 13*(4), 546–555.

ACTIVE LEARNING EXERCISE 2.2
ASSESSMENT OF DEFENSES*

According to Cramer (1987):

> [T]he study of defense mechanisms began with Freud's investigation into certain forms of psychopathology. Shortly thereafter, he began to consider defense as a category of general—i.e., nonpathological—mental mechanism(s) used by the individual in conflict situations.
>
> The term "defense mechanism" refers to any cognitive operation that functions so as to protect the individual from the disruptive effects of excessive anxiety. In this sense, defenses are adaptive; they allow the individual to continue to function in anxiety-arousing situations.
>
> This conception of defenses as a part of normal personality functioning opens the way for a consideration of the development of defense mechanisms. There is considerable consensus in the theoretical literature that some defenses are more primitive or immature, while others are more complex or mature. . . . From a developmental perspective, it makes sense to assume that the most primitive defenses would emerge earliest in the life of an individual, while the more complex defenses would not appear until later, much in the same way that other ego functions (e.g., cognitive operations or moral reasoning) emerge in a developmental, stage-related fashion. (pp. 597–598)

This exercise was designed to give you a clearer idea of how psychologists assess children's defenses. One procedure, the Thematic Apperception Test (TAT), provides opportunities for people to tell stories of situations depicted on cards. Since defenses are inferred from verbal behavior, psychologists often rely on specific guidelines to evaluate children's responses to test stimuli.

*Cramer, P. (1987, December). The development of defense mechanisms. *Journal of Personality, 55* (4), 597–614.

NAME _____

DATE _____

1. Using the following scoring guide, which was developed to assess the use of three defenses (denial, projection, and identification), score each of the TAT stories below. Each category is scored as many times as it appears in a story. All stories were responses to TAT card 17BM, which depicts a man climbing up or down a rope.

Note the predominant defense(s) in each story. (See pages 44 and 45 for scoring guide.)

    A. The following story was told by a 5-year-old girl.

        A statue . . . climbing down a rope. He falls and then breaks. And then somebody builds him back up and he does the same thing over again. The people have to build him back up and put him back up on the rope and then he swings down and breaks.
        (How is he feeling?) He's made out of clay. He doesn't.

Note the categories scored:

B. A story from a 10-year-old boy:

> A man was being chased by a bunch of soldiers who wanted to kill him. He's climbing up the rope and if he doesn't make it up he'll get chopped to death with swords. So he is hanging as tight as he can and when he gets to the top he'll be on the border—that's a secret place underground. There is this hatch that is on the border so they can't get him.

Note the categories scored:

C. A story from a high school boy:

> The people are the citizens of the U.S. and they're all trying as hard as they can to have a good life. They number between 5 and 10 in population. They have all had hard lives and they've been hardened by it. They are almost at the end of their climb to greatness. They're all thinking of the rewards they'll have for their hard work. They feel as though they have all the troubles of the world on their shoulders. Most of them reach the top, but the weak fall behind and [lose] out in life.

Note the categories scored:

SCORING GUIDE FOR DEFENSES

DENIAL

1. Statements of negation
   a. a character "does not . . ." an action, wish or intention, which if acknowledged, would cause displeasure, pain or humiliation.
   b. the storyteller negates or denies a fact or feeling.
   c. references to doubt as to what the picture is or represents.

2. Denial of reality
   a. the storyteller denies the reality of the story or situation.
   b. sleeping, daydreaming, or fainting as a way of avoiding something unpleasant.
   c. avoiding looking at (hearing, thinking about) something that would be unpleasant to see (hear, think about).
   d. any perception, attribution or implication that is blatantly false with regard to reality.

3. Reversal
   a. transformation, such as weakness into strength.
   b. any figure who takes on qualities previously stated conversely.

4. Misperception
   a. unusual or distorted perception of a figure, object or action in the picture, without support (not ominous).
   b. perception of figure as being of opposite sex from that usually perceived.

5. Omission of major characters or objects
   (Specific criteria for each TAT card.)

6. Overly maximizing the positive or minimizing the negative
   a. gross exaggeration or underestimation of a character's qualities, size, power, etc.

7. Unexpected goodness, optimism, positiveness, gentleness
   a. unexpected goodness.
   b. a drastic change of heart for the good.
   c. references to natural beauty, wonder, awesomeness.
   d. nonchalance in the face of danger.
   e. acceptance of one's (negative) fate or loss; "sour grapes."

PROJECTION

1. Attribution of aggressive or hostile feelings, emotions or intentions to a character, or of any other feelings, emotions or intentions that are normatively unusual, if such attribution is without sufficient reason.

2. Addition of people, ghosts, animals, objects, or qualities
   a. score only if the additions are of an ominous or potentially threatening nature.
   b. especially the addition of blood, serious and uncommon illnesses, nightmares.
   c. references to people, animals or objects being decrepit, falling apart, deteriorating.

3. Concern for protection against external threat
   a. fear of threat or assault and the need for protection against this, as seen in the use of disguises and the creation of protective barriers.
   b. suspiciousness, spying, anticipation of kidnap, etc.
   c. having seen something one shouldn't and the need to hide this; fear of being seen; protective hiding.
   d. defensive self-justification on the part of the storyteller.

4. Themes of pursuit, entrapment and escape
   a. one character pursuing or trapping another.
   b. escape from a physical imprisonment, danger, or threat thereof.

5. Apprehensiveness of death, injury, assault
   a. physical attack, injury, or death actually occurs.
   b. fear of going to sleep.

6. Magical, autistic, or circumstantial thinking
   a. use of magical powers, including hypnosis, in which one character controls another.
   b. animism.
   c. circumstantial reasoning with a paranoid flavor; hyper alert search for flaws or hidden meanings.

7. Bizarre or very unusual story or theme
   a. negative themes that occur very rarely, especially if there is a peculiar twist.
   b. unusual punishment, including self-punishment.

IDENTIFICATION

1. Emulation of skills

   a. one character imitating, taking over, or otherwise acquiring a skill or talent of another character, or trying to do so.

2. Emulation of characteristics

   a. imitating, taking over, or otherwise acquiring a characteristic, quality, or attitude of another character, or trying to do so.

   b. references to one character being like another, the same as another, or merged with another.

3. Regulation of motives or behavior

   a. demands, influence, guidance, prohibitions of one character over another; or the rebelling against these.

   b. self-criticism or self-reflection, on the part of the storyteller or of a character in the story.

   c. justified punishment by parents or authority.

4. Self-esteem through affiliation

   a. success or satisfaction which comes about through association with someone else (peer), or the expressed need for this kind of affiliation.

   b. being part of a special group from which some special pleasure or help derives.

5. Work, delay of gratification

   a. references to a character working.

   b. references to delay, in order to obtain some future gratification.

6. Role differentiation

   a. mention of characters in specific adult roles (non-familial).

7. Moralism

   a. moralistic outcome to story.

   b. justified punishment administered by authority figure (not parents).

2. Assuming that these stories were representative of subjects in the study, what would you conclude about the development and utilization of defense mechanisms from childhood to early adolescence?

SPOTLIGHT

HUMOR*

Freud, in his theory of humor, noted the importance of conflict. Humorous situations involve stimuli that raise arousal (anxiety, tension) and then dispel it. As Freud notes, "The essence of humor is that one spares oneself the affects to which the situation would naturally give it. . . ."

To test this theory, Arthur Shurcliff devised a very interesting experiment. He randomly assigned 36 male students in three treatment groups designed to engender different levels of anxiety.

In the low-anxiety condition, each subject was seen in a room containing three rat cages and was administered a brief questionnaire on attitudes toward small animals. The subject was then told that he would be required to pick up a rat, hold him for 5 seconds, and then put him back. He was also told that the rats were bred to be docile and easy to handle. He was then given a glove with which to hold the rat and instructed to open the cage door and pick up the rat. The task was terminated when he discovered that the rat in the cage was a toy. Following the task, the subject was asked to complete a second questionnaire that, among other questions, assessed his anxiety level (on a 4-point scale) during the task and the humorousness (on a 6-point scale) of the situation.

The procedure was similar for the moderate-and high-anxiety conditions. In the moderate-anxiety condition, there were slides for "blood samples" and a needle next to the cages. Each subject was told to extract a small blood sample from a rat and place it on a slide. The specific directions for the procedure pointed out that the task was easier than it looked. The subject was given a glove and a lab coat and instructed to open the cage door.

In the high-anxiety condition, small bottles and syringes were next to the cages. Each subject was told to extract 2 cubic centimeters of blood from a rat. In following elaborate directions stressing the difficulties involved and warnings that the rat might bite or escape, each subject was told to put on the lab coat and gloves, hold the syringe in one hand, and pick up the rat with the other.

Shurcliff reported significant relationships between humor ratings and the anxiety conditions and between humor ratings and self-reported anxiety. The greater the anxiety, the more humorous the experience was considered.

*Based on material in Shurcliff, A. (1968). Judged humor, arousal, and the relief theory. *Journal of Personality and Social Psychology, 8*(4), 360–363.

NAME _____

DATE _____

DREAM ANALYSIS

Sigmund Freud developed the first comprehensive theory of dreams. According to Freud, dreaming's significance lies in its reflection of intrapsychic forces at work. In fact, he called dreams "the royal road to the unconscious."

Freud distinguished between the text of the dream, called its *manifest* content, and what lay behind the dream, called its *latent* content. He described the task of dream analysis as transforming the manifest dream into the latent one.

To see how this process works, read the following dream and respond to the following questions.

> My husband and I are going to a gala evening. My mother-in-law, who knows I do not have an evening gown, lends me hers, a beautiful white one. My husband has no problems. He has his tails and starched shirt. While we are dressing, I find that the maid has washed the shirts but they are not starched. I show one to my husband, hoping it will do, but it is no good. Then I show him another, and that is no good either. The same thing happens with a third one. My husband says, "I've had it." Everybody goes to the party and we stay at home.
>
> (From *The psychoanalysis of dreams* by Angel Garma. Copyright © 1966 by Angel Garma.
> Reprinted by permission of Times Books, a division of Random House, Inc.)

1. What prior experience(s) may have contributed to this dream?

2. With which aspects of this dream would you most like to have the dreamer associate? Why?

3. Describe the symbolism in this dream.

4. Speculate about the latent content of this dream.

5. What is the wish fulfillment in this dream?

READING
WHAT I MEANT TO SAY*

Michael T. Motley

Editors' Note:

At one time or another, we have all said something we did not intend to say. In addition to the embarrassment we experienced, we may have wondered what prompted this slip of the tongue, or *Freudian slip*. Michael Motley, who has extensively researched this topic, explains this phenomenon.

It happens quite often. Right before an exam a student calls to ask for a postponement, giving one of several familiar excuses. It is easy to be skeptical when this happens, but I recall one occasion when my doubt was underscored with a curious slip of the tongue. The student said that she wanted the postponement because ". . . last night my grandmother lied—I mean died!"

How should I have interpreted her verbal slip? One possibility is that she had fabricated the excuse, and that her awareness of the lie prompted the error. Another possibility is that she was telling the truth but was afraid I might think that she was lying. Yet another is that she might have been feeling repressed guilt about a lie she once told her grandmother. On the other hand, the slip may have had nothing to do with lies; perhaps it was an innocent slip of the tongue in which the first "d" in "died" simply got replaced by an "l" as the result of some sort of linguistic confusion or articulatory fluke.

These interpretations hint at the wide range of explanations that psychologists, linguists and others have given for verbal slips during nearly a century of study. Almost all researchers who have examined the phenomenon agree on one thing, however. Since slips of the tongue, which we all experience from time to time, represent breakdowns in the normally efficient and error-free process of speech, they might provide a sort of window on the mind.

Linguists and cognitive psychologists investigate verbal slips for insights into how the mind processes information (including spoken language) and controls behavior. One discovery has been that slips of the tongue often seem to be the result of competition between similar verbal choices. These aren't conscious and deliberate choices, such as those that accompany delicate social situations, but are the more automatic and instantaneous choices of casual speech. A colleague, for example, once introduced a point with "Is this a rhetorical question perhaps?" when either "perchance" or "perhaps" would have fit his intention.

Almost any time we wish to express a thought, we must choose from several roughly equivalent verbal possibilities. Sometimes competition between these choices, or indecision about them, results in a slip of the tongue. This explanation has an intuitive appeal, at least in the case of some errors.

At a political event a few years ago, for instance, the featured speaker was introduced as being "as American as mother pie and applehood." Presumably, indecision over two equal choices, "apple pie and motherhood" and "motherhood and apple pie," caused the error. It is easy to imagine verbal competition as the source of numerous slips, such as "hairible" instead of "terrible" or "horrible" and "hairline crackture" instead of "hairline fracture" or "hairline crack."

*Motley, M.T. (1987, February). What I meant to say. *Psychology Today*, pp. 24–28. Reprinted with permission from *Psychology Today* magazine. Copyright © 1987 (Sussex Publishers, Inc.).

One reason for such slips could be a lapse in the mental attention normally devoted to resolving competition. Slips of the tongue are more frequent, for example, when we are speaking in public, being interviewed or are confronted with other uncomfortable communication situations. Slips at these times are probably instances of our attention being diverted enough to allow alternate verbal choices to replace intended ones.

There are several ways that verbal competition could cause slips. Some are purely linguistic. When speakers begin to utter one of the choices, they may decide to switch to another after they have passed the point of no return or have uttered a fraction of the first choice. For example, an acquaintance who said "moptimal productivity" might have switched her decision from "maximum" to "optimal" after it was too late to abort the initial "m" of "maximum." But this explanation seems somewhat limited.

A theory known as "spreading activation" offers a more versatile explanation of verbal competition. According to this theory, a person's lexicon, or mental dictionary, is organized so that each word in it is interconnected with other words associated by meaning, sound or grammar—somewhat like the interconnection of points in a complex spider web. When we prepare to speak, the relevant parts of the web are activated, causing reverberation within the system. Activation spreads first to the most closely related words, then to words associated with them and so on. Each word activates an alternate path through the web. The cumulative activation for each word is tallied by checking how often each "point" in the web "vibrates," and the word with the highest accumulated activation (the most vibration, in our web analogy) is selected. Verbal slips would be explained as the result of competing choices that have equal or nearly equal activation levels.

For example, I recently told a colleague who needed information for her son Aaron that she could get it by phoning my wife. I suggested that she "wait for about an hour, because [my wife] is running an Aaron." According to the spreading activation theory, my mental dictionary was receiving activation on the word "Aaron," because he was one of the subjects of the conversation, on "errand" as a topic of the message and on "Aaron," again, because of its association by sound with "errand." Since "Aaron" got a double dose of activation, it won the cumulative-activation competition, so to speak.

Or consider the slip of an older colleague who identified a motion-picture character as "one of the black women in *The Colored Purple*" instead of *The Color Purple*. It is easy to imagine that in this person's mental dictionary, "colored" received activation both as a variation of "color" and as an archaic synonym for "black." Thus, its cumulative activation might have been greater than that of the intended word.

Thus far, spreading activation theorists have not considered the possibility that competing words might be related by something other than meaning, sound or grammar. Sigmund Freud, however, long ago introduced the idea that verbal slips represent the hidden motives and anxieties of the speaker. We still call them "Freudian slips," and, as with the cognitive explanation, there is an intuitive sensibility to Freud's notion, at least for some verbal slips. For example, it would explain a mistake I once made when introduced to a competitor at a job interview. Intending to say "Pleased to meet you," I slipped and said instead "Pleased to beat you."

Until recently, however, Freud's explanation of verbal slips had been dismissed by most contemporary researchers. The relatively few slips that appear to be related to hidden thoughts were said to be linked by mere coincidence.

There were two arguments against the Freudian explanation. First, there was no known cognitive mechanism by which Freudian slips might operate. It is easy to imagine hidden thoughts that might prompt a local newscaster to proclaim to his voluptuous coanchor that "Bill Cosby is one of the breast bite lights on television," but it is quite difficult to explain the mental operations by which his hidden thoughts could have affected his originally intended utterance "best bright lights." Since it was difficult for many of those interested in the subject to imagine how Freudian slips might occur, it was difficult to believe that they did.

The second criticism of Freud's notion of verbal slips was that his theory was untestable. We can hypothesize, for example, that certain hidden thoughts caused a slip I once heard about a camping trip: "Ron often perks Jackie" instead of "Ron often packs jerky." But it has always seemed difficult to devise methods for testing such hypotheses objectively.

Both of these arguments have been tempered, however, with the development, over the past several years, of laboratory methods for studying slips of the tongue and Freudian hypotheses in particular.

Freud claimed that hidden thoughts can influence our choice of words, even in everyday speech without verbal slips. To test this claim, my colleagues and I asked men to read aloud and complete a series of fill-in-the-blank sentences. Half of them did this while being mildly sexually aroused—an attractive and provocatively attired woman administered the experiment—while the other half read and completed the same sentences in the presence of a man.

In line with Freud's suggestion, word choices that related to sex as well as completed the sentence were almost twice as frequent for men who were sexually aroused. For example, to complete the sentence, "The old hillbilly kept his moonshine in big . . ." most men in the nonarousal group answered "vats," "barrels" or "jars," while "jugs" was the overwhelming answer of the aroused group. In another example, given the sentence, "Tension mounted at the end, when the symphony reached its . . ." most of the men in the nonaroused group responded "finale," "conclusion" or "peak," while those in the aroused group were much more likely to answer "climax."

Spreading activation of hidden thoughts could account for these results. Both groups of men probably experienced activation on words that would complete the sentences, but it seems that in the aroused group another set of items—words related to sex and sexy women—was also activated. For those who were aroused, the double-entendre words, "jugs" and "climax," received double doses of activation and were selected. This suggests that hidden thoughts can activate our mental dictionary, much as Freud suggested.

If hidden thoughts can compete to influence deliberate word choices, might they also create competition that leads to slips of the tongue? It is possible to produce slips of the tongue by asking people to read silently pairs of words that are flashed on a screen at one-second intervals, after being instructed that if a buzzer sounds, they are to pronounce aloud the word pair then on the screen. This process can yield very interesting results. After seeing "let double" and "left decimal," for example, an attempt to say "dead level" will sometimes result in the slip "led devil."

My colleagues and I have used a variation of this procedure to test Freud's claim about verbal slips. One group of men performed the word-pair task believing that they were going to receive an electric shock at some point, while another group of men performed the task with mild sexual arousal—again in the form of a provocative female experimenter. For both groups, the lists and the words to be spoken aloud were identical. Each list contained an equal number of words that could result in slips related to electric shocks or to sexy women.

As Freud might have predicted, the two groups made quite different kinds of mistakes. The men expecting an electric shock were much more likely to make slips such as "damn shock" instead of "sham dock," and "cursed wattage" instead of "worst cottage." Those tested in the presence of the female experimenter were more likely to make slips such as "fast passion" instead of "past fashion," and "nude breasts" instead of "brood nests." Also, men who had been found to be more anxious in general about sexual matters made an especially high number of sex-related slips if they were aroused.

Experiments such as these have given support to Freud's claim that hidden thoughts and anxieties can influence verbal slips. Even more importantly, they are consistent with the spreading activation theory that explains competition between cognitively and linguistically similar choices. Apparently, choices can be activated in the network, whether they originate from the message we intend or from hidden thoughts.

While experiments add to our understanding of slips, another issue remains to be settled: Freud claimed that virtually all slips of the tongue derive from unconscious hidden thoughts. If this were true, however, hidden motives would be responsible not only for slips such as that made by a neighbor who approached a female cocktail-party guest saying, "I don't believe we've been properly seduced yet—I mean introduced yet," but for more innocuous slips, such as saying "chee kanes" instead of "key chains," or "coregaty" instead of "category."

Just as the results of experiments make it unreasonable to insist that no slips are Freudian, the spreading activation theory makes it unreasonable to insist that they all are. For many slips of the tongue, the hidden-motive interpretation seems needlessly circuitous. For example, one of three professors at a recent meeting proposed that funding for a special seminar might be available "once we get underground—I mean under way." One might argue that the "underground" slip shows some sort of guilt or surreptitiousness in the speaker's attitude toward the group's objectives. But one might argue, just as easily, the interpretation that "underground" was the innocuous outcome of competition between "once we get under way" and the colloquial "once we get off the ground," with an extra boost on "underground" coming from similarity to a third alternative, "once we're on solid ground," for example.

It seems likely then that the explanation for slips of the tongue lies between the two extremes of those who insist on Freudian interpretations and those who completely exclude them. Most slips probably are the result of verbal competition, with hidden thoughts as the source of the competition in some cases and simple message alternatives providing the competition in others. There is no need to posit hidden motives for slips such as "computer pute-out" instead of "computer printout," or "offewsional" instead of "occasional." With enough imagination, one might hypothesize hidden thoughts behind these slips, but simpler explanations can be found: "Computer printout" probably competed with "printer output," while "occasional" vied with "few."

On the other hand, hidden motives seem much more likely for slips such as that committed by a lecturer who announced his topic as "Fraud's Theories" instead of "Freud's Theories," or the embarrassing reference to an engagement ring as a "garish cheapsake" in lieu of "cherished keepsake." One might dream up competing message choices for these slips, but the most straightforward explanation is competition from hidden thoughts.

For some slips, the derivation will be impossible to determine. I remember being in an especially inelegant diner, for example, and ordering a "chilled grease sandwich" when I meant to order a "grilled cheese sandwich." While I assumed that the slip came from competition with an alternative verbal choice, "cheese sandwich," the waitress assumed that it had originated with a hidden thought, "greasy-spoon diner." Which interpretation is correct? All that can be said is that both are reasonable possibilities.

NAME _____

DATE _____

ACTIVE LEARNING EXERCISE 2.4
PERSONALITY ASSESSMENT*

As Davidson (1987) noted, personality constructs can be difficult to grasp at more than a rudimentary level. Consequently, graphic illustrations of these constructs in people's daily lifestyles can be especially enlightening.

This exercise will give you firsthand, personal experience with a personality scale based on one of Freud's constructs. More information will be provided once you complete the following scale.

Respond to each statement by circling one of the following responses: strongly disagree (**SD**), disagree(**D**), neutral (**N**), agree (**A**), strongly agree (**SA**). Then follow the directions provided at the end of the scale.

	SD	D	N	A	SA
1. I keep careful accounts of the money I spend.	SD	D	N	A	SA
2. I like to think out my own methods rather than use other people's.	SD	D	N	A	SA
3. I find more pleasure in doing things than in planning them.	SD	D	N	A	SA
4. There's nothing more infuriating than people who don't keep appointments.	SD	D	N	A	SA
5. I like to see something solid and substantial for my money.	SD	D	N	A	SA
6. I easily change my mind once I've made a decision.	SD	D	N	A	SA
7. Only a fool with his/her money does not think of the years ahead.	SD	D	N	A	SA
8. I can usually put my hand on anything I want in my room.	SD	D	N	A	SA
9. Waste not, want not: every child should have this imprinted on his/her mind.	SD	D	N	A	SA
10. I continue doing something even when I really know I'm not employing the best method.	SD	D	N	A	SA
11. It is sheepish to follow the dictates of style and fashion.	SD	D	N	A	SA
12. I have a special place for important documents.	SD	D	N	A	SA

*Exercise adapted from Davidson, W. B. (1987). Undergraduate lab project in personality assessment: Measurement of anal character. *Teaching of Psychology, 14*(2), 101–103. Scale from Kline, P. (1968). Obsessional traits, obsessional symptoms and anal eroticism. *British Journal of Medical Psychology, 41*, 299–305. Reprinted by permission.

SCORING

Each response receives a score of 1 through 5. Items 1, 2, 4, 5, 7, 8, 9, 10, 11, and 12 are scored as follows: strongly disagree = 1, disagree = 2, neutral = 3, agree = 4, and strongly agree = 5. Items 3 and 6 are scored in the reverse direction (e.g., strongly disagree = 5, strongly agree = 1).

Total your scores across the 12 items. High scores (maximum score = 60) indicate anal retentive tendencies that are characterized by three traits: frugality, orderliness, and obstinacy/individuality.

Score =

INTERPRETATION

The following table will show how you compare with other college students.

SCORE	PERCENTILE
55	99
52	95
48	90
44	80
42	70
41	60
39	50
37	40
34	30
32	20
31	10
29	5
28	1

1. How well (or poorly) did this scale assess your personality with respect to the three traits mentioned?

2. In what ways might anal retentive traits benefit us in our daily lives?

3. In what ways might they hinder us in our daily lives?

CHAPTER
3

Neo-Freudian and Contemporary Psychoanalytical Perspectives

Introduction

As you might expect, not everyone agreed with all aspects of Freud's theory. Even his followers offered modifications, alternatives, and additions to his approach. Some of the most prominent figures, like Alfred Adler, Carl Jung, and Erik Erikson, were influential in diversifying the psychoanalytic perspective.

The neo-Freudians' most noteworthy contributions included a greater emphasis on the role of environmental forces in personality development and a more flexible view of personality developing throughout the life span.

In this chapter, you will find a blend of readings and activities to give you a fuller view of some of the neo-Freudian and contemporary views of psychoanalysis. You will read a more contemporary, evolutionary interpretation of Freud's concept of repression and a detailed account of Adler's approach in an analysis of *Frankenstein*, as well as cover major concepts from Erik Erikson's, Karen Horney's, and Carl Jung's theories. Further, you will have a chance to assess your current identity status, examine your earlier recollections, and speculate about the impact of your birth order on your personality development.

READING
FRANKENSTEIN: AN ADLERIAN ODYSSEY*

R. John Huber, Joan K. Widdifield, and Charles L. Johnson

Editors' Note:

Alfred Adler was one of the most influential neoanalytical theorists. In his approach to the study of individual personality development, he stressed the importance of the family constellation, as well as such issues as feelings of inferiority, striving for superiority, and social interest. In this article, John Huber, Joan Widdifield, and Charles Johnson utilize these and other aspects of Adler's theory in their detailed analysis of Victor Frankenstein and his creation.

Upon close inspection, *Frankenstein* is not merely the horror thriller as it has been depicted by Hollywood for so many years. Popular film versions portray Frankenstein's creation as a monster who, upon receiving life, mercilessly terrorizes the world. He has few human qualities, and is hardly a character with whom one would empathize. Like many movie versions of novels, the film "Frankenstein" deviates so greatly from the original story that it can barely be recognized beyond a few characters and events. Mary Shelley's classic novel, however, can be viewed as an Adlerian Odyssey depicting the ultimate demise of an individual who has lived a life almost devoid of social interest. In the novel, Dr. Victor Frankenstein was the brilliant scientist who, without help, created life in the laboratory. It will be demonstrated, however, that Frankenstein was a man aspiring to greatness in a socially useless manner. The creation of life is indeed an achievement saved for God; Victor Frankenstein, it will be shown, attempted to compensate for deep-seated inferiority feelings that are common to one with a pampered life-style, by striving to be godlike. Adler (1964) described this unique sort of striving as being characteristic of the compulsive neurotic, who "tries to represent himself . . . as a demigod, who exalts himself above humankind . . ." (p. 117). This grandiose goal along with low social interest rendered his life futile and led to his destruction. Victor Frankenstein, moreover, helped turn his "creation" into a power-craving, self-centered monster by being what Adler would call a neglectful parent.

The being that Frankenstein created, in his attempt to be the first to give humanoid life, was larger, stronger, and more intelligent than humans. The being was superior to human beings in most aspects, but he was a victim of neglect and an organ inferiority, his offensive appearance. Unlike film versions, the "mon-ster" as depicted by Mary Shelley did have human characteristics. Upon receiving life, a poignant child-like description is given of the creation. Like human infants, he had fears, as well as biological and social needs. He, like Adler (1956) said of all humans, had a propensity for social interest and the desire for upward striving. In the beginning of his "life" these characteristics flourished, but through time they were thwarted when he suffered the pain of rejection by society because of his offensive appearance. The being eventually adopted the lifestyle of a neglected child, and his beneficent characteristics were replaced by a striving for power with low social interest. Adler would have predicted the final fate of Victor Frankenstein and his creation. When one pursues a grandiose goal which is almost devoid of social interest as a compensation for inferiority feelings, he and all that is associated with him will be destroyed. Concerning this, Adler stated, "What happened to the earthly life of those who contribute nothing, or who interfered with the developmental process? The answer is: It has disappeared. Nothing from their lives can be found. . . . Their trace on earth is lost forever" (1964, p. 27).

The remainder of this paper discusses how the events leading to the ultimate destruction of the lives of Frankenstein and his humanoid creation originated in inferiority feelings. For Victor Frankenstein it will be shown that his feelings of inferiority were related to a pampered childhood. His pampered life-style rendered him unequal to the life problems [society, work, and love—Eds.] and led him to a useless goal that brought about his demise. The creation's inferiority, it will be shown, stemmed from neglect and organ inferiority, dampening his propensity for social interest and causing him to strive for power over others, ultimately causing his destruction.

*Frankenstein: An Adlerian odyssey by R. John Huber, Joan K. Widdifield, and Charles L. Johnson (1989) in *Individual Psychology*, 45:3, pp. 267–278, reprinted by permission of the authors and the University of Texas Press.

VICTOR FRANKENSTEIN

VICTOR FRANKENSTEIN AS A PARENT

Victor Frankenstein possessed the intelligence and skill to create life, yet at his death he had accomplished little of worth. He had created a humanoid being, but did not take responsibility for his creation's welfare. After his creation received life, Frankenstein abandoned him, shunned his responsibilities, and acted as if the results of his labors would dissolve if he ignored them. Victor Frankenstein enjoyed the thoughts of being the creator of a species, but as one would expect of a pampered child who was striving for grandiosity, he responded to the demands of reality by retreating. When the being comes to life it is clear to the reader that Frankenstein's situation is not objectively hopeless. There were a gamut of constructive courses of action that Frankenstein could have chosen, but he chose to flee from his problem.

One may wonder why a man with no lack of creativity and intelligence would be at a loss to think of a common sense solution to the challenge of dealing with the life he had created. As a "parent" he proved irresponsible and indifferent to the needs of his "child." This irresponsibility and neglect is what ultimately brought about his own destruction when his creation sought revenge by destroying him and his family. The height of his neglect for his creation was his lack of empathy expressed when he would not create a mate for his "son," even when he saw his created offspring's desperate desire for companionship. That, in a sense, was Frankenstein's last chance to save the creation and himself from a wretched existence revolving around revenge and hate. However, Frankenstein's refusal to create a female mate for the being can be regarded as a vestige of social interest because he feared having more than one being in existence that would be superior to humans in strength and intellect. He feared that they would band together with their offspring and terrorize the world; from this view it can be regarded as a socially interested decision.

From the moment when his creation realized that he could not draw forth empathy even from his creator, he resorted to striving for power and revenge. The creation inflicted vengeance on Frankenstein by killing his loved ones. The being followed Frankenstein, and as he vowed, made Frankenstein's life miserable.

At the close of his life, despondency and destitution characterized Frankenstein's existence. On his deathbed on a lost arctic explorer ship, his only goal was the destruction of the creation. Again, one must question why his life resulted in such futility. He had the ability to solve many medical problems as evidenced by his success in creating life. Yet at the end of his life he had no significant achievements to his credit; his contributions could have been significant to humanity. Why does his life result in a chaotic struggle to overcome something that he created? Why would Frankenstein allow his life work to be hindered and his potential for contribution to go untapped because of his stoically remiss and nonempathic attitude toward his creation, his fellow man?

As previously mentioned, Frankenstein displayed the behavior of a pampered child, someone who wished to be the center of attention. The life-style and schema of apperception of a pampered child that he developed left him dependent on others.

THE PAMPERED LIFE-STYLE

Adler (1956) contended that pampering is likely to result in increased inferiority feelings, unrealistic self-centered compensatory goals, a lack of social interest, a consideration of others as enemies, and inadequate preparation to meet the three life problems. An examination of Victor Frankenstein's life reveals considerable evidence of a pampered upbringing.

For the first five years of his life, Frankenstein was an only child. This is the age when, according to Adler (1956, 1964), one's view of the world is established. Frankenstein referred to his relationship with his parents in his early life as beneficent. More significantly, however, he stated that he was his parents' "innocent and helpless creature bestowed on them by heaven" (p. 32), their "plaything and idol" (p. 32), and their "only care" (p. 32).

After five years of being the recipient of their "inexhaustible stores of affection from a very mine of love" (p. 32), he was dethroned from his exalted presence by Elizabeth, their adopted daughter. As might be expected of a pampered child, when Victor Frankenstein's mother told him that Elizabeth would be his "pretty present" (p. 34), he took her words literally and perceived Elizabeth as his possession. His response to Elizabeth's adoption was characteristic of a pampered child in that he saw it in terms of being beneficial to himself.

All through his life Frankenstein did not cultivate friendships easily as evidenced by his having only one friend, Henry Clerval, from his home. He felt anxious when going to a new place where he knew no one; going away to college was a test of Victor Frankenstein's social interest. At the University, his feelings of inferiority and pampered life-style were manifested.

> I, who had ever been surrounded by amiable companions, continually engaged in endeavoring to bestow mutual pleasure—I was now alone. In the university wither I was going I must form my own friends and be my own protector. My life had hitherto been remarkably secluded and domestic, and this had given me invincible repugnance to new countenances. I loved my brothers, Elizabeth, and Clerval; these were "old familiar faces," but I believe myself totally unfit for company of strangers (p. 43).

According to Adler (1956), one's low social interest and inferiority can go unexpressed and may never emerge unless tested, and to the person who has incipient inferiority feelings, tasks of all kinds appear difficult. For Frankenstein, having to adapt to a new environment and having to develop new friendships seemed intolerable. He stated, ". . . it was my temper to avoid a crowd, and to attach myself fervently to a few. I was indifferent, therefore, to my school fellows . . ." (p. 35). In his scientific endeavors he refused to seek guidance and consultation from his professors. Perhaps the feelings of inferiority evoked from being in this situation contributed to his need for the godlike goal of creating life, compensating for his inferiority and fulfilling his need for dominating others. Concerning this, Adler (1931, p. 53) stated, "To some degree or other, every neurotic restricts his field of action, his contacts with the whole situation. He tries to keep at a distance the three real confronting problems of life and confines himself to circumstances in which he feels able to dominate . . . the goal is the same—to gain a feeling of superiority without working to improve the situation."

In addition to feeling inferior when confronted with having to acquire new friends, Frankenstein was afraid of meeting the problem of love. His field of action was confined to the family circle until he was an adult. According to Adler (1931), it would not be uncommon to find sexual strivings of a sheltered person such as this to be elaborated within these limits. From feelings of insecurity, his interests remained with the few people with whom he was most familiar. In Alder's view, (1931, p. 59), one who is sheltered like this "fears that with others he would not be able to dominate in the accustomed way." In view of Adler's observations, it is significant that Victor Frankenstein married his adopted sister, Elizabeth. In marrying Elizabeth, Frankenstein attempted to maintain the atmosphere that he had at home, that is, of being pampered and treated like a god. For him, marrying Elizabeth was another self-serving behavior with the goal of maintaining his status as a child at home to his adult life. Frankenstein used every opportunity available to enhance his self-esteem.

ENHANCING SELF-ESTEEM

One of the most glaring examples of Frankenstein's desire to remain in a dominant position is that he kept the knowledge of the "monster" to himself. When his creation came to life, Frankenstein immediately perceived him as a horrid beast. Why then did he not tell others, such as his professors and the local authorities, so that a common sense solution involving the world at large could have been attempted? His private knowledge, however, gave him a feeling of omnipotence because he enjoyed the feeling that he was the sole cause of all events that transpired. Telling his professors, his friend, or the authorities about the creation would not have been concurrent with his goal of viewing himself as the center and cause of all activity.

Withholding the knowledge of the creation, in addition to boosting his self-esteem, gave Frankenstein an excuse for avoiding the problems of life. If he constantly concerned himself with the whereabouts and activities of his creation, if he suffered pain with every crime the creation committed, he could thus excuse himself from useful activity. Frankenstein thus exhibited what Adler (1956) would call the hesitating attitude by concentrating on his suffering and sensitivity.

> We will observe the so-called pleasure in suffering which finally gives the neurotic a feeling that he is unique and godlike. . . . These good intentions which may appear as feelings of guilt, are absolute; they signify nothing as to any real change in the patient . . . he makes a great display of his feelings of guilt; he has the assurance that by acknowledging his guilt and raising trivialities to a rank of importance and dignity, he can appear to be more genteel and more honest than any of his fellows (Adler, 1964, pp. 117–118).

OVERSENSITIVITY AND ENEMY TERRITORY

Throughout his life, Frankenstein displayed the typical pampered behavior of oversensitivity. "Extreme discouragement, continuing doubt, hypersensitivity, impatience, exaggerated emotion and phenomena of retreat" (Adler, 1964, p. 98) are all manifestations of the pampered lifestyle. Even before the creation received life, Frankenstein did not have a sense of pride in his undertaking, which would have been a natural feeling had he been employed cooperatively with others in contributing to the progress of humanity. Instead he had only negative feelings. As Adler would predict of a pampered child: "I became nervous to a most painful degree; the fall of a leaf startled me, and I shunned my fellow creatures as if I had been guilty of a crime" (p. 55). Frankenstein felt that he was in enemy territory, a feeling of being attacked from all sides. According to Adler (1964), people who feel they are in enemy country are those who do not cooperate with others or feel at home in the world. These persons always sense malevolence in their environment. "I shunned the face of man" (p. 90); "I abhorred society" (p. 160); "sometimes I thought that the fiend followed me and might expedite my remissness by murdering my companion" (p. 163). When the creation was at large, Frankenstein's feelings of being attacked from all sides increased. He had the threat, imagined or real, of being attacked by his creation as well as guilt feelings from any crimes the being committed. As quoted above, he reached a point where he could not raise his eyes to meet those of others, and he was always afraid of being followed by his creation. Here Shelley poignantly depicted Frankenstein's feelings by citing Coleridge's *Ancient Mariner*, "Like one who on a lonely road, doth walk in fear and dread and, having once turned round, walks on, and turns no more his head; because he knows a frightful fiend doth close behind him tread" (p. 58).

Since Victor Frankenstein felt inferior and lacked connectedness with others, it is no surprise that he pursued a grandiose goal.

GRANDIOSE GOAL

According to Adler, everyone is born with an innate upward striving and the propensity for social interest. In striving to be more, every individual has a final fiction or goal of what he or she perceives as perfection. Ideally this goal, according to Adler, should be imbued with social interest. He stated, "The goal of perfection must contain the goal of ideal community, because everything we find valuable in life, what exists and what will remain, is forever a product of social feeling" (1964, p. 35).

Victor Frankenstein's striving was useless and godlike. He chose to use his talents of intellect and skill for enhancing his self-esteem and achieving dominance. During the time in which he was creating his being, Frankenstein endured illness from improper rest and diet, neglected and avoided all social contact, and lost all appreciation for beauty that surrounded him. The idea of being godlike, a creator of life, however, spurred him on, "No one can conceive of the feeling which bore me onwards, like a hurricane, in the first enthusiasm of success . . . a new species will bless me as its creator and source; many happy and excellent natures would owe their being to me. No father could claim the gratitude of his child so completely as I should deserve theirs" (p. 52).

Frankenstein was clearly striving for a useless goal of perfection in that it was not a path for the advancement of all, although he obviously had the ability to contribute in the field of medical science. In Adler's words, the "goal of godlikeness comes out in the desire to know everything, to possess universal wisdom, or in the wish to perpetuate our life" (1931, p. 61). Frankenstein expressed his desire and pleasure in possessing "universal wisdom. . . . I was surprised that among so many men of genius who had directed their inquiries towards the same science, that I alone should be reserved to discover so astonishing a secret" (p. 51).

It is interesting that Frankenstein, while anticipating his godlike role, referred to himself as a "father" and to his creation as a "child." In the Judeo-Christian tradition, God is often referred to as *abba*, i.e., father or daddy, and people are his children. However, when Frankenstein realized that the creation would not benefit him, he abandoned the being and severed the ties that bind father and child; in essence, Victor Frankenstein was a neglectful parent.

Throughout Frankenstein's life there is a consistent theme of inferiority and compensatory behavior. Adler (1964) contended that the greater the feelings of inferiority, the more grandiose the goal. As Adler (1956) stated, "An increased insecurity feeling in childhood causes a higher and more inalterable goal setting, a striving which goes beyond human measure" (p. 245). Frankenstein's inferiority feelings must have been overwhelming as he struggled in isolation and without guidance to obtain power over death and the ability to create life.

FRANKENSTEIN, A GENIUS?

One may ask, "With his talent, intellect, and ability to create life, isn't Frankenstein a genius?" According to Adler (1931), genius is defined as usefulness for all. Contributions must have common meaning which others can share and accept as valid. When one's goal has a private meaning, it is safeguarded against challenge. If a goal makes only private sense, there is no way to assess its value. Persons of genius are those who have contributed to an enriched humanity. Poets, artists, philosophers, engineers, and composers are some examples of geniuses. "There can be no question that geniuses have been the most cooperative of all human beings" (Adler, 1931, p. 284). According to Adler's definition, Victor Frankenstein, although intellectually gifted, was not a genius. His goal had private meaning; it was an expression of personal superiority; and, most of all, it lacked connectedness with others. His achievements were not those of a genius—long-lasting and beneficial for all. They were evidence of his grandiosity; destructive and short-lived to the point that they brought about the demise of his life. According to Adler (1931, p. 9), "Life means . . . to contribute to the whole." Life goals are expressed only by achievements, not professed motives, i.e., "By their fruits, ye shall know them" (Matthew 7:16). This biblical quote expresses Adler's contentions. In Frankenstein's life, the events that occurred as a result of his work can be considered the fruits of his labor by which he can be known. Frankenstein attempted to create a humanoid with no other intention except to be exalted. As Adler would predict, these self-centered motives brought his downfall. A closer look at Frankenstein's creation will reveal the results of his self-centeredness in bringing life into the world.

THE CREATION

PROPENSITY FOR SOCIAL INTEREST AND DESIRE FOR UPWARD STRIVING

The creation who at the end of the novel acted like the Hollywood depiction of the "monster" is the epitome of what Adler would term a "neglected child with an organ inferiority." According to Adler (1956), everyone is born with a propensity for social interest and the need for upward striving. The creation, just like any other human, displayed a strong desire for fellowship. His upward striving was expressed in the beginning of his "life" by his interest in learning. The creation found safety in a hovel connected to a cottage. It was there that he was socialized vicariously by watching the cottagers. From their good examples, he developed empathy, sensitivity, and a desire to form relationships with the cottagers whom he grew to love from afar. His determination to learn the language of the cottagers reflected his upward striving as well as his social interest. According to Adler, "Language itself is a common creation of mankind, the result of social interest" (1931, p. 255). With language one can connect with others; understanding is achieved only with a common language because understanding is a common, not a private, endeavor.

As the creation learned about the cottagers, he grew to empathize with them: "The gentle manners and beauty of the cottagers greatly endeared them to me: when they were unhappy, I felt depressed; when they rejoiced, I sympathized in the joys" (p. 113). The creation wept with sensitivity when he observed displays of affection, heard of injustices to mankind, or heard beautiful music. As time went on, he developed a consciousness of his own situation. He became aware of his organ inferiority when he saw himself in the reflection of a pool: ". . . when I became fully convinced that I was in reality the monster that I am, I was filled with the bitterest sensations of despondence and mortification. Alas! I did not yet entirely know the fatal effects of this miserable deformity" (p. 114).

NEGLECT AND ORGAN INFERIORITY

The being became very conscious of his social estrangement. This led to questions about his origin and the beginnings of his resentment toward his "father." "But where were my friends and relations? No father had watched my infant days. No mother had blessed me with smiles and caresses" (p. 122).

The creation became increasingly aware of his father's neglect when he read *Paradise Lost* which he found outside of his hovel. By comparing Adam's situation to his own, the creation developed hateful, inferiority feelings toward himself and resentment toward his as-yet-unknown creator. Adam lived a blissful, happy life, blessed and protected by his creator. Adam was given a wife, a mate of his own species with whom to empathize and share love; by contrast, the creation had none of these. His creator abandoned him. "He had abandoned me, and in the bitterness of my heart I cursed him" (p. 132). In addition to being rejected the being was unable to make connections with others because of his organ inferiority.

The creation's greatest desire was to have relationships with others, a further expression of his propensity toward social interest. This need was thwarted by his offensive appearance; he was treated like a monster by those he met. He described himself with such words as "solitary and abhorred" (p. 131) and "wretched outcast" (p. 131). His only desire was to have a bond with another. "Let me see that I excite the sympathy of some existing thing" (p. 147). With this need thwarted and his feelings of inferiority heightened, the creation turned to revenge and power as a form of compensatory striving: ". . . if I cannot inspire love, I will cause fear" (p. 147).

One can hardly help empathizing with the creation when, after a year of admiring and loving the cottagers from afar, he was rejected when he tried to gain their acceptance. For months he carefully planned for the day that he would attempt to endear himself to the cottagers by presenting himself first to the blind old man who lived in the cottage who would not be affected by his appearance. He envisioned telling his whole story to the old man while the others were out. The being anticipated with rapture the old man's relaying his story to the others and his acceptance by all: ". . . my heart yearned to be known by these amiable creatures; to see their sweet looks directed toward me with affection was the utmost limit of my ambition. . . . I required kindness and sympathy; but I did not believe myself utterly unworthy of it" (p. 132). In actuality, however, before the being had finished telling his story to the old man, the rest of the family entered. They were frightened by his hideous appearance and immediately drove him off. From this time all of the creation's attempts at connecting with others were thwarted.

STRIVING FOR POWER AND REVENGE

Striving for superiority is an inherent trait in everyone which is directed by social interest in the well-adjusted individual. When there are feelings of inferiority and a lack of social interest, this striving can be generated into striving for personal power. Self-aggrandizement via power became the being's mode for striving for superiority. When the being met Frankenstein, he told his creator the whole story of his life. With one final attempt to find happiness through social connection, the being begged Frankenstein to create a mate for him: "I am alone and miserable; man will not associate with me; but one as deformed and horrible as myself would not deny herself to me" (p. 145). "You must create a female for me with whom I can live in the interchange of those sympathies necessary for my being" (p. 146). When Frankenstein refused his request, fearing that the being and a mate would wreak havoc on the world at large, the being adjured him: "I am malicious because I am miserable" (p. 146).

Frankenstein finally agreed to undertake the task of creating a mate for the being. When he was working in his laboratory, he was overwhelmed by thoughts of what could happen if a race of "devils" like the being would be propagated. With these thoughts, and perhaps a vestige of social interest, he destroyed all of his work.

From this time the being's sole purpose in life was to seek revenge and the death of his creator. "Shall each man find a wife for his bosom, and each beast have a mate, and I be alone? I had feelings of affection, and they were requited by detestation and scorn" (p. 168). The being followed Frankenstein and, one by one, brutally murdered his loved ones. At the end of both their lives, the goal of Frankenstein and his creation was mutual, i.e., each wished to destroy the other. Consequently, when Victor Frankenstein finally died from exhaustion and grief, after chasing the monster for thousands of miles, the being no longer had a goal in life. Before the being took his own life, he expressed a final vestige of social interest; he still yearned for companionship, "still I desired love and fellowship, and I was still spurned" (p. 220).

CONCLUSION

As Adler stated many times, "we refuse to recognize the isolated individual." This is to say that all behavior occurs in a social context. It is significant to note, therefore, that the selfish striving of Victor Frankenstein destroyed not one life, but many.

REFERENCES

ADLER, A. (1956). *The individual psychology of Alfred Adler*. H. L. Ansbacher & R. R. Ansbacher (Eds.). New York: Basic Books.

ADLER, A. (1958). *What life should mean to you*. New York: Capricorn. (Originally published in 1931).

ADLER, A. (1964). *Superiority and social interest*. H. L. Ansbacher & R. R. Ansbacher (Eds.). Evanston, IL: Northwestern University Press.

HUBER, R. J. (1984). Adlerian theory and its application to The Catcher In The Rye—Holden Caulfield. In J. T. Natoli (Ed.), *Psychological perspectives on literature*. Hamden, CT: Archon.

JUNG, C. G. (1953). *Two essays on analytical psychology*. H. Read, M. Fordha, & G. Adler (Eds.). New York: Pantheon. (Originally published in 1912.)

SHELLEY, M. W. (1965). *Frankenstein: A modern Prometheus*. New York: Dell.

SPOTLIGHT
MOVING AGAINST*

Horney described three neurotic styles: moving toward people, moving against people, and moving away from people, that develop during childhood as attempts to deal with anxiety, and continue to influence adult behavior. To examine the moving against style, Avshalom Caspi, Glen Elder, and Daryl Bem designed an intriguing study to address the question: "Do ill-tempered children become ill-tempered adults?"

Using previously collected data from the Berkeley Guidance Study, they identified children who exhibited a pattern of temper tantrums in childhood. Since the Berkeley Study was initiated over 50 years ago, these researchers were able to trace the continuities and consequences of the "moving against" style well into adulthood.

Childhood data were obtained from clinical interviews with the children's mothers. Children were classified as ill-tempered or even-tempered based on the *severity* and *frequency* of temper tantrums.

These children were later interviewed as adults, at age 30 and age 40. Detailed information was obtained on their education, work, marriage, and parenthood. Additional data on their marital and parenting roles were obtained from interviews with their spouses and teenage children.

Life-course continuities in the moving against behavior style were noted for both men and women. Men who were ill-tempered as children were judged to be more undercontrolled, irritable, and moody, and less ambitious, productive, and dependable as adults than their even-tempered peers. They experience lower occupational status in comparison to even-tempered peers, and even downward occupational mobility in comparison to the occupational status of their fathers. They also have more erratic work lives (e.g., more unemployment), and a higher divorce rate than even-tempered peers.

There were no significant relationships between childhood and adult ratings of temperament in women. However, interviewer data indicated that ill-tempered girls become ill-tempered women. They more frequently married men with lower occupational status than their even-tempered peers. There was a greater tendency for them to divorce, and, even if they did not divorce, to experience more marital conflict and more dissatisfaction with their marriage. They were also described by their husbands and children as less adequate, more ill-tempered mothers.

*Based on material in Casper, A., Elder, G. H., Jr., & Bem, D. J. (1987). Moving against the world: Life-course patterns of explosive children. *Developmental Psychology, 23*, 308–313.

NAME _____

DATE _____

ACTIVE LEARNING EXERCISE 3.1

BIRTH ORDER*

1. List the order of birth of all children (including yourself) in your family.

2. How did your position in the family affect your life?

*Based on Parrott, L. (1992). Earliest recollections and birth order: Two Alderian exercises. *Teaching of Psychology, 19*, 40–42.

3. How does your position continue to affect you today?

4. After identifying which category you fall into (i.e., first born, middle born, or last born), explain how you might be different if you were in each of the other two positions.

In his theory of individual psychology, Alfred Adler emphasized the importance of family constellation or birth order on the formation of personality. He noted a number of differences among the oldest, middle, and youngest children in the family.

First-born children find themselves in a unique position—temporarily. They enjoy a position of privilege and receive a great deal of attention. But, they are eventually "dethroned" with the birth of siblings. As a result, they may seek to regain this attention through exceptional achievements.

Middle children are used to sharing attention. They are in continual competition with older siblings and always striving to catch up. This engenders a sense of restlessness—a continual striving to outdo others—often at the expense of a sense of inner harmony and contentment.

Youngest children cannot be dethroned; they will always be the babies of the family. They are the most pampered and are likely to be more dependent on others. They may try to be unique and different because accomplishment has not come easy—they are younger, weaker, and less experienced than everyone in their immediate environment.

How do your experiences compare to these descriptions?

NAME _____

DATE _____

ACTIVE LEARNING EXERCISE 3.2
EARLY RECOLLECTIONS*

Before reading further, write out a detailed account of your earliest memory.

*Based on Parrott, L. (1992). Earliest recollections and birth order: Two Adlerian exercises. *Teaching of Psychology, 19*, 40–42.

Consider the following questions (Parrott, 1992, p. 41) in examining your early recollections.

a. Who is present in your early recollection?

b. How are different people portrayed (basic thoughts and feelings)?

c. What is the world like (e.g., friendly, hostile, depressing, exciting)?

d. What is your role or behavior?

e. What is the outcome of your behavior?

f. What is your primary social attitude (i.e., I or we)?

g. What is your dominant emotion (e.g., happy, worried, fearful, proud, guilty)?

h. What is your primary motive (e.g., to help, to gain attention, to exert power)?

i. What are the underlying themes?

Adler (1959) considered early recollections "the most trustworthy way of exploring personality" (p. 92) "because they often encapsulate a person's life theme or script" (Parrott, 1992, p. 40). As Parrott (1992) noted, in contrast to "Freud's belief that the past determines the future, Adler believed that the present determines the past" (p. 40). More specifically, Adler (1958) noted:

> There are no "chance memories." Out of the incalculable number of impressions which meet an individual, he must choose to remember only those which he feels, however darkly, to have a bearing on his situation. (p. 73)

Therefore, "if people live their lives believing that others are always trying to humiliate them, the memories they are likely to recall will be interpreted as humiliating experiences." (Parrott, 1992, p. 41)

Your responses to the questions above should shed some light on your life-style—that is, your view of yourself, your role in life, and the world in general.

REFERENCES

ADLER, A. (1958). *What life should mean to you.* New York: Capricorn.

ADLER, A. (1959). *The practice and theory of individual psychology.* Totowa, NJ: Littlefield Adams.

PARROTT, L. (1992). Earliest recollections and birth order: Two Adlerian exercises. *Teaching of Psychology, 19,* 40–42.

SPOTLIGHT
JUNGIAN TYPOLOGY*

Jung proposed the idea that people could be divided into two fundamental attitude types (extraverts and introverts) and four psychological functions (sensing, intuiting, thinking, and feeling). Combining the extraversion and introversion dimensions with each of the four functions yields eight personality types.

As part of a series of studies, Rae Carlson and Nissin Levy examined the "ideal type" for social service volunteers—Jung's extraverted intuitive type, "direct responsiveness to others and an intrinsic enjoyment of interpersonal relationships, an empathetic, nonjudging attitude toward others; and sufficient optimism about the possibilities for growth and about one's possible effectiveness as an instrument of change" (pp. 570–571).

They matched a group of volunteers at a halfway house for disturbed adolescents with a group of nonvolunteers and administered the Myers-Briggs Type Indicator (a self-report inventory developed to measure Jung's typology).

They found that 70% of the volunteers compared to only 10% of the nonvolunteers were extraverted intuitive types.

*Based on material in Carlson, R., & Levy, N. (1973). Studies of Jungian typology: I. Memory, social perception, and social action. *Journal of Personality, 41*, 559–576.

NAME _____

DATE _____

ACTIVE LEARNING EXERCISE 3.3

IDENTITY*

Erik Erikson proposed a theory of psychosocial development that progressed through eight stages—each important for the development of a dimension of personality (e.g., trust versus mistrust, identity versus role diffusion, generativity versus stagnation). According to Erikson, each stage reflects a conflict involving emerging personal needs and social demands. While crisis is inevitable, its positive or negative resolution has an impact on future development.

The following questionnaire was designed by Rhona Ochse and Cornelis Plug* to assess Erikson's fifth stage of development—identity versus role diffusion. It should give you an idea of where you stand in comparison to your peers with respect to resolution of the crisis.

The following questions are presented in the form of statements. Indicate the extent to which each statement applies to you by circling one of the following responses: never (**N**), occasionally (**O**), fairly often (**FO**), or very often (**VO**).

	N	O	FO	VO
1. I wonder what sort of person I really am.	___	___	___	___
2. People seem to change their opinion of me.	___	___	___	___
3. I feel certain about what I should do with my life.	___	___	___	___
4. I feel uncertain as to whether something is morally right or wrong.	___	___	___	___
5. Most people seem to agree about what sort of person I am.	___	___	___	___
6. I feel my way of life suits me.	___	___	___	___
7. My worth is recognized by others	___	___	___	___
8. I feel freer to be my real self when I am away from those who know me very well.	___	___	___	___
9. I feel that what I am doing in life is not really worthwhile.	___	___	___	___
10. I feel I fit in well in the community in which I live.	___	___	___	___
11. I feel proud to be the sort of person I am.	___	___	___	___
12. People seem to see me very differently from the way I see myself.	___	___	___	___
13. I feel left out.	___	___	___	___
14. People seem to disapprove of me.	___	___	___	___
15. I change my ideas about what I want from life.	___	___	___	___
16. I am unsure as to how people feel about me.	___	___	___	___
17. My feelings about myself change.	___	___	___	___
18. I feel I am putting on an act or doing something for effect.	___	___	___	___
19. I feel proud to be a member of the society in which I live.	___	___	___	___

*Ochse, R., & Plug, C. (1986). Cross-cultural investigation of the validity of Erikson's theory of personality development. *Journal of Personality and Social Psychology, 50*, 1240–1252. Copyright © 1986 by the American Psychological Association. Reprinted with permission.

Each response receives a score of 1 through 4. Items 3, 5, 6, 7, 10, 11, and 19 are scored as follows: never = 1, occasionally = 2, fairly often = 3, and very often = 4. Items 1, 2, 4, 8, 9, 12, 13, 14, 15, 16, 17, and 18 are scored in the reverse direction (e.g., never = 4, very often = 1).

Total your score across the 19 items.   Score =

We have found a mean of 59 and a standard deviation of 6 among college students enrolled in personality courses. The following table will allow you to compare your progress toward achieving a sense of identity to other college students.

SCORE	PERCENTILE
70	95
67	90
64	80
62	70
61	60
59	50
57	40
55	30
53	20
50	10
48	5

SPOTLIGHT
INTIMACY VERSUS ISOLATION*

Erikson's sixth psychosexual stage refers to the crisis of young adulthood centering on intimacy versus isolation. The major task of this stage is to establish lasting, satisfying intimate relationships.

Jacob Orlofsky designed an intricate study to examine more systematically Erikson's notions about intimacy. Using a semistructured interview technique to evaluate the presence or absence of close relationships with peers, commitment to an enduring heterosexual love relationship, and depth of relationships, he determined five types of resolution of this intimacy crisis: intimate, preintimate, stereotyped, pseudointimate, and isolate.

The subjects were forty-one male college students who were contacted by telephone and invited to participate in a psychological study of friendship in college students. Each subject was instructed to bring a close friend or spouse, who would be his partner in the experiment.

Each subject was interviewed and asked to complete a 115-item, two-choice questionnaire tapping a variety of content areas relevant to how he viewed himself and the world. [An example of a true-false item is "My feelings are not easily hurt." An example of a two-choice question is "Usually when I am depressed I would rather (a) be with friends who will sympathize with me or cheer me up, (b) be by myself."]

The students and their partners were asked to answer the questions first for themselves and then to predict how their partners would respond to the questions.

Significant differences were found among the intimacy statuses in subjects' accuracy and partners' accuracy in predicting responses of the other. Higher accuracy was found in more intimate relationships. The author determined that intimacy was related to two factors: sensitivity to the innermost thoughts and feelings of one's partner and the willingness to share one's private thoughts and feelings.

*Based on material in Orlofsy, J. L. (1976). Intimacy status: Relationship to interpersonal perception. *Journal of Youth and Adolescence, 5*, 73–88.

THE EVOLUTIONARY FUNCTIONS OF REPRESSION AND THE EGO DEFENSES*

Randolph M. Nesse

Editors' Note:

Scientists with an evolutionary perspective have been searching for explanations of why the human mind is so complex. Randolph Nesse applies this evolutionary approach to the psychoanalytical concept of repression and the ego defenses. He addresses such questions as: Why did natural selection shape such a complex apparatus? Does the capacity for repression offer special advantages over a simpler system? Why are there so many defenses, and why are they so elaborate?

The fact of repression is at the very core of psychodynamics. It must be the starting point for a consideration of the evolutionary functions of psychodynamic capacities. It remains an anomalous and awkward concept that has kept psychoanalysis apart from the rest of science. Attempts to understand it from an evolutionary perspective might promote the links that psychoanalysts have long sought with biology. It might convince many people who remain skeptical about the whole idea of repression, and who are thus unable to benefit from psychodynamic theories of human behavior.

. . .

A PROPOSAL ABOUT REPRESSION

Evolutionary biologists have developed a relatively specific proposal about the function of repression, but they started, not from clinical knowledge about repression, but from studies of animal relationships and communication. Whenever animals assist each other by exchanges of resources or favors, an individual who can gain a tiny advantage with every exchange will have a reproductive advantage over the individual who is exploited. Wherever a communication system has evolved, there will also be opportunities to increase fitness by the use of deception. Indeed, the more carefully biologists look, the more extensive and exquisite are the systems of deception they find. A dramatic example is the ability of predatory fireflies to mimic the light flash pattern of a female of another species (Lloyd, 1986). The alluring flashes draw males who are looking for mates. A male who cannot detect the deception is devoured; one with better discrimination skills escapes to reproduce with a female of his own species. This causes rapid selection for ability to detect such deceptions, which, in turn, causes strong selection for the ability of the predatory fireflies to deceive still better. The escalating spiral of selection for deceptive abilities and abilities to detect deception is very much like an arms race—there is no winning, only the evolution of more and more complex and costly but essential systems.

This has suggested to biologists that humans should have extensive capacities for deceiving each other. The crucial next step has been taken by Alexander (1975, 1979, 1987) and Trivers (1976, 1985). Each has argued that being aware of one's own motives might make it difficult to hide them adequately and that the capacity for repression may, therefore, offer a selective advantage by increasing the ability to deceive others about the pursuit of covert selfish motives. Thus, people who can self-deceptively believe themselves to be altruistic while they are, in fact, pursuing selfish motives will have higher Darwinian fitness, on the average, than people who are consciously aware of their real motives. In isolation, this idea seems bizarre, and unworthy of consideration. In the context of modern evolutionary biology, however, it is a short and natural extension of current ideas. . . .

. . . Biological traits require both a proximate explanation of anatomy and physiology and also an evolutionary explanation (sometimes called an ultimate explanation) of the selective forces that have shaped them to their present form. Recognition of the need for two separate kinds of explanations for biological phenomena is a broad conceptual advance, relatively unappreci-

* Nesse, R. M. (1990). The evolutionary functions of repression and the ego defenses. *The Journal of the American Academy of Psychoanalysis*, 18 (2), 260–285. Reprinted with permission.

ated in psychology, the history of which is detailed in Mayr's (1982) *Growth of Biological Thought*. . . . Mayr describes biology as two related but distinct areas of inquiry:

> . . . Proximate causes relate to the function of an organism and its parts as well as its development, from functional morphology down to biochemistry. Evolutionary, historical, or ultimate causes, on the other hand, attempt to explain why an organism is the way it is. Organisms, in contrast to inanimate objects, have two different sets of causes because organisms have a genetic program. . . . (pp. 67, 68)

For example, a complete explanation of a firefly's glow requires both a proximate explanation of how the glow organ works (its anatomy, physiology, and regulatory mechanisms), and also an evolutionary explanation of why the glow apparatus was shaped by natural selection (it increases fitness by serving the function of locating mates). Psychiatry and psychology have generally only sought proximate causes (Nesse, 1984, 1987), but this is about to change dramatically as more and more scientists recognize the major advances that an evolutionary perspective has brought to the field of animal behavior. A proximate explanation of repression will require understanding of mental function at many levels of organization—brain anatomy, neural structure and function, and cognition and the mechanisms of psychodynamics. But even if the wiring and anatomic details of every neuron were known, and psychological mechanisms were described in detail, a separate evolutionary explanation for the existence of repression would still be necessary.

. . . Evolutionary explanations of a trait are based on forces of selection in the past. The functions of a trait result in higher than average Darwinian fitness, but no goal directedness is implied. It is simply that those organisms who survive and reproduce the most effectively end up passing on more of their genes.

. . . It is perfectly legitimate to try to understand the evolutionary functions and origins of all biological traits, including psychological ones, and this often is best accomplished by assuming that they serve some specific functions, and then seeing if this conjecture parsimoniously accounts for the evidence and makes new predictions that turn out to be correct.

In the specific case of the capacity for repression, there are several reasons to think that it is not an epiphenomenon or a result of drift or other happenstance. Repression is complex, it is consistently present in people, and it is intimately connected with behaviors crucial to reproductive success. Though not foolproof, these criteria make it more likely that repression was shaped by natural selection.

. . .

DETERMINATES OF HUMAN REPRODUCTIVE SUCCESS

Before addressing repression and the defenses, we must consider the factors that determine human reproductive success. Strength, speed, and ability to resist infections are all important to survival, and therefore to Darwinian fitness. But, Darwinian fitness is determined entirely by reproductive success of the self and kin; survival is important only as it contributes to this (Nesse, 1988). Thus, it is no surprise that psychic energy is fundamentally sexual in character, that sexual thoughts are pervasive in human mental life, and that sexual pleasure is intense. In the concept of libido, Freud remarkably anticipated a perspective that has come to dominate evolutionary thinking only in recent decades. Reproduction is crucial to fitness, but what specific factors determine human reproductive success? General robustness and physical skills are important, but far more important is the ability to conduct relationships. Alexander (1989) has argued this at length and the following section depends substantially on his work. People evolved in small groups and their social skills in these groups must have been major determinants of their reproductive success. Relationships increase fitness not only by exchanges of help with kin, but also by gaining the benefits of reciprocity with others, that is, by exchanging favors when that offers a net benefit to both parties. In such circumstances, especially if the exchange is delayed or in different currencies, both flagrant defection and subtle cheating are expected and inevitable. To succeed relative to someone else, which is the only kind of success that is preserved in gene frequencies, an individual must be able to gain a little more than the average other person. This leads to an unending arms race. The system that results should simultaneously allow the individual to reap the benefits of reciprocity exchanges, to protect himself or herself from gross and subtle forms of cheating, and to practice those forms of cheating and exploitation that local conditions made adaptive. Individuals should differ, not in being altruists or cheaters, but in strategies they use to manipulate others (Trivers, 1981). These abilities to negotiate relationships successfully and to form and use alliances effectively may be the most complex human skills. In the past 100,000 years, as physical forces of selection have become less important, the ability to negotiate relationships successfully has become vastly more important. This selection pressure should be reflected in the distinctive characteristics of the human mind.

. . .

REPRESSION

An evolutionary explanation that accounts for repression must propose some benefit that comes from rigidly and completely excluding an idea from consciousness, while yet keeping it near the centers of motivation. Such a proposal has been mentioned several times by Trivers and by Alexander over the last 15 years, but it has gone almost unrecognized. . . . They propose that repression offers an advantage because it allows people to deceive themselves about their own true motives, and thus better deceive others as they unconsciously pursue these covert selfish motives. Deception is a required strategy in all relationships, and is, they argue, best pursued without even knowing it, so that others are given no clues.

. . .

This radical proposal deserves several illustrations. A man who believes that he will do anything for his new love and who can sincerely promise her his undying devotion, will be far more likely to garner her sexual favors than a man who says the same things without believing them (Symons, 1979). A person who hates an exploiting superior, but experiences only admiration and feelings of inadequacy, will have a considerable advantage over someone who is aware of rage and competitive feelings (Hartung, 1988). We tend to assume that the brain has been shaped for accurate perception of reality, but it is evident that, in some situations, distorted perceptions of reality may enhance fitness, and selection will tend to incorporate those tendencies to distortion (Trivers, 1981).

Trivers and Alexander both emphasize the benefits that come from pursuing covert motives without awareness of these motives. There are, however, many distinct ways that repression could enhance fitness. I will describe a variety of plausible benefits of repression so that they can be used to analyze the proposal that repression was shaped because of the benefits it may offer in the course of deceptive manipulations.

In addition to concealing a covert motive that is being pursued, repression may hide a fall-back strategy that is held in reserve. For instance, a dissatisfied spouse may embark on a campaign to please the mate, carefully hiding by repression the alternate strategy, simultaneously being considered and planned, of leaving for someone else. It need not be unsavory strategies that are repressed. Often it is useful to repress warm feelings. For instance, when a person threatens to leave a relationship, the threat lacks sincerity unless warm feelings are repressed. This explains the dramatic swings between intense love and bitter hatred experienced by couples who are in the process of trying either to change or leave the relationship.

A third way in which repression can increase fitness is by concealing a strategy that will never be pursued because it conflicts with fundamental values (and thus would have too great an emotional or fitness cost) or because it would just never be worthwhile. This function of repression is substantially the same as the impulse control function long recognized by psychoanalysis. Psychoanalysis emphasizes the need to maintain integrity of the ego, while an evolutionary view emphasizes the disastrous social and fitness consequences of experiencing (and thus perhaps revealing) certain motives, strategies, or fantasies. For instance, perverse sexual wishes, not uncommonly uncovered during psychoanalysis, are not repressed so they can be pursued covertly, or at some later date. They just would not increase fitness under any circumstances, and are best kept unconscious.

This third possibility is different from the original Alexander/Trivers proposal in that the strategy is never pursued. All three functions are based on deception, but in the first two the hidden motive is held close to the centers of motivation so it can be pursued when it is advantageous, while in this third case, there is no need to keep the motive close to centers of motivation because there is no benefit in pursuing the motive. The deception serves to protect the person's reputation and relationships. All three functions use deception to sustain an appearance of altruism. The difference is whether or not the selfish motives are acted on currently, possibly later, or never. If the answer is never, then concealing impulses becomes the same thing as controlling them.

A fourth function of repression is illustrated when one must repress the transgression of an ally so as to maintain an important relationship. A personal slight might have been a misunderstanding instead of a defection. Even if it was a defection, it might be better to ignore it so as to maintain the relationship. This function has been suggested by Lockard (1977) and Lloyd (1984). In this case it is not one's own motives that are repressed, but those of someone else. This is especially valuable when the other is more powerful (Hartung, 1988). Deception is still at the root of this function of repression, but the motive is to maintain long-term relationships, not to pursue short-term selfish gain.

Not only motives are repressed. Guilt can be kept unconscious just as rigidly, and with equal benefit. When it is best to fight without ambivalence, the guilty inhibited person is at a disadvantage. When benefit comes from brazenly denying that an action was self-serving, the expression of guilt is worse than useless. In many situations, however, the expression of guilt is beneficial. When a person wants to repair a relationship, and denial or excuses won't work, then expression of abject guilt is called for. A mere apology is worth little, emotional expressions of remorse are better, but tangible reparations of self-punishment are necessary for full reconciliation. This is hard for most theories to explain, but an evolutionary view of reciprocity relationships suggests that it is quite sensible to be skeptical of apologies unless the guilty party takes some action that decreases fitness by at least as much as was gained by the transgression. Such actions are convincing indicators that the transgression will not be repeated. It would not be surprising if people had a built-in tendency to try to reestablish relationships in this way. This may offer clues to the explanation of masochism.

. . .

EVOLUTIONARY FUNCTIONS OF THE DEFENSES

One general strategy of deception, well described by Slavin, is to act younger than the actual age, thus manipulating the parent into providing resources that would only be in the parent's interest to provide for a younger offspring. This offers an explanation for the capacity for regression. The notion that regression may serve as a strategy of deception is of enormous interest. It helps to account for the ubiquity of regression in stressful situations where increased investment is in the parent's best interests. The ubiquity of regression may have led to its use as a general signal of a need for aid, perhaps one used routinely and automatically by adults as well as children. Slavin provides a detailed description of the benefits of deception for both parties in parent–child interactions, and convincingly argues that the mental agencies function to modulate the use of these defenses. In adults, however, he decreases emphasis on the benefits of deception and implies that it may involve regression to earlier modes of interaction. It would be nice to find that these deceptive strategies are used mainly by children and regressed adults, but I fear that, in fact, children's ability to use repression in the service of deception may be but an early and relatively crude precursor of skills that become so smooth in adulthood that they are easily overlooked.

The suggestion that repression functions by enhancing the capacity for deception leads naturally to the supposition that other defenses may also. This may explain why the defenses are so many and so elaborate. The various ego defenses may be elaborate and specialized strategies for deception. Although the benefits of repression may mainly support long-term strategies, the benefits of the specific ego defenses may arise mainly from their support of short-term deceptive strategies.

Reaction formation, for example, may be more effective than simple repression at promoting deception in certain circumstances. The man who is aroused by a proposition from an attractive woman may loudly proclaim the next day at church that he is starting an antipornography group. Whether he pursues the sexual opportunity or not, he effectively hides his secret. If he overdoes it, of course, people will recognize that "he doth protest too much," but it is surprising how reluctant people are to consider impure motives in loud moralists. Projection is effective for similar reasons. If someone angrily accuses other people of a failing, most people are distracted from the possibility that the person is trying to conceal the same failing and they will be reluctant to accuse him or her or it. Also, the person who experiences his or her own impulses in others will often accurately anticipate the unsavory motives of others, especially if they face similar choices.

Empathy is valuable because it allows a person to experience the world as another does and, therefore, to act towards the person in ways that are especially finely tuned to the other person's special needs. This allows people to anticipate the needs of their friends. It also, however, allows them intuitively to know what will effectively deceive (and manipulate) a specific other individual. This is a far cry from the usual more benevolent view of the capacity for empathy, but it may offer at least as powerful an explanation.

Identification with the aggressor is one of the so-called "primitive defenses." The case of Patty Hearst horrified the country but exerted a fascination and sympathy as well, because many people intuitively knew that a kidnapped woman might be able to survive only by psychologically joining her captors. What most people don't know is that such kidnappings continue to be a part of everyday life in several parts of the world, and have undoubtedly been common during human evolution. A person with an unchangeable loyalty to one group would be at a substantial disadvantage in the environment of evolutionary adaptedness.

What about splitting? It is a strategy as important to adult human relationships as the ability to distinguish good and bad milk is to the infant. A person with the ability to split the affections of others has a powerful weapon, especially in situations where relationship partners are otherwise unavailable. By using splitting, a person can disrupt an established alliance and gain a chance to form an alliance with one of the previous partners. This works only if the chosen partner is idealized and thus can be deceptively flattered and promised the moon, and if the other party is depreciated so as to disengage the affections of the chosen new ally . . .

What about passive aggressive behavior? It is infuriating and often self-defeating, but it may be the best way for a powerless person to manipulate a more powerful person who would retaliate massively if any overt defiance were recognized. Whining, bitching, malingering, hypochondrias, and similar strategies are also useful when dealing with a more powerful person.

Introjection of values and beliefs serves early in life to allow the transmission of cultural norms and traditions. Later in life, unconscious introjection of the leader's wishes is likely to benefit the individual as well as the group, especially if the leader is powerful and has substantial resources to distribute. Identification with a powerful person offers profound advantages, while accurate perception of the situation might be disastrous.

The more "mature" defenses distort reality more subtly. Rationalization explains the behavior of the self and others in ways that distract from the true motives, a benefit both to deception of others and to maintaining self-esteem when a defection by another or the self must be accepted. Intellectualization keeps affect separate from the content that arouses it, so that pleasure or anger is not shown in public at moments that would lead to trouble. Then there are the defenses that are the most mature of all: humor and sublimation. Humor turns problematic confrontations into play so that neither party is required to compete seriously, with the risks that would entail. It is also a way of gracefully giving way without acknowledgment of inferior status. It can also be used to insult a third party subtly so as to define the in-group and out-group (Alexander, 1986). In sublimation, the desired activity is carried out in displacement and some derivative satisfaction is achieved. The activity offers benefits to the individual, even if they are quite distant from the original aim.

Finally we come to asceticism and altruism. It is no accident that these defenses are valued above others. What could be better or more admirable (or beneficial for us!) than the person who abjures personal pleasure and resources for the sake of helping others? These people are our saints and we admire and encourage them, even if we don't always emulate them. The defense of altruism gives the self over to the satisfactions of pride and self-esteem as substitutes for resources and sex. Our saints are poor and uninterested in money and sex, as they must be, for we quickly suspect the self-proclaimed altruist or ascetic who takes pleasure in personal satisfactions.

We all like to appear to be altruists, but neurotics try especially hard. They experience themselves as morally superior to other people and they pride themselves on their altruistic behavior. They tend to become bitter after experience with the disappointingly selfish nature of most people. Paradoxically, however, they are also wary of those who say that all people are basically motivated to pursue their self-interests one way or another. Such proposals threaten their fundamental strategy of appearing to be an ideal reciprocator and ideal relationship partner.

Just one step further is the strategy of appearing to be a naive, vulnerable person ready to be exploited. If some people are self-destructively beneficent (i.e., make altruistic mistakes), it might be profitable to try to convince others that one is such a mistake-maker so as to be accepted as a cooperator in order that the other will be beneficent in expectation of large return through "mistakes" later (Alexander, 1987). This is not a bad description of certain forms of neurosis. Such people tend to attract exploiters, but they don't end the relationship when the other tries to defect. Instead, they induce guilt, demand expensive reparations, and unconsciously inflict all kinds of subtle revenge if the partner does not comply. Both partners in such relationships are liable to exert substantial efforts to undermine the self-esteem of the other in order to induce the belief that no alternative relationships are possible and it is not possible to leave. It makes perfect sense that such people are particularly reluctant to admit any less-than-altruistic impulse in themselves. Such an admission would wreck their whole strategy.

. . .

PSYCHOANALYSIS AND EVOLUTIONARY BIOLOGY

The proposal about repression has many disturbing implications. Perhaps most disturbing is the suggestion that we cannot trust ourselves. When we experience ourselves as most generous, we may merely be manipulating others for our own benefit in especially subtle ways. When we are feeling most angry, we may be especially guilty. It has been no secret that self-knowledge is difficult to attain. Freud revealed the enormity of the task by showing that our conscious experience is just the tip of the iceberg. Now, if it is correct that the defenses serve mainly to deceive ourselves so that we can better deceive others, the task is found to be many-fold more difficult than it seemed, if not altogether impossible. Whoever would undertake the task of self-exploration would do well to begin with the task of understanding why we are so self-deceived, why, that is, people with the capacity for repression have a selective advantage.

. . .

REFERENCES

ALEXANDER, R. D. (1975). The search for a general theory of behavior, *Behav. Sci., 20,* 77–100.

ALEXANDER, R. D. (1979). *Darwinism and Human Affairs,* University of Washington Press, Seattle.

ALEXANDER, R. D. (1986). Ostracism and indirect reciprocity: The reproductive significance of humor. *Ethol. Sociobiol., 7,* 253–270.

ALEXANDER, R. D. (1987). *The Biology of Moral Systems,* Aldine de Gruyter Press, Hawthorne, NY.

ALEXANDER, R. D. (1989). Evolution of the human psyche, in P. Mellars and C. Stringer (Eds.), *Origins and Dispersal of Modern Humans,* University of Edinburgh Press, Edinburgh, pp. 455–513.

HARTUNG, J. (1988). Deceiving down, in J. S. Lockard and D. L. Paulhaus (Eds.), *Self-deception: An Adaptive Mechanism?,* Prentice Hall, Englewood Cliffs, NJ, pp. 170–185.

LLOYD, A. (1984). On the evolution of the instincts: Implications for psychoanalysis, unpublished monograph.

LLOYD, J. E. (1986). Firefly communication and deception: "Oh, what a tangled web," in R. W. Mitchell and N. S. Thompson (Eds.), *Deception: Perspectives on Human and Nonhuman Deceit,* State University of New York Press, Albany, NY.

LOCKARD, J. (1977). Panhandling as an example of sharing of resources, *Science, 198,* 858.

MAYR, E. (1982). *The Growth of Biological Thought,* Belknap Press of the Harvard University Press, Cambridge, MA.

NESSE, R. M. (1984). An evolutionary perspective on psychiatry, *Comp. Psychiat., 25,* 575–580.

NESSE, R. M. (1987). An evolutionary perspective on panic disorder and agoraphobia, *Ethol. Sociobiol., 8,* 73s–85s.

NESSE, R. M. (1988). Life table tests of evolutionary theories of senescence, *Exper. Gerontol, 23,* 445–453.

SYMONS, D. (1979). *The Evolution of Human Sexuality,* Oxford University Press, New York.

TRIVERS, R. L. (1976). Forward in R. Dawkins *The Selfish Gene,* Oxford University Press, New York.

TRIVERS, R. (1981). Sociobiology and politics, in E. White (Ed.), *Sociobiology and Politics,* D.C. Heath Co., Lexington, MA.

TRIVERS, R. L. (1985). *Social Evolution,* Benjamin/Cummings, Menlo Park, CA.

CHAPTER
4

Trait, Motive, and Need Perspectives

Introduction

When we think of personality assessment, traits, motives, and needs typically come to mind. Our descriptions of ourselves and others include characteristics that are stable over time and across situations. In other words, we attempt to identify enduring qualities of individuals.

Throughout the history of psychology there have been numerous attempts to identify important individual differences. With respect to traits, motives, and needs, these approaches follow two distinct patterns. One approach focuses on an in-depth study of individual needs and motives (e.g., achievement). The other approach seeks to categorize large numbers of characteristics into a relatively small number of dimensions or *factors*.

In this chapter you will have the opportunity to examine both approaches. Through readings and exercises, you will take a closer look at the five-factor model and assess the impact of several major motives and needs on your everyday behavior.

READING

VALIDATION OF THE FIVE-FACTOR MODEL OF PERSONALITY ACROSS INSTRUMENTS AND OBSERVERS*

Robert R. McCrae and Paul T. Costa, Jr.

Editors' Note:

Over the years, there have been a number of attempts to explain the structure of personality. Recently, however, the five-factor model has become a dominant view of personality trait structure. In this article, Robert McCrae and Paul Costa provide a detailed review of the factors that make up this model of personality.

. . . **[R]**esearchers have . . . recognized the need for a consensus on at least the general outlines of a trait taxonomy. . . . One particularly promising candidate has emerged. The five-factor model—comprising extraversion or surgency, agreeableness, conscientiousness, emotional stability versus neuroticism, and culture—of Tupes and Christal (1961) was replicated by Norman in 1963 and heralded by him as the basis for "an adequate taxonomy of personality." Although it was largely neglected for several years, variations on this model have recently begun to re-emerge. . . .

[Data on the five-factor model of personality were collected from two sources—self-reports and peer ratings—and two instruments—adjective factors and questionnaire scales.]

SUBJECTS

Individuals who provided self-reports and who were targets for peer ratings were members of the Augmented Baltimore Longitudinal Study of Aging. The Baltimore Longitudinal Study of Aging (BLSA) sample is composed of a community-dwelling, generally healthy group of volunteers who have agreed to return for medical and psychological testing at regular intervals.

PEER RATERS

Subjects were asked to nominate

> three or four individuals who know you very well as *you* are *now*. They can be friends, neighbors, or co-workers, but they should *not* be relatives. These should be people who have known you for at least one year and have seen you in a variety of situations. . . .

MEASURES

Adjective factors. On the basis of a series of analyses of English-language trait names, Goldberg (1983) developed a 40-item bipolar adjective-rating scale instrument to measure five major dimensions of personality. In subsequent work (McCrae & Costa, 1985b) we supplemented his list with an additional 40 items.

NEO Personality Inventory. A questionnaire measure of the five-factor model is provided by the NEO Personality Inventory (Costa & McCrae, 1985), which comprises the NEO [Neuroticism-Extraversion-Openness] Inventory (Costa & McCrae, 1980; McCrae & Costa, 1983a) along with newly developed scales to measure agreeableness and conscientiousness.

THE NATURE OF THE FIVE FACTORS

. . . The factors in the following Table, which so closely parallel factors found in self-reports and which show such clear evidence of convergent and discriminant validity across observers and instruments, can form a particularly useful guide to the conceptual content of the dimensions of personality.

Neuroticism versus emotional stability. There is perhaps least disagreement about neuroticism, defined here by such terms as worrying, insecure, self-conscious, and temperamental. Although adjectives describing neuroticism are relatively infrequent in English (Peabody, 1984), psychologists' concerns with psychopathology have led to the development of innumerable scales saturated with neuroticism. Indeed, neuroticism is so ubiquitous an element of personality scales that theorists sometimes take it for granted.

*McCrae, R. R. & Costa, P. T., Jr. (1987). Validation of the five-factor model of personality across instruments and observers. *Journal of Personality and Social Psychology, 52* (1), 81–90.

80 Adjective Items from Peer Ratings

ADJECTIVES	ADJECTIVES

NEUROTICISM (N)
Calm—worrying
At ease—nervous
Relaxed—high-strung
Unemotional—emotional
Even-tempered—temperamental
Secure—insecure
Self-satisfied—self-pitying
Patient—impatient
Not envious—envious/jealous
Comfortable—self-conscious
Not impulse-ridden—impulse-ridden
Hardy—vulnerable
Objective—subjective

EXTRAVERSION (E)
Retiring—sociable
Sober—fun-loving
Reserved—affectionate
Aloof—friendly
Inhibited—spontaneous
Quiet—talkative
Passive—active
Loner—joiner
Unfeeling—passionate
Cold—warm
Lonely—not lonely
Task oriented—person oriented
Submissive—dominant
Timid—bold

OPENNESS (O)
Conventional—original
Down to earth—imaginative
Uncreative—creative
Narrow interests—broad interests
Simple—complex
Uncurious—curious
Unadventurous—daring
Prefer routine—prefer variety
Conforming—independent
Unanalytical—analytical
Conservative—liberal
Traditional—untraditional
Unartistic—artistic

AGREEABLENESS VS. ANTAGONISM (A)
Irritable—good-natured
Ruthless—soft-hearted
Rude—courteous
Selfish—selfless
Uncooperative—helpful
Callous—sympathetic
Suspicious—trusting
Stingy—generous
Antagonistic—acquiescent
Critical—lenient
Vengeful—forgiving
Narrow-minded—open-minded
Disagreeable—agreeable
Stubborn—flexible
Serious—cheerful
Cynical—gullible
Manipulative—straightforward
Proud—humble

CONSCIENTIOUSNESS VS. UNDIRECTEDNESS (C)
Negligent—conscientious
Careless—careful
Undependable—reliable
Lazy—hardworking
Disorganized—well organized
Lax—scrupulous
Weak-willed—self-disciplined
Sloppy—neat
Late—punctual
Impractical—practical
Thoughtless—deliberate
Aimless—ambitious
Unstable—emotionally stable
Helpless—self-reliant
Playful—businesslike
Unenergetic—energetic
Ignorant—knowledgeable
Quitting—persevering
Stupid—intelligent
Unfair—fair
Imperceptive—perceptive
Uncultured—cultured

A provocative view of neuroticism is provided by Tellegen (in press), who views it as negative emotionality, the propensity to experience a variety of negative affects, such as anxiety, depression, anger, and embarrassment. Virtually all theorists would concur in the centrality of negative affect to neuroticism; the question is whether other features also define it. Tellegen himself (in press) pointed out that his construct of negative emotionality has behavioral and cognitive aspects. Guilford included personal relations and objectivity in his emotional health factor (Guilford, Zimmerman, & Guilford, 1976), suggesting that mistrust and self-reference form part of neuroticism. We have found that impulsive behaviors, such as tendencies to overeat, smoke, or drink excessively, form a facet of neuroticism (Costa & McCrae, 1980), and *impulse-ridden* is a definer of the neuroticism factor in self-reports, although not in ratings. Others have linked neuroticism to irrational beliefs (Teasdale & Rachman, 1983; Vestre, 1984) or to poor coping efforts (McCrae & Costa, 1986).

What these behaviors seem to share is a common origin in negative affect. Individuals high in neuroticism have more difficulty than others in quitting smoking because the distress caused by abstinence is stronger for them. They may more frequently use inappropriate coping responses like hostile reactions and wishful thinking because they must deal more often with disruptive emotions. They may adopt irrational beliefs like self-blame because these beliefs are cognitively consistent with the negative feelings they experience. Neuroticism appears to include not only negative affect, but also the disturbed thoughts and behaviors that accompany emotional distress.

Extraversion or surgency. Sociable, fun-loving, affectionate, friendly, and talkative are the highest loading variables on the extraversion factor. This is not Jungian extraversion (see Guilford, 1977), but it does correspond to the conception of H. J. Eysenck and most other contemporary researchers, who concur with popular speech in identifying extraversion with lively sociability.

However, disputes remain about which elements are central and which are peripheral to extraversion. Most writers would agree that sociability, cheerfulness, activity level, assertiveness, and sensation seeking all covary, however loosely. But the Eysencks have at times felt the need to distinguish between sociability and what they call impulsiveness (S. B. G. Eysenck & Eysenck, 1963) . . . Hogan (1983) believed that the five-factor model was improved by dividing extraversion into sociability and assertiveness factors. In Goldberg's analyses, surgency (dominance and activity) were the primary definers of extraversion, and terms like warm-cold were assigned to the agreeableness-antagonism factor. Tellegen (in press) emphasized the complementary nature of neuroticism and extraversion by labeling his extraversion factor positive emotionality.

These distinctions do seem to merge at a high enough level of analysis (H. J. Eysenck & Eysenck, 1967; McCrae & Costa, 1983a), and sociability—the enjoyment of others' company—seems to be the core. What is essential to recall, however, is that liking people does not necessarily make one likable. Salesmen, those prototypic extraverts, are generally happier to see you than you are to see them.

Openness to experience. The reinterpretation of Norman's culture as openness to experience was the focus of some of our previous articles (McCrae & Costa, 1985a, 1985b), and the replication of results in peer ratings was one of the purposes of the present article. According to adjective-factor results, openness is best characterized by original, imaginative, broad interests, and daring. In the case of this dimension, however, questionnaires may be better than adjectives as a basis for interpretation and assessment. Many aspects of openness (e.g., openness to feelings) are not easily expressed in single adjectives, and the relative poverty of the English-language vocabulary of openness and closedness may have contributed to confusion about this domain (McCrae & Costa, 1985a). We know from questionnaire studies that openness can be manifest in fantasy, aesthetics, feelings, actions, ideas, and values (Costa & McCrae, 1978, 1980), but only ideas and values are well represented in the adjective factor. Interestingly, questionnaire measures of openness give higher validity coefficients than do adjective-factor measures. . . .

Perhaps the most important distinction to be made here is between openness and intelligence. Open individuals tend to be seen by themselves and others as somewhat more intelligent. . . . However, joint factor analyses using Army Alpha intelligence subtests and either adjectives (McCrae & Costa, 1985b) or NEO Inventory scales (McCrae & Costa, 1985a) show that intelligence scales define a factor clearly separate from openness. Intelligence may in some degree predispose the individual to openness, or openness may help develop intelligence, but the two seem best construed as separate dimensions of individual differences.

Agreeableness versus antagonism. As a broad dimension, agreeableness-antagonism is less familiar than extraversion or neuroticism, but some of its component traits, like trust (Stark, 1978) and Machiavellianism (Christie & Geis, 1970), have been widely researched. The essential nature of agreeableness-antagonism is perhaps best seen by examining the disagreeable pole, which we have labeled antagonism. . . . [A]ntagonistic people seem always to set themselves against others. Cognitively they are mistrustful and skeptical; affectively they are callous and unsympathetic; behaviorally they are uncooperative, stubborn, and rude. It would appear that their sense of attachment or bonding with their fellow human beings is defective, and in extreme cases antagonism may resemble sociopathy (cf. H. J. Eysenck & Eysenck's, 1975, psychoticism).

An insightful description of antagonism in its neurotic form is provided by Horney's account of the tendency to move against people (1945, 1950). She theorized that a struggle for mastery is the root cause of this tendency and that variations may occur, including narcissistic, perfectionistic, and arrogant vindictive types. Whereas some antagonistic persons are overtly aggressive, others may be polished manipulators. The drive for mastery and the overt or inhibited hostility of antagonistic individuals suggest a resemblance to some formulations of Type A personality (Dembroski & MacDougall, 1983), and systematic studies of the relations between agreeableness-antagonism and measures of coronary-prone behavior should be undertaken.

Unappealing as antagonism may be, it is necessary to recognize that extreme scores on the agreeable pole may also be maladaptive. The person high in agreeableness may be dependent and fawning, and agreeableness has its neurotic manifestation in Horney's self-effacing solution of moving toward people.

Antagonism is most easily confused with dominance. Amelang and Borkenau (1982), working in German and apparently unaware of the Norman taxonomy, found a factor they called *dominance*. Among its key definers, however, were Hartnäckigkeit (*stubbornness*) and Erregbarkeit (*irritability*); scales that measure agreeableness and cooperation defined the opposite pole in their questionnaire factor. Clearly, this factor corresponds to antagonism. In self-reports (McCrae & Costa, 1985b), submissive-dominant is a weak definer of extraversion; from the peers' point of view, it is a definer of antagonism. The close etymological relationship of *dominant* and *domineering* shows the basis of the confusion.

Agreeableness-antagonism and conscientiousness-undirectedness are sometimes omitted from personality systems because they may seem too value laden. Indeed, the judgment of character is made largely along these two dimensions: Is the individual well or ill intentioned? Is he or she strong or weak in carrying out those intentions? Agreeableness-antagonism, in particular, has often been assumed to be an evaluative factor of others' perceptions rather than a veridical component of personality (e.g., A. Tellegen, personal communication, March 28, 1984).

However, the fact that a trait may be judged from a moral point of view does not mean that it is not a substantive aspect of personality. The consensual validation seen among peers and between peer-reports and self-reports demonstrates that there are some observable consistencies of behavior that underlie attributions of agreeableness and conscientiousness. They may be evaluated traits, but they are not mere evaluations.

Conscientious versus undirectedness. Conscientious may mean either governed by conscience or careful and thorough (Morris, 1976), and psychologists seem to be divided about which of these meanings best characterizes the last major dimension of personality. Amelang and Borkenau (1982) labeled their factor self-control versus impulsivity, and Conley (1985) spoke of impulse control. This terminology connotes an inhibiting agent, as

Cattell (Cattell, Eber, & Tatsuoka, 1970) recognized when he named his Factor G *superego strength*. A conscientious person in this sense should be dutiful, scrupulous, and perhaps moralistic.

A different picture, however, is obtained by examining the adjectives that define this factor. In addition to conscientious and scrupulous, there are a number of adjectives that suggest a more proactive stance: hardworking, ambitious, energetic, persevering. Digman and Takemoto-Chock (1981) labeled this factor *will to achieve*, and it is notable that one of the items in the questionnaire measure of conscientiousness, "He strives for excellence in all he does," comes close to the classic definition of need for achievement (McClelland, Atkinson, Clark, & Lowell, 1953).

At one time, the purposefulness and adherence to plans, schedules, and requirements suggested the word *direction* as a label for this factor, and we have retained that implication in calling the opposite pole of conscientiousness *undirectedness*. In our view, the individual low in conscientiousness is not so much uncontrolled as undirected, not so much impulse ridden as simply lazy.

It seems probable that these two meanings may be related. Certainly individuals who are well organized, habitually careful, and capable of self-discipline are more likely to be able to adhere scrupulously to a moral code if they choose to—although there is no guarantee that they will be so inclined. An undirected individual may have a demanding conscience and a pervasive sense of guilt but be unable to live up to his or her own standards for lack of self-discipline and energy. In any case, it is clear that this is a dimension worthy of a good deal more empirical attention than it has yet received. Important real-life outcomes such as alcoholism (Conley & Angelides, 1984) and academic achievement (Digman & Takemoto-Chock, 1981) are among its correlates, and a further specification of the dimension is sure to be fruitful.

Some personality theorists might object that trait ratings, in whatever form and from whatever source, need not provide the best foundation for understanding individual differences. Experimental analysis of the psychophysiological basis of personality (H. J. Eysenck & Eysenck, 1984), examination of prototypic acts and act frequencies (Buss & Craik, 1983), psychodynamic formulations (Horney, 1945), or behavioral genetics (Plomin, DeFries, & McClearn, 1980) provide important alternatives. But psychophysiological, behavioral, psychodynamic, and genetic explanations must eventually be related to the traits that are universally used to describe personality, and the five-factor model can provide a framework within which these relations can be systematically examined. The minor conceptual divergences noted in this article suggest the need for additional empirical work to fine-tune the model, but the broad outlines are clear in self-reports, spouse ratings, and peer ratings; in questionnaires and adjective factors; and in English and in German (Amelang & Borkenau, 1982; John, Goldberg, & Angleitner, 1984). Deeper causal analyses may seek to account for the structure of personality, but the structure that must be explained is, for now, best represented by the five-factor model.

REFERENCES

AMELANG, M., & BORKENAU, P. (1982). Uber die faktorielle Struktur und externe. Validitat einiger Fragebogen-Skalen zur Erfussung von Dimensionen der Extraversion und emotionales Labilitat [On the factor structure and external validity of some questionnaire scales measuring dimensions of extraversion and neuroticism]. *Zeitschrift fur differentielle und Diagnostische Psychologie, 3*, 119–146.

BUSS, D. M., & CRAIK, K. H. (1983). The act frequency approach to personality. *Psychological Review, 90*, 105–126.

CATTELL, R. B., EBER, H. W., & TATSUOKA, M. M. (1970). *The handbook for the sixteen personality factor questionnaire.* Champaign, IL: Institute for Personality and Ability Testing.

CHRISTIE, R., & GEIS, R. L. (EDS.). (1970). *Studies in Machiavellianism,* New York: Academic Press.

CONLEY, J. J. (1985). Longitudinal stability of personality traits. A multi-trait–multimethod–multioccasion analysis. *Journal of Personality and Social Psychology, 49,* 1266–1282.

CONLEY J. J., & ANGELIDES, M. (1984). *Personality antecedents of emotional disorders and alcohol abuse in men: Results of a forty-five year prospective study.* Manuscript submitted for publication.

COSTA, P. T., JR., & McCRAE, R. R. (1978). Objective personality assessment. In M. Storandt, I. C. Siegler, & M. F. Elias (Eds.), *The clinical psychology of aging* (pp. 119–143). New York: Plenum Press.

COSTA, P. T., JR., & McCRAE, R. R. (1980). Still stable after all these years: Personality as a key to some issues in adulthood and old age. In P. B. Bales & O. G. Brim, Jr. (Eds.), *Life span development and behavior* (Vol. 3, pp. 65–102). New York: Academic Press.

COSTA, P. T., JR., & McCRAE, R. R. (1985). *The NEO personality inventory manual.* Odessa, FL: Psychological Assessment Resources.

DEMBROSKI, T. M., & MacDOUGALL, J. M. (1983). Behavioral psychophysiological perspectives on coronary-prone behavior. In T. M. Dembroski, T. H. Schmidt, & G. Blumchen (Eds.), *Biobehavioral bases of coronary heart disease* (pp. 106–129). New York: Karger.

DIGMAN, J. M., & TAKEMOTO-CHOCK, N. K. (1981). Factors in the natural language of personality: Re-analysis, comparison, and interpretation of six major studies. *Multivariate Behavioral Research, 16,* 149–170.

EYSENCK, H. J., & EYSENCK, M. (1984). *Personality and individual differences.* London: Plenum Press.

EYSENCK, H. J., & EYSENCK, S. B. G. (1967). On the unitary nature of extraversion. *Acta Psychologica, 26,* 383–390.

EYSENCK, H. J., & EYSENCK, S. B. G. (1975). *Manual of the Eysenck personality questionnaire.* San Diego, CA: EDITS.

EYSENCK, S. B. G., & EYSENCK, H. J. (1963). On the dual nature of extraversion. *British Journal of Social and Clinical Psychology, 2,* 46–65.

GOLDBERG, L. R. (1983, June). The magical number five, plus or minus two: Some considerations on the dimensionality of personality descriptors. Paper presented at a research seminar, Gerontology Research Center, NIA/NIH, Baltimore, MD.

GUILFORD, J. P. (1977). Will the real factor of extraversion-introversion please stand up? A Reply to Eysenck. *Psychological Bulletin, 84,* 412–416.

GUILFORD, J. S., ZIMMERMAN, W. S., & GUILFORD, J. P. (1976). *The Guilford-Zimmerman temperament survey handbook: Twenty-five years of research and application.* San Diego, CA: EDITS.

HOGAN, R. (1983) Socioanalytic theory of personality. In M. M. Page (Ed.), *1982 Nebraska symposium on motivation: Personality—current theory and research* (pp. 55–89). Lincoln: University of Nebraska Press.

HORNEY, K. (1945). *Our inner conflicts.* New York: Norton.

HORNEY, K. (1950). *Neurosis and human growth.* New York: Norton.

JOHN, O. P., GOLDBERG, L. R., & ANGLEITNER, A. (1984). Better than the alphabet: Taxonomies of personality-descriptive terms in English, Dutch, and German. In H. J. C. Bonarius, G. L. M. van Hec, & N. G. Smid (Eds.), *Personality psychology in Europe: Theoretical and empirical developments.* Lisee, Switzerland: Sweets & Zeitlinger.

McCLELLAND, D. C., ATKINSON, J. W., CLARK, R. A., & LOWELL, E. L. (1953). *The achievement motive.* New York: Appleton-Century-Crofts.

McCRAE, R. R., & COSTA, P. T., JR. (1983a). Joint factors in self-reports and ratings: Neuroticism, extraversion, and openness to experience. *Personality and Individual Differences, 4,* 245–255.

McCRAE, R. R., & COSTA, P. T., JR. (1983b). Social desirability scales: More substance than style. *Journal of Consulting and Clinical Psychology, 51,* 882–888.

McCRAE, R. R., & COSTA, P. T., JR. (1985a). Openness to experience. In R. Hogan & W. H. Jones (Eds.), *Perspectives in personality: Theory, measurement, and interpersonal dynamics* (Vol. 1). Greenwich, CT: JAI Press.

McCRAE, R. R., & COSTA, P. T., JR. (1985b). Updating Norman's "adequate taxonomy": Intelligence and personality dimensions in natural language and in questionnaires. *Journal of Personality and Social Psychology, 49,* 710–721.

McCRAE, R. R., & COSTA, P. T., JR. (1986). Personality, coping, and coping effectiveness in an adult sample. *Journal of Personality, 54,* 385–405.

MORRIS, W. (Ed.). (1976). *The American heritage dictionary of the English language.* Boston: Houghton Mifflin.

NORMAN, W. T. (1963). Toward an adequate taxonomy of personality attributes: Replicated factor structure in peer nomination personality ratings. *Journal of Abnormal and Social Psychology, 66,* 574–583.

PEABODY, D. (1984). Personality dimensions through trait inferences. *Journal of Personality and Social Psychology, 46,* 384–403.

PLOMIN, R., DeFRIES, J. C., & McCLEARN, G. E. (1980). *Behavior genetics: A primer.* San Francisco: Freeman.

STARK, L. (1978). Trust. In H. London & J. E. Exner, Jr. (Eds.), *Dimensions of personality* (pp. 561–599). New York: Wiley.

TEASDALE, J. D., & RACHMAN, S. (Eds.) (1983). Cognitions and mood: Clinical aspects and applications [Special issue]. *Advances in Behavior Research and Therapy, 5,* 1–88.

TELLEGEN, A. (in press). Structures of mood and personality and their relevance to assessing anxiety, with an emphasis on self-report. In A. H. Tuma & J. D. Maser (Eds.), *Anxiety and the anxiety disorders.* Hillsdale, NJ: Erlbaum.

TUPES, E. C., & CHRISTAL, R. E. (1961). Recurrent personality factors based on trait ratings. *USAF ASD Technical Report* (No. 61-97).

VESTRE, N. D. (1984). Irrational beliefs and self-reported depressed mood. *Journal of Abnormal Psychology, 93,* 239–341.

SPOTLIGHT
NEUROTICISM*

A recent research project by Niall Bolger and Elizabeth Schilling examined the mechanism through which personality influences health and psychological well-being. Specifically, they investigated the chief determinant of psychological distress—neuroticism, and addressed the following major questions:

1. Are people high in neuroticism more distressed on average than people low in neuroticism?

2. Do people high in neuroticism report greater exposure to daily stressors than people low in neuroticism?

3. Are people high in neuroticism more emotionally reactive to the daily stressors they experience?

Three hundred thirty-nine married people who were determined to be either high or low in neuroticism based on the Neuroticism Scale of the Eysenck Personality Inventory [sample item: Would you call yourself a nervous person?] completed diaries every day for 42 consecutive days. A list of stressors evaluated in the daily diaries included nine categories: overload at home, overload at work, family demand, other demand, transportation problems, financial problems, argument with spouse, argument with child, and argument with others. Subjects also indicated on a 4-point scale (from "not at all" to "a lot") how strongly they had felt each of 18 emotions drawn from the anxiety, depression, and hostility subscales of the Affect Balance Scale over the previous 24 hours.

They found that, on average, people high in neuroticism were indeed more distressed than people low in neuroticism over the 6-week period. They also experienced more stressors (especially arguments with spouse and arguments with others). And they reported greater reactivity or distress in response to stressors (the difference between a person's distress on days when a stressor occurs compared to days when it does not).

*Based on material in Bolger, N., & Schilling, E. A. (1991). Personality and the problems of everyday life: The role of neuroticism in exposure and reactivity to daily stressors. *Journal of Personality, 59*, 355–386.

READING
HOTHEADS AND HEART ATTACKS*

Edward Dolnick

Editors' Note:

Research on the hard-driving Type A personality has been linked to heart disease for decades. Recent research, however, has begun to examine the relative contributions of individual components of the Type A personality to heart disease. Edward Dolnick examines hostility as a risk factor in heart disease and offers suggestions on how to reduce this risk.

Jaw clenched, voice rising, sturdy finger jabbing furiously as if to impale her victim, Mary Brown pauses momentarily to catch her breath. "She's my grandmother, for God's sake!" she yells at the nursing home supervisor. "We're paying all this money, and nobody even checks on her? Don't you tell me you can't do it. You went into this business to take care of people. If you can't do it, get out of the business!"

The anger is real, but little else in the scene is genuine. Brown, though she seems to have forgotten it, is a volunteer in a study designed to gauge the impact of anger on the heart. Hooked up to a blood pressure cuff and heart monitors in a physiology lab at Baltimore's V.A. hospital, she is simply acting a role, though it helps that her own grandmother was once neglected by the staff at a nearby nursing home.

Brown has focused all her attention on the young man playing the role of the nursing supervisor. She has ignored the true source of her torment, a small figure standing quietly at the edge of the room. He is Aron Siegman, a soft-spoken 66-year-old psychologist with a slight paunch and a fringe of white hair.

His mild appearance to the contrary, Siegman spends his days stirring up trouble—coaxing a college student to recall a spouse's adulterous affair, for example, or repeatedly interrupting a volunteer's answer to a question he has posed about her aging father. A connoisseur of anger, he is as caught up in the nuances of his favorite subject as any wine collector. The reason is simple: A host of studies seem to show that we have become a nation of Rumplestiltskins, so much more likely to lose our cool than we were even a few decades ago that we have pushed our bodies to the breaking point.

It's not a pretty picture. Too many of us overreact to the countless provocations of everyday life—traffic jams and surly clerks and brutish bosses—by boiling over. Heart pounding, blood pressure skyrocketing, adrenaline surging, we are doing ourselves in prematurely, the experts say, by pushing our bodies beyond what they can take. One of the leading proponents of this new theory summarizes it with a succinctness more common on bumper stickers than in science. Current wisdom, declares Duke University stress researcher Redford Williams, is that "anger kills."

Fortunately, a simple remedy may be at hand. Siegman is now testing a theory that anger in itself isn't bad for your heart; the unhealthy consequences only kick in, he says, if you act out that anger. If he is right, the cry from the sixties to "let it all hang out" had it exactly backwards. It's perfectly okay, says the University of Maryland psychologist, to think that the nitwit who just turned left from the right lane shouldn't be let outdoors without a keeper; what's not okay is to scream at him and pound the steering wheel.

The Mary Brown experiment, for example, has two halves. First, Siegman wants to show that expressing anger sets the heart racing and blood pressure soaring. The lab's recording devices make that clear. Her blood pressure alone, normally 176/75, has skyrocketed to 213/98 since her tirade began. The experiment's second half involves coaxing Brown to replay the same infuriating scene, but this time without any outward displays of anger. What physiological changes do the various monitors reveal when a person feels angry but chooses not to express it? "Virtually nothing," says Siegman. "We don't get anything."

Here no news truly is good news. Heart disease is the nation's leading killer, and anger is emerging as a risk factor as important as smoking or high cholesterol or any of the other well-known villains. If Siegman is right that anger can be tamed, and tamed fairly simply, he's on to something big.

The kind of hostile personality that may put people at especially high risk for heart disease does not yet have a name. For the moment, let's call it Type H, for hostility, and to acknowledge its link to the famous Type A personality.

Type A behavior is a mix of impatience, aggressiveness, anger, and competitiveness. Mix Donald Trump with Margaret Thatcher, stir in Murphy Brown, and you have a Type A. For decades, everyone living this high-strung, fast-paced life was seen as a heart attack waiting (impatiently) to happen.

By 1981, the Type A theory had earned an official stamp of approval. An all-star panel appointed by the National Heart, Lung, and Blood Institute to evaluate the evidence had come back with a hearty endorsement.

This was major news. Medicine had long paid lip service to the idea that the mind affects the body—no one who has ever blushed could deny it—but this was more. After years in the shadows, psychology had suddenly leapt onstage. In predicting heart disease, a psychological trait seemed as important as any biological measure.

But no sooner had the experts committed their enthusiasm for Type A to print than a slew of new and authoritative studies appeared. Their message: Type A's faced no higher risk of heart disease than anyone else. Two studies that looked at patients who already had heart disease came to an even more unwelcome conclusion. Type A's, it seemed, fared *better* than their laid-back counterparts.

Oops!

The Type H theory salvages something important from that wreckage. Indeed, it seems Type A theorists weren't entirely off the mark, after all. Type A was a package, and though most of its ingredients were irrelevant to heart disease, one component—hostility—may truly be toxic. Impatience and competitiveness, on the other hand, seem to have been innocents who got a bad reputation by hanging out with the wrong crowd.

Type H theory rests on some compelling findings. In one study, for example, 255 doctors who had taken a standard personality test while attending the University of North Carolina's medical school were tracked down 25 years later. Those whose hostility scores had been in the top half were four to five times as likely to have developed heart disease in the intervening decades as were those whose hostility scores had been in the lower half.

A similar study that looked at 118 lawyers found equally striking results. Of those lawyers who had scored in the top quarter for hostility, nearly one in five was dead by age 50. Of those in the lowest quarter, only one in 25 had died. What's more, say the Type H proponents, such findings have a straightforward biological explanation. Evolution, they note, has designed the human body to respond to acutely stressful situations with a cascade of changes. In crises, your heart pumps faster and harder, arteries that carry blood to your muscles dilate so that blood flow increases still more, your platelets become stickier so that you are less likely to bleed to death if an attacker takes a bite out of you.

It's a fine system if you're running from a lion. If you start the whole process up every time the elevator is late, though, everyday life will soon lay you low. As blood surges through your arteries and stress hormones pour from your adrenal glands, once-smooth artery walls begin to scar and pit. Then fatty cells clump on that pocked surface, like mineral deposits in an old water pipe. Arteries narrow, blood flow decreases, and your body is starved of oxygen. The downward spiral eventually ends in chest pain or strokes or heart attacks.

The mechanism behind Type A, in contrast, was a good deal harder to picture. Exactly how would competitiveness, say, put the body at risk? Even in its heyday, Type A had other problems as well. For one, it seemed to call for a personality transplant. To teach his frazzled patients mellowness, for example, one Type-A pioneer had them wait in the longest line at the bank and drive all day in the right-hand lane. It sounds brutal, the brainstorm of a malicious researcher who had grown bored with harassing rats and was looking for bigger game.

"With the original Type A," says David Krantz, a psychologist at Uniformed Services University of the Health Sciences, in Bethesda, Maryland, "people would say, 'You're telling me I can't be competitive? I shouldn't meet deadlines? How am I going to explain that to my boss?' Now the message is more manageable: 'Ambition is not the problem. Aggressiveness is not the problem. Hostility is the problem.'"

"What your boss wants is for you to get a hell of a lot of work done," Krantz adds. "He doesn't necessarily want you to act like a son of a bitch."

The Type H theory differs from its forebearer in one other important way—it specifically includes women. In theory, Type A did, too, but in practice it focused heavily on males. In part, the reason was a matter of convenience for the researchers: Most men have their heart attacks ten years earlier than women; in larger part, the reason was that when scientists thought Type A, the stereotype that came to mind was a male executive.

They might have thought of Mary Brown instead. She is a delightful woman, lively and down-to-earth and a good storyteller. It's just that, as the Pompeians said about Vesuvius, there is this one tiny quirk. Brown is in her sixties now and works hard to keep her temper in bounds, but for as long as she can remember she has erupted at the slightest provocation. "I'm real proud if I can go two days without getting upset," she says. "I blow up. I know it's terrible, but I just do."

If someone cuts ahead of her in the supermarket line, Brown tells them off. "I'd like to see someone try to butt in front of me," she boasts. If they venture into the express line with a dozen items rather than the legal ten, Brown dresses them down and makes sure the cashier knows of their sin, too. On the freeway, preparing to exit, she sticks close to the car in front of her so that no one else can cut in. "I'm not going to let you in," she snarls at anyone trying it. "You should have moved in way back there."

Mary Brown is no tyrant. She's funny, and, once the storm has passed, she can laugh at her tirades. She has been married to the same man for 50 years. "It's incredible, some of what he's had to put up with," she says with a rueful smile. And she is close to her son and daughter.

Outsiders are more at risk. Brown cannot abide injustice, and she sees it in every driver who runs a yellow light, in every shopper with an extra can of soup. "To me," she says, "silence is acceptance. If I don't say anything, I'm agreeing with something that's wrong, and"—she hammers out the last words, like a general exhorting the troops to defend their homeland—"that cannot happen."

The medical establishment tends to wrinkle its nose in distaste at this whole subject. Many cardiologists concede that a diseased heart can be undone by such sudden stresses as winning the lottery or getting robbed at gunpoint; in ways that are not well understood, stress somehow sets the heart's ventricles to chaotic quivering. But they question whether chronic stress in general, or hostility in particular, can undo a healthy heart.

Look again, for example, at the study that showed a high number of deaths among hostile lawyers. It's tempting, critics say, to conclude that hostility gradually undermined their healthy hearts. But maybe not. Maybe heart disease strikes randomly at the hostile and the pleasant alike, and hostility serves only to speed up the dying process in those who are already vulnerable. In large measure, this is simply "show me" skepticism. Where, doubters ask, is clear-cut proof?

Part of the problem is that a theory based on hostility is harder to pin down than one based on something as easy to measure as blood pressure. Even Siegman concedes that the case for Type H is far from airtight. "Look," he says, "it's a complicated story. It was the same with cholesterol. That started out, Cholesterol is bad. Then somebody found out cholesterol levels alone didn't predict so well, and then there was HDL and LDL, and then the ratio between them. It's an ongoing story."

But even if Siegman and his colleagues are right that hostility is bad for the heart, is there anything we can do about it?

To begin with, everyone agrees that we cannot banish anger. Even if we wanted to, we could no more stop getting angry than we could stop getting hungry. But who would want to? Anger has its place. There is injustice in the world, after all, and righteous indignation is an honorable emotion.

In a rare lyric moment, psychologists have dubbed the real problem free-floating hostility. An occasional flash of temper is fine, they say; a permanent snarl is not. Hostile people are perpetually suspicious, wary, and snappish, forever tense and on edge. They see every sales clerk as determined to linger on the phone for hours, every compliment as a dig in disguise, every colleague as a rival in waiting.

That's bad for two reasons, says Timothy Smith, a psychologist at the University of Utah in Salt Lake City. First, hostility is harmful for all the Type H reasons. Second, hostility feeds on itself, typically leaving its "victims" precariously alone. That's worrisome because a variety of studies have shown that people with friends and families, or even pets, fare better than those without such support.

So what is a hostile person to do? The advice from the experts is surprisingly straightforward: Relax, take a deep breath, decide whether this latest injustice really merits a battle. Give in to your anger, they say, and you become all the more angry. Resist it, by keeping your voice down or your teeth ungritted, and the anger seeps away.

"Anger is not just emotion, it's physiology, too," Siegman says. "Your blood pressure goes up, your voice gets loud, you clench your jaws"—he has worked himself into a mini-tirade, bellowing at the top of his voice, windmilling his arms, thrusting his chin out belligerently—"but then, if you lower your voice, speak more slowly, relax your muscles"—he has followed his own instructions and collapsed weakly into his seat, like a balloon with a slow leak—"if you do that, if you eliminate any part of the cycle, then you weaken the whole performance, and you can't sustain the feelings of anger."

Siegman's experiments seem to support this theory. In its own way, Hollywood has tested the same idea. Audiences watching an actor in a supposed rage see and hear all the familiar signs of anger—we recognize *bad* acting precisely because there is a dissonance between spoken words and body language—and actors, by their own report, feel the emotions they simulate. Similarly, studies on laughter and smiling have shown that simulated merriment offers the same benefits—increased blood flow, reduced levels of hormones that create stress, reduced pain perception—as the genuine article.

But even among those who believe that Type H's are putting themselves at risk, Siegman's strategy for taming anger is controversial. "What if your anger is unresolved?" asks Lynda Powell, a psychologist at Chicago's Rush-Presbyterian-Saint Luke's Medical Center. "What if it's inside and you haven't dealt with it? Sometimes when you express it, you get it out and get beyond it. If you've just stuffed it inside, then the question is, Could that do just as much damage to your heart?"

Siegman is impatient with such objections, which he sees as smacking of an outdated Freudianism. "The psychoanalysts thought that anger was like physical energy," he complains. "They thought it couldn't be dissipated—the only choice was to express it or to repress it.—But anger is not like physical energy," he says. "An angry person who chooses to divert his attention will no longer be angry. We have a lot of evidence to show that."

Siegman tries to head off the doubters by making a distinction between suppressing the outward expressions of anger, which he favors, and repressing anger itself, which he warns against. The difference, he says, is that people who repress their anger don't merely stifle it; they hide it so well that they themselves are unaware of it. The person who follows Siegman's advice walks a middle road; she neither denies her rage nor gives in to it. Instead she simply decides that the matter isn't worth the theatrical fireworks—whether expressed in pounded fists and shouting or in the seething language of gritted teeth—

and calmly talks it out or lets it go. The result is that the anger neither festers nor explodes, but gradually loses its hold.

Despite skeptics' objections, the hostility–heart disease connection is undeniably tantalizing. For one thing, it seems suspicious that so many studies of heart disease in the past few years have fingered hostility as a culprit. Where there's smoke, there's ire.

So if we are a long way from proof beyond a reasonable doubt, we may still have enough evidence to justify a small bet.

What seems called for, in fact, is a mundane version of Pascal's wager. The French philosopher opted to believe in God, on the grounds that he had everything to gain if he was right and nothing to lose by being wrong.

When it comes to hostility, there doesn't seem to be much downside in taking the experts' advice to ease up a bit. This is unusual. With most medical advice—quit eating chocolate cake, say—the risks are considerable. Giving up cake cuts out part of life's pleasure, first of all, and the loss could be even worse. In five years, researchers might come back and say, "It turns out we had it wrong. It's really, the more cake the better. Sorry about that."

Here, the experts' advice amounts to every grandmother's list of maxims: Take a deep breath and count to ten, look on the bright side, don't say anything if you can't say anything nice, and so on. What's the risk? At best, you'll live longer and better. At worst, you'll be better company.

SPOTLIGHT
MEN, WOMEN, AND ANGER*

WE ALL GET ANGRY

According to a number of studies, women and men tend to get angry equally often (about six or seven times a week), equally intensely, and for more or less the same reasons. Tests designed to reveal aggressive feelings, hidden anger, or hostility turned inward haven't discovered any sex differences at all.

MEN EXPLODE, WOMEN MOSTLY SEETHE

Some angry women do shout and pound their fists, of course—just as some men do. But in general, studies show, women and men have very different styles when it comes to getting angry. Women are more likely to express anger by crying, for example, or to keep their anger under wraps. "Women have cornered the market on the seething, unspoken fury that is always threatening to explode," says Anne Campbell, a psychologist at England's Durham University. Women are also more likely to express their anger in private. They might get angry at a boss or coworker, but chances are they'll wait until they're alone or with a spouse or close friend to show their anger.

IN WOMEN, AN ANGRY OUTBURST, THEN REGRET

Surveys show that anger itself means different things to men than it does to women. Men's anger tends to be uncomplicated by restraint and guilt, says Campbell. It is straightforwardly about winning and losing. Women are more likely to feel embarrassed when they show anger, equating it with a loss of control, she says. Women are also more likely than men to believe their anger is out of proportion to the events that caused it. "After an outburst," she says, "women tell themselves, 'Whoa! Get a grip.' Men say, 'That ought to show him.'" According to one study, the more furious a woman gets, the longer it takes her to get over the episode. That's not true for men—at least not to the same degree.

The way women and men view crying is different, too. According to Campbell and other researchers, men often see women's crying as a sign of remorse or contrition—or as a tactic used to win a fight. Women are more likely to view crying as a sign of frustration or rage—a way to release tension. According to one study, 78 percent of women who cried during fights did so out of frustration.

So what does all this mean for women's risk of heart disease? Researchers say that whether anger is expressed through clenched teeth or raised voices, in public or in private, it appears to wreak the same havoc on the heart.

*Dolnick, E. (1995), July/August). Hotheads and heart attacks. *Health*, pp. 58–64. Reprinted from *Health*, Copyright © 1995, with permission.

NAME _____

DATE _____

ACTIVE LEARNING EXERCISE 4.1

HOSTILITY*

Gauging your hostility quotient isn't as simple as measuring blood pressure or cholesterol. But the following 12 questions—supplied by Redford Williams, director of behavioral research at Duke University and the author of *Anger Kills*—could indicate whether a hostile temperament is getting the best of you. Circle yes or no for each of the questions.

Y   N   **1.** Have you ever been so angry at someone that you've thrown things or slammed a door?

Y   N   **2.** Do you tend to remember irritating incidents and get mad all over again?

Y   N   **3.** Do little annoyances have a way of adding up during the day, leaving you frustrated and impatient?

Y   N   **4.** Stuck in a long line at the express checkout in the grocery store, do you often count to see if anyone ahead of you has more than ten items?

Y   N   **5.** If the person who cuts your hair trims off more than you wanted, do you fume about it for days afterward?

Y   N   **6.** When someone cuts you off in traffic, do you flash your lights or honk your horn?

Y   N   **7.** Over the past few years, have you dropped any close friends because they just didn't live up to your expectations?

Y   N   **8.** Do you find yourself getting annoyed at little things your spouse does that get under your skin?

Y   N   **9.** Do you feel your pulse climb when you get into an argument?

Y   N   **10.** Are you often irritated by other people's incompetence?

Y   N   **11.** If a cashier gives you the wrong change, do you assume he's probably trying to cheat you?

Y   N   **12.** If someone doesn't show up on time, do you find yourself planning the angry words you're going to say?

SCORING

To gauge your level of hostility, add up your yes responses. If you scored three or less, consider yourself one cool cucumber. A score of four to eight is a warning sign that anger may be raising your risk of heart disease. A score of nine or more puts you squarely in the hot zone for hostility, significantly increasing your risk of dying prematurely.

Score =

THE CURE

A few simple strategies can cool down even the hottest temper. First, when you feel yourself getting angry, stop long enough to ask yourself three questions: Is this really serious enough to get worked up over? Am I justified in getting angry? And is getting angry going to make any difference? If the answer to all three is yes, experts say, go ahead and get mad—it just might make you feel better. If not—the answer to any of the questions is no—cool out. Often, just asking reasonable questions is enough to take the edge off anger. But if you're still simmering, distract yourself by picking up a magazine, turning on music, taking a walk. Or simply close your eyes and concentrate on your breathing.

NAME _____

DATE _____

ACTIVE LEARNING EXERCISE 4.2

PERSONAL BELIEFS AND ATTITUDES*

Before reading further, answer the following questions about your personal beliefs and attitudes by circling either true or false.

T F **1.** Before voting, I would thoroughly investigate the qualifications of all the candidates.

T F **2.** I never hesitate to go out of my way to help someone in trouble.

T F **3.** It is sometimes hard for me to go on with my work if I am not encouraged.

T F **4.** I have never intensely disliked anyone.

T F **5.** On occasion I have had doubts about my ability to succeed in life.

T F **6.** I sometimes feel resentful when I don't get my way.

T F **7.** I am always careful about my manner of dress.

T F **8.** My table manners at home are as good as when I eat out in a restaurant.

T F **9.** If I could get into a movie without paying and be sure I was not seen, I would probably do it.

T F **10.** On a few occasions, I have given up doing something because I thought too little of my ability.

T F **11.** I like to gossip at times.

T F **12.** There have been times when I felt like rebelling against people in authority even though I knew they were right.

T F **13.** No matter who I'm talking to, I'm always a good listener.

T F **14.** I can remember "playing sick" to get out of something.

T F **15.** There have been occasions when I took advantage of someone.

T F **16.** I'm always willing to admit it when I make a mistake.

T F **17.** I always try to practice what I preach.

T F **18.** I don't find it particularly difficult to get along with loud-mouthed, obnoxious people.

T F **19.** I sometimes try to get even rather than forgive and forget.

T F **20.** When I don't know something I don't at all mind admitting it.

T F **21.** I am always courteous, even to people who are disagreeable.

T F **22.** At times I have really insisted on having things my own way.

T F **23.** There have been occasions when I felt like smashing things.

T F **24.** I would never think of letting someone else be punished for my wrongdoings.

T F **25.** I never resent being asked to return a favor.

T F **26.** I have never been irked when people expressed ideas very different from my own.

T F **27.** I never make a long trip without checking the safety of my car.

T F **28.** There have been times when I was quite jealous of the good fortune of others.

T F **29.** I have almost never felt the urge to tell someone off.

T F **30.** I am sometimes irritated by people who ask favors of me.

T F **31.** I have never felt that I was punished without cause.

T F **32.** I sometimes think when people have a misfortune they only got what they deserved.

T F **33.** I have never deliberately said something that hurt someone's feelings.

*Crowne, D. P., & Marlowe, D. (1960). A new scale of social desirability independent of psychopathology. *Journal of Consulting Psychology, 24,* 349–354. Reprinted with permission.

This questionnaire is widely used in psychological research as a measure of the social desirability response tendency.

To calculate your score, add the number of *true* responses to questions 1, 2, 4, 7, 8, 13, 16, 17, 18, 20, 21, 24, 25, 26, 27, 29, 31, and 33 and the number of *false* responses to questions 3, 5, 6, 9, 10, 11, 12, 14, 15, 19, 22, 23, 28, 30, and 32.

Score =

INTERPRETATION

The following table will show you how you compare with other college students.

SCORE	PERCENTILE
25	99
22	95
20	90
18	80
16	70
15	60
13	50
10	40
8	30
7	20
5	10
4	5
2	1

Research on the scale has shown that the desire to appear socially desirable is not merely a test-taking response, but reflects a more pervasive determinant of individual behavior. Crowne and Marlowe (1964) and Brannigan (1977) described a diverse series of experiments on the behavior correlates of what has been termed the *approval motive*. Findings show that higher scores are associated with enhanced sensitivity to the evaluations of others, greater compliance to social norms, and more protectiveness of the self-image. See the following article for a more detailed account of approval motivation.

REFERENCES

BRANNIGAN, G. G. (1977). Dimensions of approval motivation: Sensitivity, conformity, and defensiveness. *Psychological Reports, 40,* 1155–1159.

CROWNE, D. P., & MARLOWE, D. (1964). *The approval motive.* New York: Wiley.

READING

WHAT SOME PEOPLE WON'T DO FOR APPROVAL*

Gary G. Brannigan and Stanley W. Johnson

Editors' Note:

The past 35 years have seen extensive research on approval motivation. Gary Brannigan and Stanley Johnson offer some thoughts on the basis for our reliance on approval from others and explore the research demonstrating how approval motivation influences our behavior across a wide spectrum of situations.

Inflation may have dampened the enthusiasm of those who say, "I'd do anything for money," but don't be discouraged. Social scientists have found potent substitutes—incentives as strong as or stronger than the "All Mighty Dollar." One of the most powerful of these incentives is *social approval*.

Though social approval may be far less tangible than legal tender—often consisting of such fleeting manifestations as words, gestures, or facial expressions—it is not to be taken lightly. It is a complex and powerful phenomenon.

Beginning in infancy, we learn to associate reinforcements, such as food, drink, and relief from discomfort, with the sight, sound, and touch of significant people in our lives, most noticeably Mom and Dad. Very often, parents combine feeding, watering, and changing tasks with behaviors that express their own pleasurable feelings. They smile, speak softly, and fondly caress us. Since, as Edward Thorndike pointed out long ago, we all tend to function as *hedonists*, especially when very young, these supplementary stimuli presented by parents easily become associated with more primary pleasurable sensations and eventually take on meaning themselves. Most often the "meaning" which they acquire is of a positive valence.

Once this conditioning occurs, the stage is set for "social" variables to assume powerful control over our behavior. We quickly learn to value behavior followed by approval. And, we learn, equally well, to devaluate or even disregard behavior which does not appear to elicit approval.

In 1960, Douglas Crowne and David Marlowe developed a *Social Desirability Scale* based on the premise that *people describe themselves in favorable terms in order to gain the approval of others*. This short assessment instrument (only 33 true and false items) relies upon two types of behaviors and attitudes: (1) those culturally sanctioned and approved though occurring infrequently and (2) those culturally disapproved though they occur frequently.

Using this scale, these two researchers conducted an extensive series of experiments on the behavioral correlates of the "approval motive." Their findings suggest that the desire to appear socially acceptable is much more than a test taking phenomenon; it is a pervasive determinant of individual behavior. Indications are that approval seekers manifest extreme *sensitivity* and *conformity* to the evaluations of others.

At about the same time Crowne was exploring *social desirability* with Marlowe, he and another colleague, Bonnie Strickland, were conducting the initial formal investigations of *approval motivation*. Working under the assumption that social reinforcement would facilitate the learning behavior of approval seekers, they compared the performance of high and low approval motivated groups on a simple verbal learning task.

Subjects who were interviewed in this experiment were asked to "say words"—all the words they could think of without using sentences, phrases or numbers. Key words—in this case plural nouns—were arbitrarily followed by either favorable (mm-hmm) or unfavorable (uh-uh) verbal and head shake cues.

As expected, approval seekers were found to respond differentially to varying reinforcement conditions—responses receiving positive evaluations increased and those followed by unfavorable cues decreased. Low approval motivated groups, on the other hand, showed no significant changes in response rate under comparable conditions. The clinical importance of this phenomenon has been clearly demonstrated in simulated interviews in which the emission of such verbalizations as negative self-references, hostile verbs, and counter-attitudinal statements in approval seeking groups was altered significantly.

In addition to extreme sensitivity to the expectations of others regarding their own behavior, there is evidence that approval seekers shape their behavior to fit such expectations. In fact, they apparently ignore the reality of the world about them in favor of compliance which gains approval. In another experiment by Strickland and Crowne, college students were exposed to an *Asch* type conflict situation where an objective fact and statements of a physically present majority differed. In this simply designed study, individuals identified as high approval "types" (in comparison with those labeled as low approval "types") more often chose to ignore easily evaluated auditory stimuli—the number of knocks they heard from a recorded tape—in favor of compliance with deliberately inaccurate reports by experimental stooges.

The person on the street might explain such apparent lack of independence by saying, "If you can't lick 'em, join 'em." But psychologists see this increased sensitivity and conformity to the evaluations of others as involving an avoidance system which attempts to avert threat to self-esteem—a less parsimonious explanation to be sure, but one which receives support from the data of many other studies.

Researchers in this area feel that approval seeking behavior serves the function of maintaining or enhancing self-esteem through actively seeking approval and avoiding disapproval of others. Such an explanation incorporates a third dimension to approval motivated behavior—*defensiveness*.

Support for inclusion of this defensiveness dimension comes from a diverse group of studies ranging from avoidance of obscenity and inhibition of aggression, to premature termination of psychotherapy.

Bartel and Crowne—in one of the more interesting of these studies—reasoned that if any common behavior area was inherently loaded with traditional social evaluation it would be obscenity. In an experimental setting in which the individual was asked to recognize and report obscene material, subjects were faced with a choice between (1) inhibition of recognition responses to comply with expected social approval codes or (2) fast, accurate reporting of perceived stimulus words. High and low approval motivated college students were shown both neutral and taboo (e.g. whore, penis, bitch, screw) words. The researchers found that approval seekers, who interpreted this task as one involving social approval rather than perceptual speed, had higher recognition thresholds for the taboo words. They interpreted this to mean that approval seekers were attempting to avert disapproval by prolonged avoidance of the stimulus words.

Similarly, there are several studies which show that when approval seekers are frustrated they tend to be less aggressive than *low-approval* peers. Again, the suggested rationale for this behavior is their concern over social rejection and the resulting loss of self-esteem.

In a more applied setting, high-approval motivated patients at an outpatient psychiatric clinic were found to terminate psychotherapy earlier than low approval motivated patients. In addition to showing less improvement, they were also characterized by their therapists as being defensive. Their premature termination was regarded as an avoidant and defensive maneuver to protect their self-concepts.

Singer, in *Key Concepts in Psychotherapy*, pointed out that reliance on external guides is one of the prime expressions of psychopathology:

> "Man is all too prone to search for external guidelines and conditioners because freedom of choice and action, and the awareness of such freedom and the responsibility associated with this awareness, are frequently unbearable. But this very search for external motivators and this very abandoning of freedom are the essential expressions of psychopathology itself. Escape from freedom, as Fromm among others has shown so well, is giving up one's humanness, represents self-oblivion, leads to willing submission to totalitarian domination, and is therefore pathological. . . ."

We live in an other-directed society, one that encourages us to define ourselves according to the appraisal of others. We therefore become accustomed to looking to others for evaluation. We lose the ability to determine for ourselves when we are right. Everyone, it seems, does this to some extent. However, there are individuals who may rely *too* heavily upon social approval. These people are generally labeled as *dependent personality types*.

The distinguishing features of the dependent personality are a marked need for affection and a willingness to alter one's life in accordance with the values and desires of others. Theodore Millon, in *Modern Psychopathology*, described two basic dependent personality types—the *submissive* personality and the *gregarious* personality.

Submissive personality types are willing to give in to others, complying at any cost to the desires and demands made of them. They tend to be "self-effacing, obsequious, ever-agreeable, docile and ingratiating." The behavior of gregarious personality types is strikingly different in many ways. Rather than passively submitting to the wishes, whims, and tastes of others, they use their talents, charms, and cleverness to maneuver the approval and affection they crave. Through these devious manipulations they are capable of engaging, fascinating, and seducing those whose approval they seek. These types of individuals, although outwardly exemplifying traditional values of American middle-class culture, are, in the opinion of psychologists, actually harboring considerable social and personal conflict.

On the other hand, emotionally healthy individuals acknowledge the fact that they are "unique"—independently acting units, consciously experiencing the choices at their disposal and making responsible decisions.

Viktor Frankl, in *Man's Search for Meaning*, considered the assumption that people need to be in a state of equilibrium, a dangerous misconception of mental health. What people actually need is not a tensionless state but rather the striving and struggling for some goal worthy of them. People do not simply exist, but always decide what their existence will be, what they will become in the next moment. This way one "copes" with others without losing individual identity, generating a feeling of self-respect through a sense of pride. Unfortunately, "pride" has traditionally been considered to be a character flaw—pride goeth before destruction (Proverbs 16:18). As a society we are threatened by pride—associating it with selfishness, arrogance, and egocentrism. We even give it preeminence as the *first* of the cardinal sins.

Whenever a premium is placed upon conformity, compromise, and acquiescence (e.g., in school), pride is actually discouraged. The proud person is *not* readily accepting. He or she causes dissension and fights against those who would deny dignity and worthwhileness. In short, these individuals are more difficult to manage than their approval seeking peers . . . but, *they may be healthier*!

SPOTLIGHT
THE LEADERSHIP MOTIVE*

David McClelland identified a particular pattern of motives that was associated with effective managing within organizations. This pattern, referred to as the *leadership motive pattern*, consists of high need for power, low need for affiliation, and high self-control.

McClelland and Richard Boyatzis designed a longitudinal study of this leadership motive pattern in nontechnical managers at AT&T. Using Thematic Apperception Test data originally collected on entry-level managers from 1956 to 1960, they identified managers as either having or not having the leadership motive pattern based on a specially designed coding system to score their stories. Level of management attainment in the organization was determined by a 7-point scale (1 = lowest level of management, 7 = president of the company) at 8- and 16-year follow-ups.

As predicted, level of management at both follow-ups was associated with the leadership motive pattern. The researchers speculated that the leadership pattern is associated with success because "High need for power . . . means the person is interested in the influence game, . . . low need for affiliation enables the person to make tough decisions without worrying about being disliked, and high self-control means that the person is likely to be concerned with maintaining organizational systems and following orderly procedure" (p. 737).

*Based on material in McClelland, D. C., & Boyatzis, R. E. (1982). Leadership motive pattern and long term success in management. *Journal of Applied Psychology, 67,* 737–743.

NAME _____

DATE _____

ACTIVE LEARNING EXERCISE 4.3

SELF-MONITORING AND DATING RELATIONSHIPS*

This exercise is designed to demonstrate how a personality characteristic can relate to social behavior. Specifically, the relationship between self-monitoring orientation and commitment in dating relationships will be studied.

Self-monitoring orientation is assessed by the 18-item true/false scale developed by Mark Snyder and Steve Gangestad (1986). The scale identifies persons "whose behavior tends to be guided by what is socially appropriate in a given situation (high self-monitors) and persons whose behavior tends to be guided by their own attitudes, beliefs, and feelings, regardless of the situation at hand (low self-monitor)" (Simpson, 1988, p. 31). Mark Snyder and Jeffrey Simpson (1984) hypothesized important differences between high and low self-monitors in their dating behavior. The results of this exercise should shed some light on the nature of these differences.

You and your classmates will be collecting data from two unmarried individuals (one male and one female) who have dating histories (not necessarily with each other). Ask your subjects to complete the scale on the following page and then respond to the questions in the Dating Survey. They need only identify themselves by gender.

In class, you can combine the data.

*Adapted from Simpson, J. A. (1988). Self-monitoring and commitment to dating relationships: A classroom demonstration. Teaching of Psychology, 15, 31–33.

SELF-MONITORING SCALE*

The statements below concern your personal reactions to a number of different situations. No two statements are exactly alike, so consider each statement carefully before answering. If a statement is TRUE or MOSTLY TRUE as applied to you, circle the "T." If a statement is FALSE or NOT USUALLY TRUE as applied to you, circle the "F."

T   F   **1.** I find it hard to imitate the behavior of other people.

T   F   **2.** At parties and social gatherings, I do not attempt to do or say things that others will like.

T   F   **3.** I can only argue for ideas when I already believe.

T   F   **4.** I can make impromptu speeches even on topics about which I have almost no information.

T   F   **5.** I guess I put on a show to impress or entertain people.

T   F   **6.** I would probably make a good actor.

T   F   **7.** In a group of people I am rarely the center of attention.

T   F   **8.** In different situations and with different people, I often act like very different persons.

T   F   **9.** I am not particularly good at making other people like me.

T   F   **10.** I'm not always the person I appear to be.

T   F   **11.** I would not change my options (or the way I do things) in order to please someone else or win their favor.

T   F   **12.** I have considered being an entertainer.

T   F   **13.** I have never been good at games like charades or improvisational acting.

T   F   **14.** I have trouble changing my behavior to suit different people and different situations.

T   F   **15.** At a party I let others keep the jokes and stories going.

T   F   **16.** I feel a bit awkward in company and do not show up quite so well as I should.

T   F   **17.** I can look anyone in the eye and tell a lie with a straight face (if for a right end).

T   F   **18.** I may deceive people by being friendly when I really dislike them.

*From Snyder, M. & Gangestad, S. (1986). On the nature of self-monitoring: Matters of assessment, matters of validity. *Journal of Personality and Social Psychology, 51* (1), 125–139. Copyright © 1986 by the American Psychological Association. Reprinted with permission.

DATING SURVEY

1. Are you currently dating someone *exclusively* (that is, one person and no one else)? (Check one.)

Yes _____   No _____

2. If yes, how many *months* have you dated this person?

_____

3. If you are *not* dating one person exclusively at the present time, have you dated at least two different people in the past year? (Check one.)

Yes _____   No _____

4. If yes, how many different persons have you dated in the past year?

_____

Gender: M F

SELF-MONITORING SCALE*

The statements below concern your personal reactions to a number of different situations. No two statements are exactly alike, so consider each statement carefully before answering. If a statement is TRUE or MOSTLY TRUE as applied to you, circle the "T." If a statement is FALSE or NOT USUALLY TRUE as applied to you, circle the "F."

T   F   **1.** I find it hard to imitate the behavior of other people.

T   F   **2.** At parties and social gatherings, I do not attempt to do or say things that others will like.

T   F   **3.** I can only argue for ideas when I already believe.

T   F   **4.** I can make impromptu speeches even on topics about which I have almost no information.

T   F   **5.** I guess I put on a show to impress or entertain people.

T   F   **6.** I would probably make a good actor.

T   F   **7.** In a group of people I am rarely the center of attention.

T   F   **8.** In different situations and with different people, I often act like very different persons.

T   F   **9.** I am not particularly good at making other people like me.

T   F   **10.** I'm not always the person I appear to be.

T   F   **11.** I would not change my options (or the way I do things) in order to please someone else or win their favor.

T   F   **12.** I have considered being an entertainer.

T   F   **13.** I have never been good at games like charades or improvisational acting.

T   F   **14.** I have trouble changing my behavior to suit different people and different situations.

T   F   **15.** At a party I let others keep the jokes and stories going.

T   F   **16.** I feel a bit awkward in company and do not show up quite so well as I should.

T   F   **17.** I can look anyone in the eye and tell a lie with a straight face (if for a right end).

T   F   **18.** I may deceive people by being friendly when I really dislike them.

*From Snyder, M. & Gangestad, S. (1986). On the nature of self-monitoring: Matters of assessment, matters of validity. *Journal of Personality and Social Psychology, 51* (1), 125–139. Copyright © 1986 by the American Psychological Association. Reprinted with permission.

DATING SURVEY

1. Are you currently dating someone *exclusively* (that is, one person and no one else)? (Check one.)

        Yes _____   No _____

2. If yes, how many *months* have you dated this person?

            _____

3. If you are *not* dating one person exclusively at the present time, have you dated at least two different people in the past year? (Check one.)

        Yes _____   No _____

4. If yes, how many different persons have you dated in the past year?

            _____

SCORING

To score the scale, give one point for each of the following questions answered True: 4, 5, 6, 8, 10, 12, 17, and 18, and one point for each of the following questions answered False: 1, 2, 3, 7, 9, 11, 13, 14, 15, and 16. Total the score. High scores indicate higher self-monitoring.

MALE   **FEMALE**

Score =

In class, determine the median score for the total sample:

Median =

Those scoring above the median are *high* self-monitors. Those scoring below the median are *low* self-monitors.

Once subjects have been classified as high or low self-monitors, the following comparisons can be made.

1. As a class, determine the proportion of high versus low self-monitors who are dating someone exclusively (i.e., answered "yes" to question 1 of the Dating Survey).

PROPORTION OF EXCLUSIVE DATERS

YES   **NO**

high self-monitor

low self-monitor

2. As a class, determine the proportion of high versus low self-monitors who have dated multiple partners (i.e., answered "no" to question 1 and "yes" to question 3 of the Dating Survey).

PROPORTION OF MULTIPLE DATES

YES   **NO**

high self-monitor

low self-monitor

3. As a class, compare the number of months high and low self-monitoring exclusive daters have dated their current partners.

MONTHS DATING CURRENT PARTNER

high self-monitoring

exclusive daters

low self-monitoring

exclusive daters

4. As a class, determine the number of partners high and low self-monitoring multiple daters have dated in the past year.

NUMBER OF PARTNERS

high self-monitoring

multiple daters

low self-monitoring

multiple daters

5. What would you conclude from the results of this study?

REFERENCES

SIMPSON, J. A. (1988). Self-monitoring and commitment to dating relationships: A classroom demonstration. *Teaching of Psychology, 5*, 31–33.

SNYDER, M. & GANGESTAD, S. (1986). On the nature of self-monitoring: Matters of assessment, matters of validity. *Journal of Personality and Social Psychology, 51* (1), 125–139.

SNYDER, M., & SIMPSON, J. A. (1984). Self-monitoring and dating relationships. *Journal of Personality and Social Psychology, 47*, 1281–1291.

CHAPTER
5

Genetic
and
Evolutionary
Perspectives

Introduction

While genetic theories of personality have been proposed for many years, it is only in recent decades that significant research has begun the process of understanding the ways in which genes impact our personality. Evolutionary psychology has also proposed a number of important views about personality.

In this chapter, you will read about the Human Genome Project, the genetic impact on mental illness, obesity, homosexuality, and personality traits; sensation seeking, an interesting personality variable that appears to be biologically based; and a provocative theory about sexual attraction and mating. You will also have a chance to test what you think about these concepts by participating in the Active Learning Exercises. You will have an opportunity to assess your own level of sensation seeking, and to measure a number of interesting evolutionary concepts related to how we form human relationships.

READING

MY GENES MADE ME DO IT!*

Stanton Peele and Richard DeGranpre

Editors' Note:

The age-old issue of whether our behavior is determined by genetic or environmental causes (i.e., the nature–nurture debate) often leads us to think in simplistic ways. Stanton Peele and Richard DeGranpre present us with a comprehensive view of this issue, with many examples of important topics in personality and behavior.

Just about every week now, we read a newspaper headline about the genetic basis for breast cancer, homosexuality, intelligence, or obesity. In previous years, these stories were about the genes for alcoholism, schizophrenia, and manic-depression. Such news stories may lead us to believe our lives are being revolutionized by genetic discoveries. We may be on the verge of reversing and eliminating mental illness, for example. In addition, many believe, we can identify the causes of criminality, personality, and other basic human foibles and traits.

But these hopes, it turns out, are based on faulty assumptions about genes and behavior. Although genetic research wears the mantle of science, most of the headlines are more hype than reality. Many discoveries loudly touted to the public have been quietly refuted by further research. Other scientifically valid discoveries—like the gene for breast cancer—have nonetheless fallen short of initial claims.

Popular reactions to genetic claims can be greatly influenced by what is currently politically correct. Consider the hubbub over headlines about a genetic cause for homosexuality and by the book The Bell Curve, which suggested a substantial genetic basis for intelligence. Many thought the discovery of a "gay gene" proved that homosexuality is not a personal choice and should therefore not lead to social disapproval. The Bell Curve, on the other hand, was attacked for suggesting [that] differences in IQ measured among the races are inherited.

The public is hard pressed to evaluate which traits are genetically inspired based on the validity of scientific research. In many cases, people are motivated to accept research claims by the hope of finding solutions for frightening problems, like breast cancer, that our society has failed to solve. At a personal level, people wonder about how much actual choice they have in their lives. Accepting genetic causes for their traits can relieve guilt about behavior they want to change, but can't.

These psychological forces influence how we view mental illnesses like schizophrenia and depression, social problems like criminality, and personal maladies like obesity and bulimia. All have grown unabated in recent decades. Efforts made to combat them, at growing expense, have made little or no visible progress. The public wants to hear that science can help, while scientists want to prove that they have remedies for problems that eat away at our individual and social well-being.

Meanwhile, genetic claims are being made for a host of ordinary and abnormal behaviors, from addiction to shyness and even to political views and divorce. If who we are is determined from conception, then our efforts to change or to influence our children may be futile. There may also be no basis for insisting that people behave themselves and conform to laws. Thus, the revolution in thinking about genes has monumental consequences for how we view ourselves as human beings.

THE HUMAN GENOME PROJECT

Today's scientists are mapping the entire genome—the DNA contained in the 23 pairs of human chromosomes. This enterprise is enormous. The chromosomes of each person contain 3 billion permutations of four chemical bases arrayed in two interlocking strands. This DNA may be divided into between 50,000 and 100,000 genes. But the same DNA can function in more than one gene, making the concept of individual genes something of a convenient fiction. The mystery of how these genes, and the chemistry underlying them, cause specific traits and diseases is a convoluted one.

The Human Genome Project has, and will continue to, advance our understanding of genes and suggest preventive and therapeutic strategies for many diseases. Some diseases, like Huntington's, have been linked to a single gene. But the search for single genes for complex human traits, like sexual orientation or antisocial behavior, or mental disorders like schizophrenia or depression, is seriously misguided.

Most claims linking emotional disorders and behaviors to genes are *statistical* in nature. For example, differences in the correlations in traits between identical twins (who inherit identi-

*Peele, S. & DeGranpre, R. (1995, July/August). My genes made me do it! *Psychology Today*, pp. 50–53, 62, 64, 66, 68. Reprinted by permission of the authors.

cal genes) and fraternal twins (who have half their genes in common) are examined with the goal of separating the role of environment from that of genes. But this goal is elusive. Research finds that identical twins are treated more alike than fraternal twins. These calculations are therefore insufficient for deciding that alcoholism or manic-depression is inherited, let alone television viewing, conservatism, and other basic, everyday traits for which such claims have been made.

THE MYTH OF MENTAL ILLNESS

In the late 1980s, genes for schizophrenia and manic-depression were identified with great fanfare by teams of geneticists. Both claims have now been definitively disproved. Yet, while the original announcements were heralded on TV news and front pages of newspapers around the country, most people are unaware of the refutations.

In 1987, the prestigious British journal *Nature* published an article linking manic-depression to a specific gene. This conclusion came from family linkage studies, which search for gene variants in suspect sections on the chromosomes of families with a high incidence of a disease. Usually, an active area of DNA (called a genetic marker) is observed to coincide with the disease. If the same marker appears only in diseased family members, evidence of a genetic link has been established. Even so, this does not guarantee that a gene can be identified with the marker.

One genetic marker of manic-depression was identified in a single extended Amish family. But this marker was not apparent in other families that displayed the disorder. Then, further evaluations placed several members of the family without the marker in the manic-depressive category. Another marker detected in several Israeli families was subjected to more detailed genetic analysis, and a number of subjects were switched between the marked and unmarked categories. Ultimately, those with and without the putative markers had similar rates of the disorder.

Other candidates for a manic-depression gene will be put forward. But most researchers no longer believe a single gene is implicated, even within specific families. In fact, genetic research on manic-depression and schizophrenia has rekindled the recognition of the role of environment in emotional disorders. If distinct genetic patterns can't be tied to the disorders, then personal experiences are most likely crucial in their emergence.

Epidemiologic data on the major mental illnesses make it clear that they can't be reduced to purely genetic causes. For example, according to psychiatric epidemiologist Myrna Weissman, Ph.D., Americans born before 1905 had a 1 percent rate of depression by age 75. Among Americans born a half century later, 6 percent become depressed by *age 24*! Similarly, while the average age at which manic-depression first appears was 32 in the mid 1960s, its average onset today is 19. Only social factors can produce such large shifts in incidence and age of onset of mental disorders in a few decades.

GENES AND BEHAVIOR

Understanding the role of our genetic inheritance requires that we know how genes express themselves. One popular conception is of genes as templates stamping out each human trait whole cloth. In fact, genes operate by instructing the developing organism to produce sequences of biochemical compounds.

In some cases, a single, dominant gene *does* largely determine a given trait. Eye color and Huntington's disease are classic examples of such Mendelian traits (named after the Austrian monk, Gregor Mendel, who studied peas). But the problem for behavioral genetics is that complex human attitudes and behavior—and even most diseases—are not determined by single genes.

Moreover, even at the cellular level, environment affects the activity of genes. Much active genetic material does not code for any kind of trait. Instead it regulates the speed and direction of the expression of other genes; it modulates the unfolding of the genome. Such regulatory DNA reacts to conditions inside and outside the womb, stimulating different rates of biochemical activity and cellular growth. Rather than forming a rigid template for each of us, most genes form part of a lifelong give-and-take process with the environment.

The inextricable interplay between genes and environment is evident in disorders like alcoholism, anorexia, or overeating that are characterized by abnormal behaviors. Scientists spiritedly debate whether such syndromes are more or less biologically driven. If they are mainly biological—rather than psychological, social, and cultural—then there may be a genetic basis for them.

Therefore, there was considerable interest in the announcement of the discovery of an "alcoholism gene" in 1990. Kenneth Blum, Ph.D., of the University of Texas, and Ernest Noble, M.D., of the University of California, Los Angeles, found an allele of the dopamine receptor gene in 70 percent of a group of alcoholics—these were cadavers—but in only 20 percent of a non-alcoholic group. (An allele is a variant of a gene.)

The Blum-Noble discovery was broadcast around the country after being published in the *Journal of the American Medical Association* and touted by the AMA on its satellite news service. But, in a 1993 *JAMA* article, Joel Gelernter, M.D., of Yale and his colleagues surveyed all the studies that examined this allele and alcoholism. Discounting Blum and Noble's research, the combined results were that 18 percent of non-alcoholics, 18 percent of problem drinkers, and 18 percent of severe alcoholics *all* had the allele. There was simply no link between this gene and alcoholism!

Blum and Noble have developed a test for the alcoholism gene. But, since their own data indicate that the majority of people who have the target allele are not alcoholics, it would be foolhardy to tell those who test positive that they have an "alcoholism gene."

The dubious state of Blum and Noble's work does not disprove that a gene—or set of genes—could trigger alcoholism. But scientists already know that people do not inherit loss-of-control drinking whole cloth. Consider this: Alcoholics do not drink uncontrollably when they are unaware that they are drinking alcohol—if it is disguised in a flavored drink, for example.

A more plausible model is that genes may affect how people experience alcohol. Perhaps drinking is more rewarding for alcoholics. Perhaps some people's neurotransmitters are more activated by alcohol. But although genes can influence reactions to alcohol, they cannot explain why some people continue drinking to the point of destroying their lives. Most people find orgasms rewarding, but hardly any engage in sex uncontrollably. Rather, they balance their sexual urges against other forces in their lives.

Jerome Kagan, Ph.D., a Harvard developmental psychologist, was speaking about more than genes when he noted, "we also inherit the human capacity for restraint."

OF (FAT) MICE AND MEN

Public interest was aroused by the 1995 announcement by Rockefeller University geneticist Jeffrey Friedman, M.D., of a genetic mutation in obese mice. The researchers believe this gene influences development of a hormone that tells the organism how fat or full it is. Those with the mutation may not sense when they have achieved satiety or if they have sufficient fatty tissue, and thus can't tell when to stop eating.

The researchers also reported finding a gene nearly identical to the mouse obesity gene in humans. The operation of this gene in humans has not yet been demonstrated, however. Still, professionals like University of Vermont psychologist Esther Rothblum, Ph.D., reacted enthusiastically: "This research indicates that people really are born with a tendency to have a certain weight, just as they are to have a particular skin color or height."

Actually, behavioral geneticists believe that less than half of total weight variation is programmed in the genes, while height is almost entirely genetically determined. Whatever role genes play, America is getting fatter. A survey by the Center for Disease Control found that obesity has increased greatly over the last 10 years. Such rapid change underlines the role of environmental factors, like the abundance of rich foods, in America's overeating. The CDC has also found that teens are far less physically active than they were even a decade ago.

Certainly people metabolize food differently and some gain weight more easily than others. Nonetheless, anyone placed in a food-rich environment that encourages inactivity will gain weight, whatever fat genes the person has. But, in nearly all environments, highly motivated people can maintain lower weight levels. We thus see that social pressure, self-control, specific situations—even seasonal variations—combine with physical make-up to influence diet and determine weight.

Accepting that weight is predetermined can relieve guilt for overweight people. But people's belief that they cannot control their weight can itself contribute to obesity. No test will ever be performed that can tell you how much you must weigh. Personal choices will always influence the equation. And anything that inspires positive efforts at weight control can help people lose weight, or avoid gaining more.

The case of obesity—along with schizophrenia, depression, and alcoholism—raises a striking paradox. At the same time that we now view these conditions as diseases that should be treated medically, their prevalence is growing precipitously. The very reliance on drugs and other medical treatments has created a cultural milieu that seeks external solutions for these problems. Relying on external solutions may itself be exacerbating matters; it may be teaching us a helplessness that is at the root of many of our problems. Instead of reducing the incidence of these problems, this seems to have fueled their growth.

HOW TO INTERPRET GENETIC DISCOVERIES

1. Nature of the study

Does the study involve humans or lab animals? If animals, additional factors will almost certainly affect the same aspect of human behavior. If humans, is the study a statistical exercise or an actual investigation of the genome? Statistical studies apportioning variation in behavior between genes and environment can't tell us whether individual genes actually cause a trait.

2. Mechanism

How exactly is the gene claimed to affect the proposed trait to which it is linked? That is, does the gene affect people in a way that leads logically to the behavior or trait in question? For example, to say that a gene makes some people welcome alcohol's effects doesn't explain why they would regularly drink until they became unconscious, destroying their lives along the way.

3. Representativeness

Are the populations studied large and diverse, and does the same genetic result appear in different families and groups? Are those studied selected randomly? Early claims about manic-depression, schizophrenia, and alcoholism were made with limited groups and didn't hold up. Findings about homosexuality will likely suffer a similar fate.

4. Consistency

Are the results of the study consistent with other studies? Have other studies found a similar genetic loading for the behavior? Have gene studies identified the same gene or area of the chromosome? If every positive study implicates a different section of DNA as the major determinant of the behavior, the likelihood is that none will hold up.

5. Predictive power

How closely linked are gene and trait? One measure of power is the likelihood [that] a syndrome or disease will appear given a genetic disposition. With Huntington's gene, the disease may be inevitable. In other cases, only a small minority with a claimed genetic predisposition may express a trait. For example, accepting the original Blum–Noble figures for the A1 Allele, many more of those with the gene would not be alcoholic than would be.

6. Usefulness

What use can be made of the proposed discovery? Simply warning people [that] they will have a problem may be little help to them. Teenagers with an "alcoholism gene" who are told they are genetically predisposed to alcoholism may believe they cannot drink normally. Since most of them nonetheless will drink, they are then set up for a self-fulfilling prophecy in which they act as they have been told they would. If a proposed genetic discovery is not useful, it is merely a curiosity or, worse, a distraction from real solutions.

HARNESSING DISCOVERIES

In 1993, the gene that determines the occurrence of Huntington's disease, an irreversible degeneration of the nervous system, was discovered. In 1994, a gene was identified that leads to some cases of breast cancer. Utilizing these discoveries, however, is proving more difficult than anticipated.

Finding a gene for breast cancer was cause for elation. But of all the women with breast cancer, only a tenth have family histories of the disease. Furthermore, only half of this group has the gene mutation. Scientists also hoped that breast cancer victims without family histories would show irregularities at this same site on the DNA. But only a small minority do.

The section of the DNA involved in inherited breast cancers is enormously large and complex. There are probably several hundred forms of the gene. The task of determining which variations in the DNA cause cancer, let alone developing therapies to combat the disease, is tremendous. Right now, women who learn that they have the gene defect know they have a high (85 percent) likelihood of developing the disease. But the only decisive response available to them is to have their breasts removed before the disease appears. And even this does not eliminate the possibility of cancer.

The failure to translate genetic discoveries into treatments has also been true for Huntington's disease. Scientists have been unable to detect how the flawed gene switches on dementia and palsy. These difficulties with a disease created by an individual gene show the monumental complexity involved in unraveling how genes determine human traits.

When a distinct gene is not involved, linking genes to traits may well be an absurdity. Any possible link between genes and traits is exponentially more complex with elaborate behavior patterns like overdrinking, personality characteristics like shyness or aggressiveness, or social attitudes such as political conservatism and religiousness. Many genes might be involved in all such traits. It is impossible to separate the contributions environment and DNA make to attitudes and behaviors.

BEHAVIORAL GENETICS: METHODS AND MADNESS

The research discussed so far searches for genes implicated in specific problems. But research relating behavior and genetics rarely involves actual examination of the genome. Instead, psychologists, psychiatrists, and other nongeneticists calculate a heritability statistic by comparing the similarity in behaviors among different sets of relatives. This statistic expresses the old nature–nurture division by representing the percentage of a behavior due to genetic inheritance versus the percentage due to environmental causes.

Such research purports to show a substantial genetic component to alcoholism. For example, some studies have compared the incidence of alcoholism in adopted children with that of their adoptive parents and with their natural parents. When the similarities are greater between the offspring and absent biologic parents, the trait is thought to be highly heritable.

But children are often adopted by relatives or people from the same social background as the parents. The very social factors related to placement of a child—particularly ethnicity and social class—are also related to drinking problems, for example, thus confusing efforts to separate nature and nurture. A team led by University of California sociologist Kaye Fillmore, Ph.D., incorporated social data on adoptive families in the reanalysis of two studies claiming a large genetic inheritance for alcoholism. Fillmore found that the educational and economic level of the receiving families had the greater influence, statistically erasing the genetic contribution from the biological parents.

Another behavioral genetics methodology compares the prevalence of a trait in monozygotic (identical) twins and dizygotic (fraternal) twins. On average, fraternal twins have only half their genes in common. If the identical twins are more alike, it is believed that genetic inheritance is more important, because the two types of twins are supposedly brought up in identical environments. (To eliminate the confounding influence of gender differences, only same sex fraternal twins are compared.)

But if people treat identical twins more similarly than they treat fraternal twins, the assumptions of the heritability index dissolve. Much research shows that physical appearance affects how parents, peers, and others react to a child. Thus, identical twins—who more closely resemble one another—will experience a more similar environment than fraternal twins. University of Virginia psychologist Sandra Scarr, Ph.D., has shown that fraternal twins who resemble one another enough to be *mistaken* for identical twins have more similar personalities than other such twins.

Heritability figures depend upon a number of factors, such as the specific population being studied and where. For example, there will be less variation in weight in a food-deprived environment. Studying the inheritance of weight in deprived settings rather than [in] an abundant food environment can greatly influence the heritability calculation.

Heritability figures in fact vary widely from study to study. Matthew McGue, Ph.D., and his colleagues at the University of Minnesota calculated a zero heritability of alcoholism in women, while at the same time a team led by Kenneth Kendler, M.D., at Virginia Medical College calculated a 60 percent heritability with a different group of female twins! One problem is that the number of female alcoholic twins is small, which is true of most abnormal conditions we study. As a result, the high heritability figure Kendler's team found would be reduced to nothing with a shift in the diagnoses of as few as four twins.

CATEGORIES OF TRAITS IN RELATION TO GENES

Physical Traits

Non-pathological physical traits that are purely genetic (eye color).

Non-pathological traits with some environmental influence (height).

Abnormal physical traits caused by combinations of genetic disposition and behavior (obesity).

Illnesses

Physical illnesses with no known environmental influence (Huntington's disease).

Physical illnesses with environmental/behavioral influences (breast cancer, heart disease).

Mental illness involving genetic/environmental interactions (schizophrenia, manic depression).

Behaviors

Abnormal behavioral syndromes in which genetic predisposition may affect behavior (bulimia, overeating, alcoholism).

Personal traits that involve genetic/environmental interactions (shyness, aggressiveness, intelligence).

Personal traits in which biological correlates are remote (TV watching, ring wearing).

Personal dispositions with no identified biological correlates (conservatism, religiosity).

Shifting definitions also contribute to variations in the heritability measured for alcoholism. Alcoholism may be defined as any drinking problems, or only physiological problems such as DTs, or various combinations of criteria. These variations in methodology explain why heritability figures for alcoholism in different studies vary from zero to almost 100 percent!

THE INHERITANCE OF HOMOSEXUALITY

In the debate over homosexuality, the data supporting a genetic basis are similarly weak. One study by Michael Bailey, Ph.D., a Northwestern University psychologist, and Richard Pillard, M.D., a psychiatrist at Boston University, found that about half the identical twins (52 percent) of homosexual brothers were homosexual themselves, compared with about a quarter (22 percent) of fraternal twins of homosexuals. But this study recruited subjects through ads in gay publications. This introduces a bias toward the selection of overtly gay respondents, a minority of all homosexuals.

Moreover, other results of their study do not support a genetic basis for homosexuality. Adopted brothers (11 percent) had as high a "concordance rate" for homosexuality as ordinary brothers (9 percent). The data also showed that fraternal twins were more than twice as likely as ordinary brothers to share homosexuality, although both sets of siblings have the same genetic relationship. These results suggest the critical role of environmental factors.

One study that focused on a supposed homosexual gene was conducted by Dean Hamer, Ph.D., a molecular biologist at the National Cancer Institute. Hamer found a possible genetic marker on the X chromosome in 33 of 40 brothers who were both gay (the number expected by chance was 20). Earlier Simon LeVay, M.D., a neurologist at the Salk Institute, noted an area of the brain's hypothalamus that was smaller among gay than heterosexual men.

Although both these findings were front-page stories, they provide quite a slender basis for the genetics of homosexuality. Hamer did not check for the frequency of the supposed marker in heterosexual brothers, where it could conceivably be as prevalent as in gay siblings. Hamer has noted that he doesn't know how the marker he found could cause homosexuality, and LeVay likewise concedes he hasn't found a brain center for homosexuality.

But for many, the politics of a homosexual gene outweigh the science. A genetic explanation for homosexuality answers bigots who claim homosexuality is a choice that should be rejected. But to accept that nongenetic factors contribute to homosexuality does not indicate prejudice against gays. David Barr, of the Gay Men's Health Crisis, puts the issue this way: "It doesn't really matter why people are gay. . . . What's really important is how they're treated."

EVERYDAY PSYCHOLOGICAL TRAITS

By assigning a simple percentage to something very complex and poorly understood, behavioral geneticists turn heritability into a clear-cut measurement. Behavioral geneticists have employed these same statistical techniques with ordinary behaviors and attitudes. The resulting list of traits for which heritability has been calculated extends from such well-known areas as intelligence, depression, and shyness to such surprising ones as television viewing, divorce, and attitudes like racial prejudice and political conservatism.

Such heritability figures may seem quite remarkable, even incredible. Behavioral geneticists report that half of the basis of divorce, bulimia, and attitudes about punishing criminals is biologically inherited, comparable to or higher than the figures calculated for depression, obesity, and anxiety. Almost any trait seemingly yields a minimum heritability figure around 30 percent. The heritability index acts like a scale that reads 30 pounds when empty and adds 30 pounds to everything placed on it!

Believing that basic traits are largely predetermined at birth could have tremendous implications for our self conceptions and public policies. Not long ago, an announcement of a government conference, for example, suggested that violence could be prevented by treating with drugs children with certain genetic profiles. Or parents of children with an alcoholic heritage may tell the children never to drink because they're destined to be alcoholics. But such children, in expecting to become violent or drink excessively, may enact a self-fulfilling prophecy. Indeed, this is known to be the case. People who believe they are alcoholic drink more when told a beverage contains alcohol—even if it doesn't.

Believing the heritability figures developed by behavioral geneticists leads to an important conclusion: Most people must then be overestimating how much daily impact they have on important areas of children's development. Why ask Junior to turn off the TV set if television viewing is inherited, as some claim? What, exactly, can parents accomplish if traits such as prejudice are largely inherited? It would not seem to matter what values we attempt to convey to our children. Likewise, if violence is mostly inbred, then it doesn't make much sense to try to teach our kids to behave properly.

FROM FATALISM TO DEPRESSION

The vision of humanity generated by statistical research on behavioral genetics seems to enhance the passivity and fatalism many people are already saddled with. Yet evidence gathered by University of Pennsylvania psychologist Martin Seligman, Ph.D., and others indicates that "learned helplessness"—or believing one can't influence one's destiny—is a major factor in depression. The opposite state of mind occurs when people believe they control what happens to them. Called self-efficacy, it is a major contributor to psychological well-being and successful functioning.

Is there a connection between the increase in depression and other emotional disorders in 20th-century America and our outlook as a society? If so, then the growing belief that our behavior is not ours to determine could have extremely negative consequences. As well as attacking our own sense of personal self-determination, it may make us less able to disapprove of the misbehavior of others. After all, if people are born to be alcoholic or violent, how can they be punished when they translate these dispositions into action?

Jerome Kagan, whose studies provide a close-up of the interaction of nature and nurture and how it plays out in real life, worries that Americans are too quick to accept that behavior is predetermined. He has studied the temperaments of infants and children and found distinctive differences from birth—and even before. Some babies are outgoing, seemingly at home in the world. And some recoil from the environment; their nervous systems are overly excitable in response to stimulation. Do such findings mean [that] children born with a highly reactive nervous system will grow into withdrawn adults? Will extremely fearless children grow into violent criminals?

In fact, less than half of the reactive infants (those who more frequently fret and cry) are fearful children at the age of two. It all depends on the actions parents take in response to their infant.

Kagan fears people may read too much into children's supposedly biological dispositions, and make unwarranted predictions about how they will develop: "It would be unethical to tell parents that their three-year-old son is at serious risk for delinquent behavior." People who are more fearful or fearless than average have choices about the paths their lives will take, like everyone else.

NATURE, NURTURE: LET'S CALL THE WHOLE THING OFF

How much freedom each person has to develop returns us to the issue of whether nature and nurture can be separated. Thinking of traits as being either environmentally or genetically caused cripples our understanding of human development. As Kagan puts it, "To ask what proportion of personality is genetic rather than environmental is like asking what proportion of a blizzard is due to cold temperature rather than humidity."

A more accurate model is one in which chains of events split into further layers of possible paths. Let's return to alcoholism. Drinking produces greater mood change for some people. Those who find alcohol to serve a strong palliative function will be more likely to use it to calm themselves. For example, if they are highly anxious, alcohol may tranquilize them. But even this tranquilizing effect, we should recognize, is strongly influenced by social learning.

Among drinkers who are potentially vulnerable to alcohol's addictive effects, most will nonetheless find alternatives to drinking to deal with anxiety. Perhaps their social group disapproves of excessive drinking, or their own values strongly rule out drunkenness. Thus, although people who find that alcohol redresses their anxiety are more likely to drink addictively than others, they are not programmed to do so.

MIRROR, MIRROR

The goal of determining what portion of behavior is genetic and environmental will always elude us. Our personalities and destinies don't evolve in this straightforward manner. Behavioral genetics actually shows us how the statistical plumbing of the human spirit has reached its limits. Claims that our genes cause our problems, our misbehavior, even our personalities are more a mirror of our culture's attitudes than a window for human understanding and change.

NAME _____

DATE _____

ACTIVE LEARNING EXERCISE 5.1

SENSATION-SEEKING SCALE*

The following questionnaire is a brief version of the Sensation-Seeking Scale. For each of the 13 items, circle the choice, A or B, that best describes your likes or dislikes or the way you feel. Instructions for scoring appear at the end of the test.

1. **A.** I would like a job that requires a lot of traveling.
   B. I would prefer a job in one location.

2. **A.** I am invigorated by a brisk, cold day.
   B. I can't wait to get indoors on a cold day.

3. **A.** I get bored seeing the same old faces.
   B. I like the comfortable familiarity of everyday friends.

4. **A.** I would prefer living in an ideal society in which everyone is safe, secure, and happy.
   B. I would have preferred living in the unsettled days of our history.

5. **A.** I sometimes like to do things that are a little frightening.
   B. A sensible person avoids activities that are dangerous.

6. **A.** I would not like to be hypnotized.
   B. I would like to have the experience of being hypnotized.

7. **A.** The most important goal of life is to live it to the fullest and experience as much as possible.
   B. The most important goal of life is to find peace and happiness.

8. **A.** I would like to try parachute-jumping.
   B. I would never want to try jumping out of a plane, with or without a parachute.

9. **A.** I enter cold water gradually, giving myself time to get used to it.
   B. I like to dive or jump right into the ocean or a cold pool.

10. **A.** When I go on a vacation, I prefer the comfort of a good room and bed.
    B. When I go on a vacation, I prefer the change of camping out.

11. **A.** I prefer people who are emotionally expressive even if they are a bit unstable.
    B. I prefer people who are calm and even-tempered.

12. **A.** A good painting should shock or jolt the senses.
    B. A good painting should give one a feeling of peace and security.

13. **A.** People who ride motorcycles must have some kind of unconscious need to hurt themselves.
    B. I would like to drive or ride a motorcycle.

SCORING

Count one point for each of the following items that you have circled: 1A, 2A, 3A, 4B, 5A, 6B, 7A, 8A, 9B, 10B, 11A, 12A, 13B. Add up your total and compare it with the norms below.

Score =

1–8	Very low on sensation-seeking	10–11	High
4–5	Low	12–13	Very High
6–9	Average		

*Reprinted with permission from *Psychology Today* magazine. Copyright © 1978 (Sussex Publishers, Inc.).

READING

THE SEARCH FOR HIGH SENSATION*

Marvin Zuckerman

Editors' Note:

Marvin Zuckerman traces the development of his concept of sensation-seeking. You have already

completed Active Learning Exercise 5.1, which gives you an idea of your own rating on this dimension

of personality. Zuckerman views this trait as biologically based but certainly recognizes the impact of

various sociocultural factors.

We are living in what has been called the Age of Sensation, although for most it is only the age of vicarious sensation. The sex and aggression in films and television produce only brief excitement and respite from boredom for the routinized urban worker. Football and hockey spectacles are a pallid substitute for the gory productions of the Roman Colosseum. In past centuries, war, conquest, and exploration, along with saturnalias, tournaments, public executions, and orgiastic feasts, fed the hunger for unusual and arousing experience. The knights rode out on their Crusades to enjoy new sights and to rape, plunder, and fight, while back at the castles their wives played with the troubadours and composed love lyrics. The peasants sought more earthy pleasures when they had the time or energy.

In 19th-century America, the more adventurous struck out for the frontier when life on the Eastern seaboard became tame and predictable. Ever since our ancestors settled in permanent locations, boredom has been a problem that varies inversely with the need for survival. In every society, there are some persons who are more susceptible to boredom than others. For them, security is not a goal in life, it is their nemesis. As life becomes more secure, some men and women feel compelled to search for new, nonvicarious sources of excitement and novel experience.

"Boredom" is the term we use to describe the negative feeling produced by lack of change in the environment. When we are bored, we may be inclined to indulge in risky adventures, artistic creation, adulterous sex, alcohol, drugs, and sometimes even aggression. I call this demand for stimulation and varied experience "sensation-seeking." It is one of man's primary needs and the source of much of our creativity as well as much of our discontent and destructiveness. I also believe that it has a biological basis we share with other mammals.

When our basic survival needs for food, drink, and warmth are satisfied, we do not simply hibernate until driven into action by the next upswing of our internal-need cycles. Like other mammals, humans spend a great deal of time in play and in exploration of their physical and social environment. Even the lowly rat will explore a new environment, work to turn lights on and off, and vary the paths it follows to get to the same place. Curiosity and exploration seem to increase in mammals that are higher up on the evolutionary scale. Studies that have been done on monkeys and cats also show striking individual differences in the animals' tendency to approach novel stimuli and to explore new environments.

Sensation-seekers may be identified on a scale of 40 items that I have been developing since the 1960s and that asks subjects to rate themselves on a wide variety of interests and experiences. More than 10,000 persons in countries around the world have taken the test, which includes such paired choices as: (a) I enter cold water gradually, giving myself time to get used to it; and (b) I like to dive or jump right into the ocean or a cold pool. The Sensation-Seeking Scale has gone through five versions, and will be further refined as we test more subjects in my laboratory at the University of Delaware.

I have concluded that sensation-seeking is a general trait that is not restricted to any one sensory modality. In other words, people who tend to crave more visual stimulation than others, for instance, also want more stimulation from other senses. The high sensation-seekers are likely to have not just one but a number of adventurous tastes, from an eagerness to try risky sports such as sky-diving to a desire for variety in sexual partners. As a group, they rate the dangers of such activities lower than those who generally seek less stimulation. Even when high and low sensation-seekers appraise the risk in the same way, the highs contemplate the activity with more pleasure than anxiety, while the low sensation-seekers experience nothing but anxiety.

Like many traits, sensation-seeking may rest on a biological foundation and yet may depend for its particular expression on a range of environmental possibilities. Still, if some humans have an innate need for more stimulation than others, knowing whether one is a "high" or a "low" can be important: it may be the crucial conditions in choosing an occupation, a mate, or a style of living.

*Zuckerman, M. (1978, February). The search for high sensation. *Psychology Today, 11*, pp. 38–41, 43, 46, 96–99.

My interest in sensation-seeking stems from my experiments on sensory deprivation in humans, which were done in the 1960s. In a sensory-deprivation experiment, a person spends from 40 minutes to two weeks in a room or water tank where his visual and auditory stimulation is severely restricted. In extended experiments, his basic physical needs are taken care of: food, drink, and a toilet are provided

Not many persons in such a situation consider it nirvana. Emotional reactions range from boredom to panic. About a third of the subjects cannot stay more than two days in an isolation room, and hardly anyone can stay more than 10 hours in a water-tank "womb." If subjects are allowed to do something for stimulation, like pressing a lever that produces random patterns of light and sound, they work as hard as any rat in a Skinner box trying to earn its dinner or stimulate pleasure centers in its brain.

I developed the first Sensation-Seeking Scale with the idea that it might predict the reactions to sensory deprivation. It was developed from the theory that consistent differences between people in their optimal levels of stimulation and arousal were the basis of the wide individual differences in reactions to sensory deprivation. In writing items for the first test, I thought of friends who seemed to embody the extremes of the trait in their preferences, attitudes, and behavior.

I did find a very broad trait in the first test, with items ranging from preferences for spicy foods to desires to try risky sports such as parachuting or drugs such as hallucinogens. Applying the scale to our sensory-deprivation experiments, I found that high sensation-seekers got very restless when they were confined in any isolation condition, although they were quite happy when there was another person in the room and lots of slides to look at and music to listen to. Under these more stimulating conditions, it was the low sensation-seekers who became uncomfortable and disturbed.

Sensory deprivation became too confining as a model, and in the early 1970s, I began to ask questions about what kind of experiences sensation-seekers were having in the real world. It was a good time to look at sensation-seeking behavior. The early 1970s represented the peak of the middle-class student drug cult, the middle of a second sexual revolution after the first revolution in the 1920s, and the beginning of the end for the hippie phenomenon.

Sensation-seekers, as defined by my test, were experimenting extensively with drugs, particularly the more stimulating kinds such as marijuana, hashish, amphetamines, and LSD. Low sensation-seekers avoided even marijuana in the first two years of college, but a minority of them smoked it occasionally in their senior year, possibly because of social pressures. The relationships between the sensation-seeking traits and drug use have been confirmed by large-scale studies at other universities such as Yale and Murray State University in Kentucky. Polydrug users

in noncollege populations also have high scores on the Sensation-Seeking Scale, in contrast to alcoholics, occasional drinkers, or abstainers. Most people who abstain from both drugs and alcohol score extremely low on the scale.

I also found that high sensation-seekers in the early years of college have more varied heterosexual experiences, with more sexual partners, than do the lows. The highs are more likely than the lows to have had sexual intercourse and to have experimented with oral-genital sex. Seymour Fisher, a psychology professor at the SUNY Upstate Medical Center, used an early version of the Sensation-Seeking Scale in his study, *The Female Orgasm*. The young married women in his study who were rated high on sensation-seeking reported frequent intercourse, masturbation, multiple orgasms, and copious vaginal lubrication during intercourse. They were so easily aroused that they even became sexually excited during a laboratory session that did not involve direct erotic stimulation.

It is not hard to find sensation-seekers on college campuses: they are attracted in large numbers to any unusual experiment or activity that promises some kind of new experience. The highs tend to volunteer for sensory deprivation, hypnosis, and drug experiments, but not for learning or sleep experiments. I used to wonder why so many high sensation-seekers were volunteering for my experiments in sensory deprivation. The question was answered one day when a long-haired young man emerged after eight hours in the isolation room, complaining that he had not had any hallucinations. He had heard that sensory deprivation was a new kind of "trip."

The sensation-seekers also "flock" to courses in gambling, sensitivity training, alpha-wave control, meditation, and encounter groups. They do well in encounter groups and leaderless discussion groups, which enable them to assume dominant roles. But they do not usually persist in isolated activities such as meditation, which they find boring.

Although there is a low positive correlation between intelligence and sensation-seeking, the highs are not often achievers in high school and college. A closer analysis reveals that even in high school, they tend to cut classes and drink. Although studies have shown evidence of creativity in highs, they frequently are distracted by more hedonistic pursuits and do not realize their potential. The typical large high-school or college class is not conducive to the kind of creative interchange that would stimulate them. Instead of the usual lectures, sensation-seekers might benefit from spirited debates and assignments that would involve them in new experiences outside the classroom.

As more and more people took the sensation-seeking test, I added new items and analyzed patterns in the responses. After one experimental version, which was tested in Great Britain and the U.S., I, together with other researchers, found the items fell into four clusters, which I consider primary expressions of sensation-seeking.

SENSATION-SEEKERS: THEIR UPS AND DOWNS

Just what drives a person who likes to parachute from airplanes on weekends, fight as a mercenary in Angola, or go on vacations to the most remote, exotic corners of the earth? People who do not feel alive without such novel stimulation have described their experiences and emotions in a variety of ways.

Jacques Cousteau, one of these fortunate individuals who are able to gratify their taste for adventure in their work, once explained to an interviewer why he does what he does. "It's fun to do things you're not made to do, like going to the moon or living under the ocean," Cousteau said. "I was playing when I invented the Aqua-lung. I'm still playing. I think play is the most serious thing in the world."

An article in the *New York Times* described the background of an American mercenary captured in Angola: "In a short time, while working in a semi-skilled job he apparently regarded as menial, he took up skydiving . . . joined the National Guard, and took out a learner's permit for a 'motorcycle'." Evidently, this man was still not satisfied because he then advertised his availability as a soldier of fortune in a magazine for "professional adventures." The *Times* article continued: "His wife believed that he never seriously considered the danger to himself, that he was not blindly courageous, but simply naive and single-minded."

When "streaking" became a fad on college campuses in 1974, a study by Ronald Bone, professor of psychology at West Virginia Wesleyan College, showed that students who took part, or wanted to, were high sensation-seekers. A newspaper report described the rewards as seen by one group of streakers. "Like other participants, they discovered the heady exhilaration that is said to accompany streaking, first the sense of daring, then the nervous anticipation as you undress, the last fleeting moment of fear before you start, the wet grass underfoot, the pounding heart during the dash, the smiles of spectators flashing by, the wind brushing against your cheeks [*sic*], and the warm sense of accomplishment as you dress—uncaptured—at your goal."

This account suggests the moderate fear arousal that actually adds to the pleasure of sensation-seeking. Fear, anger, and even pain can have some attractive aspects for a sensation-seeker. For instance, actor Walter Matthau once described the curious motivation of the compulsive gambler this way: "Pain is what he's searching for—the emotion of pain," Matthau said, in all seriousness. "It's much greater than the emotion of pleasure. Bigger, larger, stronger. Therefore, more interesting."

The conflict between sensation-seeking and anxiety is very real for people who like to travel but are afraid of it. One traveler described the agony: "So there is this real fear, I think, a fear of new things where you're off your own ground, which means you're out of your body; out of your own self. There's the chance that you'll just be taken over, like the heart of darkness, where you'll go so deeply into this new experience, and away from what has defined your life in the past, that you run the risk of losing it all."

Is it any wonder that some people prefer to spend their vacations at home, or in the same place every summer? An article on Alfred Hitchcock noted that the famous director, who is known for his suspenseful films, dreads traveling. When he must go someplace, Hitchcock books the same rooms in the same hotels he has stayed in before "to preserve some sense of continuity." —**M.Z.**

Thrill- and Adventure-Seeking. The desire to seek excitement in risky but socially acceptable activities, such as parachute-jumping, diving, [or] driving fast, is a form of sensation-seeking that had been obvious from the start. Most of those who take the scale have never engaged in activities such as parachute-jumping, but their expression of a desire to do so is enough to predict their behavior in many other areas.

Experience-Seeking. The desire to seek sensation through the mind and the senses and through a nonconforming lifestyle was a less obvious element. Informally, I call this the "hippie fac-tor." Although the term is almost anachronistic, going the way of "bohemian" and "beatnik," there will always be some part of the population who cannot live in a conventional middle-class way and seeks a freer existence, with unusual friends, frequent travel, or artistic expression of some sort.

Disinhibition. For those who choose the middle-class life and find it tedious, there is an escape in social drinking, partying, gambling, and variety in sexual partners. This is a kind of extraverted sensation-seeking. "Disinhibitors" need people as sources of stimulation. They drink to free themselves from whatever social inhibitions they may have, as the Dionysians among us have for many centuries.

Boredom Susceptibility. The fourth factor is not another mode of sensation-seeking but rather a low tolerance for experience that is repetitious or constant. Not all sensation-seekers are incapable of facing long periods of time with little external stimulation, but the boredom-susceptible person gets extremely restless under such conditions.

It must be emphasized that people who have high scores on one of these factors are likely to be high on the others as well. Sometimes an individual may be high on one and just average on others; for instance, he might find all his stimulation in risky outdoor activities, and, at the same time, lead a quiet, conventional social life. But studies of people with extensive drug and sexual experience, and people who engage in physically risky activities, find that they tend to be high on all the scales. This is why I believe that sensation-seeking is a broad, unitary trait, rather than a trait that reflects learned preferences for one type of activity or another.

Sensation-seekers are not led into their activities by peers or driven to them by compulsive neurotic needs. Actually, there is no correlation between sensation-seeking and neuroticism. Therapists who do not understand this may run into problems. If they are low sensation-seekers themselves, they may not recognize the strength of the disposition in the high sensation-seeking patients, and may expect their patients' needs to disappear after treatment.

Freud viewed sensation-seeking behavior as either an attempt to master anxiety or a disguised expression of the sexual motive that had, as its ultimate aim, the reduction of tension. In contrast, the theory I propose suggests that the sexual motive becomes differentiated from a broader sensory motive, one involving all of the senses, that requires changing stimulation to activate the brain. The increase of tension, not its reduction, is the sensation-seekers' aim.

But is there a biological basis for this disposition? Much of my recent research has been devoted to this question, and has required collaboration with scientists in other fields. One of the best ways to investigate the relative contributions of nature and nurture is to compare identical or fraternal twins with each other. One such study in England grew out of my work with David Fulker, a behavioral geneticist, and Hans and Sybil Eysenck, pioneers in the biological approach to personality. We compared the differences in scores between identical twins (with the same genes) and fraternal twins (who are as genetically similar as ordinary siblings). We found that the scores of the identicals on the Sensation-Seeking Scale were much closer than the scores of the fraternals. Using new biometrical methods on the data, we concluded that somewhere between one-half and two-thirds of the variability in this general trait can be accounted for by heredity.

Studies in my laboratory have shown that high sensation-seekers have a stronger physiological response to novel stimuli of moderate intensity, as measured by galvanic skin response, than low sensation-seekers. They may need constant variety in stimuli in order to reach their own high optimal level of arousal, the level that "feels best" or where they perform most efficiently. But although they are highly aroused by a novel stimulus, they tend to stop responding when it is repeated and show about the same level of response as the lows. This responsivity to novel stimuli was called the "orienting reflex" by Pavlov. Behaviorally, the strong orienting reflexes of the highs were evident in their curiosity about the experiment and their own ratings of their degree of interest in it.

Monte Buchsbaum, a research scientist at the National Institute of Mental Health, has developed a method of measuring the brain's electrical responses (or "evoked potentials") to low- and high-intensity stimulation. He finds that some people have brains that keep pace with stimulation intensities: the stronger the stimulus, the more the brain responds. Such persons are called "augmenters." Other persons have some kind of inhibition that actually diminishes their brain response at high intensities. They are called "reducers."

Buchsbaum and I have shown that high sensation-seekers, particularly those high on the "disinhibition" factor, tend to be augmenters. This means that they continue to respond to high intensities of stimulation and lack a natural protective mechanism that is found in the reducers. The lack of such protection, Buchsbaum and other researchers have found, is a characteristic of manic-depressives, who are subject to extreme swings of mood from deep depression on the one hand to states of high excitement and overactivity on the other.

The behavior of manics represents sensation-seeking out of control. During manic attacks, they develop extraordinary self-esteem and euphoria. They tend to be constantly on the move, traveling from place to place on "missions of great importance." Hypersexuality and extreme sociability are typical. Great plans are made, deals consummated, and great sums of money spent [often in the form of bad checks].

We have not been able to test a sample of manics on the Sensation-Seeking Scale. But the highest correlate of sensation-seeking on the Minnesota Multiphasic Personality Inventory is a scale called "hypomania," which was actually developed using clinical cases of mania. This does not mean that most high sensation-seekers are vulnerable to manic-depressive disorder. There are probably other genetic factors that make some high sensation-seekers vulnerable and others not.

One of these may be fluctuations in the levels of chemical neurotransmitters in the brain and at the nerve synapses, such as nonadrenaline and dopamine. The levels of these neurotransmitters determine the excitability of brain centers that govern mood and motivation. Other chemicals in the brain regulate the supply of neurotransmitters, and one of the most important is monoamine oxidase (MAO). Chemicals that block MAO (MAO inhibitors) have been used to improve the mood of depressed patients. However, if these MAO inhibitors are given to manic-depressives in their depressed phase, nondepressed patients, or normals, they may actually cause manic-like behavior. By inference, we suspect that brain MAO controls the activity of the neurotransmitters.

If sensation-seeking is related to the supply of neurotransmitters in crucial brain areas, then high sensation-seekers should have low MAO levels and low sensation-seekers should have high MAO levels. Dennis Murphy, Buchsbaum, and other scientists at the National Institute of Mental Health have just found such a negative relationship between platelet MAO and sensation-seeking in several samples of normal subjects. While platelet MAO, obtained from the blood, is not the same as brain MAO, there are grounds for inferring that high levels of the platelet MAO indicate high levels of the brain MAO.

A more direct test of our hypothesis would involve the chemical neurotransmitters themselves. While levels of brain chemicals are difficult to measure in living organisms, one experiment suggests that large amounts of a metabolite, or chemical byproduct of brain noradrenaline, is related to high sensation-seeking. If this relationship can be replicated in larger samples, it will provide more direct evidence for this biological basis of sensation-seeking.

Another biochemical link has been discovered in sex hormones. Androgens, or male hormones, and estrogens, female hormones, are found in both sexes in different proportions. Reid Daitzman, who started this research for a doctoral dissertation at the University of Delaware, has found that high sensation-seekers among college students have high levels of both types of sex hormones. Interestingly, there is a theory that sex hormones have a role in activating neurotransmitters such as noradrenaline, by counterbalancing the effect of MAO.

While such evidence is strongly suggestive, many no doubt will be skeptical about this rather biologically biased approach to a behavioral trait. What about the influence of family examples, the role of culture, learning, and early environmental experience? I sympathize with their objections. Studies show that monkeys reared in social isolation or a dull environment are much more cautious in approaching novel stimuli, including other monkeys.

They also tend to have problems with some basic social behavior, such as mating and care of the young. In contrast, monkeys raised in normal circumstances prefer complex to simple visual stimuli and, without much hesitancy, will investigate novel objects in a new environment. They also have few social problems.

Social forces undoubtedly play a crucial role in shaping a behavioral trait. The problem in testing a social influence

hypothesis on humans is that we would not want to raise them in such severely restricted environments. There are also problems in looking at sensation-seeking among children in their home environments. Parents who provide stimulating environments for their children are likely to be high sensation-seekers themselves. If their children turn out the same way, was it the influence of genes that is most responsible or the example and stimulation that the parents provided? Ultimately, I hope we develop some method for controlling the social influences and studying their interaction with hereditary tendencies.

Many people seem to know just how much stimulation they want and need: whether they are high or low sensation-seekers no doubt plays a part in their life choices. For instance, the highs among our study subjects, who filled out vocational-interest scales, showed a preference for occupations that would bring them into varied kinds of "helping" social contacts with people, such as psychiatry and psychology. Men interested in business occupations such as accounting, and women interested in taking on a traditionally female occupation, such as homemaker, school teacher, or dietitian, tend to be low sensation-seekers. Physicians, psychologists, and paraprofessionals who volunteer for crisis intervention—for instance, responding to calls on suicide or drug hotlines—tend to be high sensation-seekers.

But sometimes the individual's choices are limited, and his environment and temperament may be ill-matched. When a high sensation-seeker is tied down to a dull, routine kind of job for eight hours a day, he builds up a terrible kind of tension that can lead to the abuse of alcohol or drugs. Some former drug abusers I've treated in a therapeutic community, for example, described how they would have to get drunk or high in order to face a day on the assembly line. Eventually, they came to prefer the risky excitement of drug-related crime to the grinding monotony of their jobs. After they had resolved not to return to drugs, they asked me, "What will we do for excitement?" Some former heroin users in California found one answer to this problem. According to a report in the *News-Journal* of Wilmington, Delaware: "Twelve former heroin users have been getting high these days by parachuting from airplanes at 2,800 feet. . . . 'Getting high naturally is the high of highs' became the unofficial motto of the 'Bridge Over Troubled Waters' correctional drug-abuse house, after the sky-jumping debuts this month."

High sensation-seekers born into middle-class, educated families may also become bored with their work, of course. Unlike the poor, however, they have a range of outlets for their needs, from sports such as skiing and scuba diving, to travel and other recreation, to sexual adventures. None of these activities is illegal, but low sensation-seekers may consider some of them reprehensible, foolish, and even crazy. The highs, for their part, consider the caution of the lows prudish, stuffy, timid, or inhibited. High and low sensation-seekers do not understand one another and this can be an unfortunate state of affairs if they are therapist and patient, or husband and wife.

NAME _____

DATE _____

EVOLUTIONARY PERSPECTIVES QUESTIONNAIRE*

Complete the following questions before reading further about this exercise.

1. You are on a boat that overturns. It contains your 5-year-old and your 1-year-old children (of the same sex). The boat sinks and you can save only one. Whom do you choose to save? Circle one.

   5-year-old   1-year-old

2. That same boat (you are slow to learn lessons) contains your 40-year-old and 20-year-old children (both of the same sex). Neither can swim. As the boat sinks, whom do you choose to save? Circle one.

   40-year-old   20-year-old

3. You and your spouse are the proud parents of a new child. The grandparents are ecstatic. Who do you think will be kinder to the child? Circle one.

   the mother of the mother   the mother of the father

4. Who will mourn more at the death of a child? Circle the answer in each pair.

   a. father   mother

   b. parents of the father   parents of the mother

   c. younger parents   older parents

5. Which will elicit more grief? Circle the answer in each pair.

   a. death of a son   death of a daughter

   b. death of an unhealthy child   death of a healthy child

*Weiner, B. (1992). *Human motivation: Metaphors, theories, and research* (p. 51). Thousand Oaks, CA: Sage.

The questionnaire you completed will allow you to become familiar with the major concepts of evolutionary psychology, a new and important method of viewing personality. Evolutionary thinking suggests that humans are basically motivated to extend their own genetic makeup. Basically our genes influence us to behave in a manner that facilitates our chance of surviving and reproducing. The following analysis is based on Weiner's (1992) presentation.

ANALYZING THE EVOLUTIONARY PERSPECTIVES QUESTIONNAIRE

Questions #1 and #2: Most respondents will select the 5-year-old (#1) and the 20-year-old (#2) for their answers. The evolutionary reasoning for this is that children are more likely to die between 1 and 5, and the 5-year-olds are more likely to live and reproduce. Selecting an older child in #1 will lead to a better chance of continuation of the gene pool. Using the same reasoning, a 20-year-old would be a better candidate for reproduction than a 40-year-old and therefore would in the same way perpetuate the gene pool.

Question #3: Men cannot be sure that women have positively given birth to their offspring, whereas women are always sure that the baby they bear is theirs. The woman's parents (baby's maternal grandparents) therefore are sure that they are contributing 25% of the child's genetic endowment. The man's parents (baby's paternal grandparents) cannot be certain that they have contributed any genetic material to the child and therefore may be less ecstatic and kinder.

Question #4: Evolutionary views predict that the greater the genetic investment, the greater will be the joy and the greater will be the grief should the child die. Therefore, those individuals with the greater genetic ties will feel the most significant loss (mother, parents of mother and older parents). Older parents are selected over younger because they are less likely to have more offspring.

Question #5: The death of a healthy son will yield the greatest grief. Why is this so from an evolutionary perspective?

NAME _____

DATE _____

EVOLUTIONARY PERSPECTIVES ON CHOOSING A MATE

Please complete the following questions before reading the Buss article.

YOUR VIEWS ON MATE SELECTION

1. If you are in a relationship now, or were formerly in a relationship, or plan to be in a relationship, please list the attributes you are looking for in a potential mate.

2. If you were to place an ad in the Relationship Want Ads in the newspaper, how would you describe yourself and how would you describe the kind of person you are seeking?

   Yourself:

   Seeking:

3. Review the Relationship Want Ads, and list the qualities used by men and women to describe themselves and the qualities they are looking for in a mate.

MEN SEEKING WOMEN:

Self Description

Description of Women Sought

WOMEN SEEKING MEN:

Self Description

Description of Men Sought

How well are the evolutionary personality research data supported by the personal and newspaper data you have collected?

The following article by Buss (1994) summarizes the evolutionary viewpoint on mate selection. Evolutionary research basically suggests that women see physical attractiveness and youth in themselves as significant variables, and that they are looking for men who are older and well off. Men see financial security in themselves as significant and are looking for women who are younger and physically attractive. This exercise will give you the opportunity to evaluate this research by looking at these issues in your own life and in the lives of others.

READING

THE STRATEGIES OF HUMAN MATING*

DAVID M. BUSS

Editors' Note:

The search for a mate is one of the most important decisions in our lives. David Buss, using an evolutionary perspective, presents an analysis of mate selection. Since you have completed Active Learning Exercise 5.3, this article will broaden your understanding of the mate selection process.

What do men and women want in a mate? Is there anything consistent about human behavior when it comes to the search for a mate? Would a Gujarati of India be attracted to the same traits in a mate as a Zulu of South Africa or a college student in the midwestern United States?

As a psychologist working in the field of human personality and mating preferences, I have come across many attempts to answer such questions and provide a coherent explanation of human mating patterns. Some theories have suggested that people search for mates who resemble archetypical images of the opposite-sex parent (á la Freud and Jung), or mates with characteristics that are either complementary or similar to one's own qualities, or mates with whom to make an equitable exchange of valuable resources.

These theories have played important roles in our understanding of human mating patterns, but few of them have provided specific predictions that can be tested. Fewer still consider the origins and functions of an individual's mating preferences. What possible function is there to mating with an individual who is an archetypical image of one's opposite-sex parent? Most theories also tend to assume that the processes that guide the mating preferences of men and women are identical, and no sex-differentiated predictions can be derived. The context of the mating behavior is also frequently ignored; the same mating tendencies are posited regardless of circumstances.

Despite the complexity of human mating behavior, it is possible to address these issues in a single, coherent theory. David Schmitt of the University of Michigan and I have recently proposed a framework for understanding the logic of human mating patterns from the standpoint of evolutionary theory. Our theory makes several predictions about the behavior of men and women in the context of their respective sexual strategies. In particular, we discuss the changes that occur when men and women shift their goals from short-term mating (casual sex) to long-term mating (a committed relationship).

Some of the studies we discuss are based on surveys of male and female college students in the United States. In these instances, the sexual attitudes of the sample population may not be reflective of the behavior of people in other cultures. In other instances, however, the results represent a much broader spectrum of the human population. In collaboration with 50 other scientists, we surveyed the mating preferences of more than 10,000 men and women in 37 countries over a six-year period spanning 1984 through 1989. Although no survey, short of canvassing the entire human population, can be considered exhaustive, our study crosses a tremendous diversity of geographic, cultural, political, ethnic, religious, racial and economic groups. It is the largest survey ever on mate preferences.

What we found is contrary to much current thinking among social scientists, which holds that the process of choosing a mate is highly culture-bound. Instead, our results are consistent with the notion that human beings, like other animals, exhibit species-typical desires when it comes to the selection of a mate. These patterns can be accounted for by our theory of human sexual strategies.

COMPETITION AND CHOICE

Sexual-strategies theory holds that patterns in mating behavior exist because they are evolutionarily advantageous. We are obviously the descendants of people who were able to mate successfully. Our theory assumes that the sexual strategies of our ancestors evolved because they permitted them to survive and produce offspring. Those people who failed to mate successfully because they did not express these strategies are not our ancestors. One simple example is the urge to mate, which is a universal desire among people in all cultures and which is undeniably evolutionary in origin.

Although the types of behavior we consider are more complicated than simply the urge to mate, a brief overview of the relevant background should be adequate to understand the evolutionary logic of human mating strategies. As with many issues in

*Buss, D. (1994). The strategies of human mating. *American Scientist, 82*, 238–250. Reprinted by permission of *American Scientist*, magazine of Sigma Xi, The Scientific Research Society.

evolutionary biology, the background begins with the work of Charles Darwin.

Darwin was the first to show that mate preferences could affect human evolution. In his seminal 1871 treatise, *The Descent of Man and Selection in Relation to Sex*, Darwin puzzled over characteristics that seemed to be perplexing when judged merely on the basis of their relative advantage for the animal's survival. How could the brilliant plumage of a male peacock evolve when it obviously increases the bird's risk of predation? Darwin's answer was sexual selection, the evolution of characteristics that confer a reproductive advantage to an organism (rather than a survival advantage). Darwin further divided sexual selection into two processes: Intrasexual competition and preferential mate choice.

Intrasexual competition is the less controversial of the two processes. It involves competition between members of the same sex to gain preferential access to mating partners. Characteristics that lead to success in these same-sex competitions—such as greater strength, size, agility, confidence or cunning—can evolve simply because of the reproductive advantage gained by the victors. Darwin assumed that this is primarily a competitive interaction between males, but recent studies suggest that human females are also very competitive for access to mates.

Preferential mate choice, on the other hand, involves the desire for mating with partners that possess certain characteristics. A consensual desire affects the evolution of characteristics because it gives those possessing the desired characteristics an advantage in obtaining mates over those who do not possess the desired characteristics. Darwin assumed that preferential mate choice operates primarily through females who prefer particular

males. (Indeed, he even called this component of sexual selection *female choice*.)

Darwin's theory of mate-choice selection was controversial in part because Darwin simply assumed that females desire males with certain characteristics. Darwin failed to document how such desires might have arisen and how they might be maintained in a population.

The solution to the problem was not forthcoming until 1972, when Robert Trivers, then at Harvard University, proposed that the relative parental investment of the sexes influences the two processes of sexual selection. Specifically, the sex that invests more in offspring is selected to be more discriminating in choosing a mate, whereas the sex that invests less in offspring is more competitive with members of the same sex for sexual access to the high-investing sex. Parental-investment theory accounts, in part, for both the origin and the evolutionary retention of different sexual strategies in males and females.

Consider the necessary *minimum* parental investment by a woman. After internal fertilization, the gestation period lasts about nine months and is usually followed by lactation, which in tribal societies typically can last several years. In contrast, a man's minimum parental investment can be reduced to the contribution of sperm, an effort requiring as little time as a few minutes. This disparity in parental investment means that the replacement of a child who dies (or is deserted) typically costs more (in time and energy) for women than men. Parental-investment theory predicts that women will be more choosy and selective about their mating partners. Where men can provide resources, women should desire those who are able and willing to commit those resources to her and her children.

SEXUAL STRATEGIES

Our evolutionary framework is based on three key ingredients. First, human mating is inherently strategic. These strategies exist because they solved specific problems in human evolutionary history: It is important to recognize that the manifestation of these strategies need not be through conscious psychological mechanisms. Indeed, for the most part we are completely unaware of *why* we find certain qualities attractive in a mate. A second component of our theory is that mating strategies are context-dependent. People behave differently depending on whether the situation presents itself as a short-term or long-term mating prospect. Third, men and women have faced different mating problems over the course of human evolution and, as a consequence, have evolved different strategies.

As outlined here, sexual strategies theory consists of nine hypotheses. We can test these hypotheses by making several predictions about the behavior of men and women faced with a particular mating situation. Even though we make only a few predictions for each hypothesis, it should be clear that many more pre-

dictions can be derived to test each hypothesis. We invite the reader to devise his or her own tests of these hypotheses.

Hypothesis 1: *Short-term mating is more important for men than women.* This hypothesis follows from the fact that men can reduce their parental investment to the absolute minimum and still produce offspring. Consequently, short-term mating should be a key component of the sexual strategies of men, and much less so for women. We tested three predictions based on this hypothesis in a sample of 148 college students (75 men and 73 women) in the midwestern United States.

First, we predict that men will express a greater interest in seeking a short-term mate than will women. We asked the students to rate the degree to which they were currently seeking a short-term mate (defined as a one-night stand or a brief affair) and the degree to which they were currently seeking a long-term mate (defined as a marriage partner). They rated their interests on a 7-point scale, where a rating of 1 corresponds to a complete lack of interest and a 7 corresponds to a high level of interest.

We found that although the sexes do not differ in their stated proclivities for seeking a long-term mate (an average rating of about 3.4 for both sexes), men reported a significantly greater interest (an average rating of about 5) in seeking a short-term sexual partner than did women (about 3). The results also showed that at any given time men are more interested in seeking a short-term mate rather than a long-term mate, whereas women are more interested in seeking a long-term mate than a short-term mate.

Second, we predict that men will desire a greater number of mates than is desired by women. We asked the same group of college students how many sexual partners they would ideally like to have during a given time interval and during their lifetimes. In this instance men consistently reported that they desired a greater number of sex partners than reported by the women for every interval of time. For example, the average man desired about eight sex partners during the next two years, whereas the average woman desired to have one sex partner. In the course of a lifetime, the average man reported the desire to have about 18 sex partners, whereas the average woman desired no more than 4 or 5 sex partners.

A third prediction that follows from this hypothesis is that men will be more willing to engage in sexual intercourse a shorter period of time after first meeting a potential sex partner. We asked the sample of 148 college students the following question: "If the conditions were right, would you consider having sexual intercourse with someone you viewed as desirable if you had known that person for (*a time period ranging from one hour to five years*)?" For each of 10 time intervals the students were asked to provide a response ranging from -3 (definitely not) to 3 (definitely yes).

After a period of 5 years, the men and women were equally likely to consent to sexual relations, each giving a score of about 2 (probably yes). For all shorter time intervals, men were consistently more likely to consider sexual intercourse. For example, after knowing a potential sex partner for only one week, the average man was still positive about the possibility of having sex, whereas women said that they were highly unlikely to have sex with someone after knowing him for only one week.

The issue was addressed in a novel way by Russell Clark and Elaine Hatfield of the University of Hawaii. They designed a study in which college students were approached by an attractive member of the opposite sex who posed one of three questions after a brief introduction: "Would you go out on a date with me tonight?" "Would you go back to my apartment with me tonight?" or "Would you have sex with me tonight?"

Of the women who were approached, 50 percent agreed to the date, 6 percent agreed to go to the apartment and none agreed to have sex. Many women found the sexual request from a virtual stranger to be odd or insulting. Of the men approached, 50 percent agreed to the date, 69 percent agreed to go back to the woman's apartment and 75 percent agreed to have sex. In contrast to women, many men found the sexual request flattering. Those few men who declined were apologetic about it, citing a fiancé or an unavoidable obligation that particular evening. Apparently, men are willing to solve the problem of partner number by agreeing to have sex with virtual strangers.

Hypothesis 2: *Men seeking a short-term mate will solve the problem of identifying women who are sexually accessible.* We can make at least two predictions based on this hypothesis. First, men will value qualities that signal immediate sexual accessibility in a short-term mate highly, and less so in a long-term mate. When we asked men in a college sample of 44 men and 42 women to rate the desirability of promiscuity and sexual experience in a mate, both were significantly more valued in a short-term mate. Although men find promiscuity mildly desirable in a short-term mate, it is clearly undesirable in a long-term mate. It is noteworthy that women find promiscuity extremely undesirable in either context.

We also predict that qualities that signal sexual inaccessibility will be disliked by men seeking short-term mates. We asked men to rate the desirability of mates who have a low sex drive, who are prudish or who lack sexual experience. In each instance men expressed a particular dislike for short-term mates with these qualities. A low sex drive and prudishness are also disliked by men in long-term mates, but less so. In contrast, a lack of sexual experience is slightly valued by men in a long-term mate.

Hypothesis 3: *Men seeking a short-term mate will minimize commitment and investment.* Here we predict that men will find undesirable any cues that signal that a short-term mate wants to extract a commitment. We asked the same group of 44 men to rate the variable *wants a commitment* for short-term and long-term mates. Of all the qualities we addressed, this one showed the most striking dependence on context. The attribute of wanting a commitment was strongly desirable in a long-term mate but strongly undesirable in a short-term mate. This distinction was not nearly so strong for women. Although women strongly wanted commitment from a long-term mate, it was only mildly undesirable in a short-term mate.

Hypotheses 4 and 5: *Men seeking a short-term mate will solve the problem of identifying fertile women, whereas men seeking a long-term mate will solve the problem of identifying reproductively valuable women.* Because these hypotheses are closely linked it is useful to discuss them together. Fertility and reproductive value are related yet distinct concepts. Fertility refers to the probability that a woman is *currently* able to conceive a child. Reproductive value, on the other hand, is defined actuarially in units of expected future reproduction. In other words, it is the extent to which persons of a given age and sex will contribute, on average, to the ancestry of future generations. For example, a 14-year-old woman has a higher reproductive value than a 24-year-old woman, because her *future* contribution to the gene pool is higher on average. In contrast, the 24-year-old woman is more fertile than the 14-year-old because her *current* probability of reproducing is greater.

Since these qualities cannot be observed directly, men would be expected to be sensitive to cues that might be indicative of a woman's fertility and reproductive value. One might expect that men would prefer younger women as short-term and long-term mates. Again, since age is not something that can be observed directly, men should be sensitive to physical cues that are reliably linked with age. For example, with increasing age, skin tends to wrinkle, hair turns gray and falls out, lips become thinner, ears become larger, facial features become less regular and muscles lose their tone. Men could solve the problem of identifying reproductively valuable women if they attended to physical features linked with age and health, *and* if their standards of attractiveness evolved to correspond to these features.

As an aside, it is worth noting that cultures do differ in their standards of physical beauty, but less so than anthropologists initially assumed. Cultural differences of physical beauty tend to center on whether relative plumpness or thinness is valued. In cultures where food is relatively scarce, plumpness is valued, whereas cultures with greater abundance value thinness. With the exception of plumpness and thinness, however, the physical cues to youth and health are seen as sexually attractive in all known cultures that have been studied. In no culture do people perceive wrinkled skin, open sores and lesions, thin lips, jaundiced eyes, poor muscle tone and irregular facial features to be attractive.

A woman's reproductive success, however, is not similarly dependent on solving the problem of fertility in mates. Because a man's reproductive capacity is less closely linked with age and cannot be assessed as accurately from appearance, youth and physical attractiveness in a mate should be less important to women than they are to men.

Among our sample of American college students we asked men and women to evaluate the relative significance (on a scale from 0, unimportant, to 3, important) of the characteristics *good looking* and *physically attractive* in a short-term and a long-term mate. We found that men's preference for physical attractiveness in short-term mates approached the upper limit of the rating scale (about 2.71). Interestingly, this preference was stronger in men seeking short-term mates than in men seeking long-term mates (about 2.31). The results are a little surprising to us because we did not predict that men would place a greater significance on the physical attractiveness of a short-term mate compared to a long-term mate.

Women also favored physical attractiveness in a short-term mate (2.43) and a long-term mate (2.10). Here again, physical attractiveness was more important in short-term mating than in long-term mating. In both contexts, however, physical attractiveness was significantly less important to women than it is to men.

We also tested these predictions in our international survey of 37 cultures. My colleagues in each country asked men and women to evaluate the relative importance of the characteristics *good looking* and *physically attractive* in a mate. As in our American college population, men throughout the world placed a high value on physical attractiveness in a partner.

In each of the 37 cultures men valued physical attractiveness and good looks in a mate more than did their female counterparts. These sex differences are not limited to cultures that are saturated with visual media, Westernized cultures or racial, ethnic, religious or political groups. Worldwide, men place a premium on physical appearance.

A further clue to the significance of reproductive value comes in an international study of divorce. Laura Betzig of the University of Michigan studied the causes of marital dissolution in 89 cultures from around the world. She found that one of the strongest sex-linked causes of divorce was a woman's old age (hence low reproductive value) and the inability to produce children. A woman's old age was significantly more likely to result in divorce than a man's old age.

Hypothesis 6: *Men seeking a long-term mate will solve the problem of paternity confidence.* Men face an adaptive problem that is not faced by women—the problem of certainty in parenthood. A woman can always be certain that a child is hers, but a man cannot be so sure that his mate's child is his own. Historically, men have sequestered women in various ways through the use of chastity belts, eunuch-guarded harems, surgical procedures and veiling to reduce their sexual attractiveness to other men. Some of these practices continue to this day and have been observed by social scientists in many parts of the world.

Most of these studies have considered three possibilities: (1) the desire for chastity in a mate (cues to *prior* lack of sexual contact with others), (2) the desire for fidelity in mates (cues to no *future* sexual contact with others), and (3) the jealous guarding of mates to prevent sexual contact with other men. We have looked at these issues ourselves in various studies.

In our international study, we examined men's and women's desire for chastity in a potential marriage partner. It proved to be a highly variable trait across cultures. For example, Chinese men and women both feel that it is indispensable in a mate. In the Netherlands and Scandinavia, on the other hand, both sexes see chastity as irrelevant in a mate. Overall, however, in about two-thirds of the international samples, men desire chastity more than women do. Sex differences are especially large among Indonesians, Iranians and Palestinian Arabs. In the remaining one-third of the cultures, no sex differences were found. In no cultures do women desire virginity in a mate more than men. In other words, where there is a difference between the sexes, it is always the case that men place a greater value on chastity.

Although we have yet to examine the desire for mate fidelity in our international sample, in her cross-cultural study Betzig found that the more prevalent cause of divorce was sexual infidelity, a cause that was highly sex-linked. A wife's infidelity was considerably more likely to result in a divorce than a husband's infidelity. Compromising a man's certainty in paternity is apparently seen worldwide as a breach so great that it often causes the irrevocable termination of the long-term marital bond.

We have examined the issue of fidelity among American college students. Indeed, Schmitt and I found that fidelity is the characteristic most valued by men in a long-term mate. It is also highly valued by women, but it ranks only third or fourth in importance, behind such qualities as honesty. It seems that American men are concerned more about the future fidelities of a mate than with her prior abstinence.

Our studies of jealousy reveal an interesting qualitative distinction between men and women. Randy Larsen, Jennifer Semmelroth, Drew Westen and I conducted a series of interviews in which we asked American college students to imagine two scenarios: (1) their partner having sexual intercourse with someone else or (2) their partner falling in love and forming a deep emotional attachment to someone else. The majority of the men reported that they would be more upset if their mate had sexual intercourse with another man. In contrast, the majority of the women reported that they would be more upset if their mate formed an emotional attachment to another woman.

We also posed the same two scenarios to another group of 60 men and women, but this time we recorded their physiological responses. We placed electrodes on the corrugator muscle in the brow (which contracts during frowning), on two fingers of the right hand to measure skin conductance (or sweating), and the thumb to measure heart rate.

The results provided a striking confirmation of the verbal responses of our earlier study. Men became more physiologically distressed at the thought of their mate's sexual infidelity than their mate's emotional infidelity. In response to the thought of sexual infidelity, their skin conductances increased by an average of about 1.5 microSiemens, the frowning muscle showed 7.75 microvolt units of contraction and their hearts increased by about five beats per minute. In response to the thought of emotional infidelity, men's skin conductance showed little change from baseline, their frowning increased by only 1.16 units, and their heart rates did not increase. Women, on the other hand, tended to show the opposite pattern. For example, in response to the thought of emotional infidelity, their frowning increased by 8.12 units, whereas the thought of sexual infidelity elicited a response of only 3.03 units.

Hypothesis 7: *Women seeking a short-term mate will prefer men willing to impart immediate resources.* Women confront a different set of mating problems than those faced by men. They need not consider the problem of partner number, since mating with 100 men in one year would produce no more off-

spring than mating with just one. Nor do they have to be concerned about the certainty of genetic parenthood. Women also do not need to identify men with the highest fertility since men in their 50s, 60s and 70s can and do sire children.

In species where males invest parentally in offspring, where resources can be accrued and defended, and where males vary in their ability and willingness to channel these resources, females gain a selective advantage by choosing mates who are willing and able to invest resources. Females so choosing afford their offspring better protection, more food and other material advantages that increase their ability to survive and reproduce. Do human females exhibit this behavior pattern? If so, we should be able to make a few predictions.

In short-term contexts, women especially value signs that a man will immediately expend resources on them. We asked 50 female subjects to evaluate the desirability of a few characteristics in a short-term and a long-term mate: *spends a lot of money early on, gives gifts early on*, and *has an extravagant lifestyle*. We found that women place greater importance on these qualities in a short-term mate than in a long-term mate, despite the fact that women are generally less exacting in short-term mating contexts.

We would also predict that women will find undesirable any traits that suggest that a man is reluctant to expend resources on her immediately. When we tested this prediction with the same sample population, we found that women especially dislike men who are stingy early on. Although this attribute is undesirable in a long-term mate as well, it is significantly more in a short-term mate.

Hypothesis 8: *Women will be more selective than men in choosing a short-term mate.* This hypothesis follows from the fact that women (more than men) use short-term matings to evaluate prospective long-term mates. We can make several predictions based on this hypothesis.

First, women (more than men) will dislike short-term mates who are already in a relationship. We examined the relative undesirability of a prospective mate who was already in a relationship to 42 men and 44 women, using a scale from −3 (extremely undesirable) to 3 (extremely desirable). Although men were only slightly bothered (averaging a score of about −1.04) by this scenario, women were significantly more reluctant to engage in a relationship with such a mate (average score about −1.70).

We would also predict that women (more than men) will dislike short-term mates who are promiscuous. To a woman, promiscuity indicates that a man is seeking short-term relationships and is less likely to commit to a long-term mating. We tested this prediction in the same sample of 42 men and 44 women using the same rating scale as before. Although men found promiscuity to be of neutral value in a short-term mate, women rated the trait as moderately undesirable (an average of about −2.00).

Finally, because one of the hypothesized functions for female short-term mating is protection from aggressive men, women should value attributes such as physical size and strength in short-term mates more than in long-term mates. When we asked men and women to evaluate the notion of a mate being *physically strong*, we found that women preferred physically strong mates in all contexts more than men did, and that women placed a premium on physical strength in a short-term mate. This was true despite the higher standards women generally hold for a long-term mate.

Hypothesis 9: *Women seeking a long-term mate will prefer men who can provide resources for their offspring.* In a long-term mating context, we would predict that women (more than men) will desire traits such as a potential mate's ambition, earning capacity, professional degrees and wealth.

In one study we asked a group of 58 men and 50 women to rate the desirability (to the average man and woman) of certain characteristics that are indicators of future resource-acquisition potential. These included such qualities as *is likely to succeed in profession, is likely to earn a lot of money*, and *has a reli-*

able future career. We found that in each case women desired the attribute more in a long-term mate than in a short-term mate. Moreover, women valued each of these characteristics in a long-term mate more than men did.

In our international study, we also examined men's and women's preferences for long-term mates who can acquire resources. In this case we looked at such attributes as *good financial prospects, social status* and *ambition-industriousness*—attributes that typically lead to the acquisition of resources. We found that sex differences in the attitudes of men and women were strikingly consistent around the world. In 36 of the 37 cultures, women placed significantly greater value on financial prospects than did men. Although the sex differences were less profound for the other two qualities, in the overwhelming majority of cultures, women desire *social status* and *ambition-industriousness* in a long-term mate more than their male counterparts do.

Finally, in her international study of divorce, Betzig found that a man's failure to provide proper economic support for his wife and children was a significant sex-linked cause of divorce.

CONCLUSION

The results of our work and that of others provide strong evidence that the traditional assumptions about mate preferences—that they are arbitrary and culture-bound—are simply wrong. Darwin's initial insights into sexual selection have turned out to be scientifically profound for people, even though he understood neither their functional-adaptive nature nor the importance of relative parental investment for driving the two components of sexual selection.

Men and women have evolved powerful desires for particular characteristics in a mate. These desires are not arbitrary, but are highly patterned and universal. The patterns correspond closely to the specific adaptive problems that men and women have faced during the course of human evolutionary history. These are the problems of paternity certainty, partner number and reproductive capacity for men, and the problems of willingness and ability to invest resources for women.

It turns out that a woman's physical appearance is the most powerful predictor of the occupational status of the man she marries. A woman's appearance is more significant than her intelligence, her level of education or even her original socio-

economic status in determining the mate she will marry. Women who possess the qualities men prefer are most able to translate their preferences into actual mating decisions. Similarly, men possessing what women want—the ability to provide resources—are best able to mate according to their preferences.

Some adaptive problems are faced by men and women equally: identifying mates who show a proclivity to cooperate and mates who show evidence of having good parenting skills. Men do not look at women simply as sex objects, nor do women look at men simply as success objects. One of our most robust observations was that both sexes place tremendous importance on mutual love and kindness when seeking a long-term mate.

The similarities among cultures and between sexes implies a degree of psychological unity or species typicality that transcends geographical, racial, political, ethnic and sexual diversity. Future research could fruitfully examine the ecological and historical sources of diversity, while searching for the adaptive functions of the sexual desires that are shared by all members of our species.

CHAPTER
6

Behavioral Perspectives

Introduction

Behaviorism, in its most radical expression, focuses on how forces outside the individual operate to mold, modify, and build behaviors. The power of the environment is stressed as the major determinant of personality development and operation.

Our society is absorbed with the impact that media such as TV, films, and the World Wide Web have on our children. We are concerned with developing more effective modes of living together harmoniously. We also struggle to understand and change maladaptive personality features.

In this chapter you will experience the efforts directed toward these goals. You will examine early behavioral studies based on a classical conditioning framework, explore how Skinnerian principles fared in the development of an experimental community, and discover the roots of observational learning. You will also do a behavioral analysis of one of your own behaviors and evaluate your own assertive behavior.

READING
CONDITIONED EMOTIONAL REACTIONS*
John B. Watson and Rosalie Rayner

Editors' Note:

In this early classic study, John Watson and Rosalie Rayner show us how classical conditioning can lead to the development of problematic behavior patterns. In reading this article, think about how fears developed in your own life.

In recent literature various speculations have been entered into concerning the possibility of conditioning various types of emotional response, but direct experimental evidence in support of such a view has been lacking. If the theory advanced by Watson and Morgan to the effect that in infancy the original emotional reaction patterns are few, consisting so far as observed of fear, rage and love, then there must be some simple method by means of which the range of stimuli which can call out these emotions and their compounds is greatly increased. Otherwise, complexity in adult response could not be accounted for. These authors without adequate experimental evidence advanced the view that this range was increased by means of conditioned reflex factors. It was suggested there that the early home life of the child furnishes a laboratory situation for establishing conditioned emotional responses. The present authors have recently put the whole matter to an experimental test.

Experimental work has been done so far on only one child, Albert B. This infant was reared almost from birth in a hospital environment; his mother was a wet nurse in the Harriet Lane Home for Invalid Children. Albert's life was normal: he was healthy from birth and one of the best developed youngsters ever brought to the hospital, weighing twenty-one pounds at nine months of age. He was on the whole stolid and unemotional. His stability was one of the principal reasons for using him as a subject in this test. We felt that we could do him relatively little harm by carrying out such experiments as those outlined below.

At approximately nine months of age we ran him through the emotional tests that have become a part of our regular routine in determining whether fear reactions can be called out by other stimuli than sharp noises and the sudden removal of support. In brief, the infant was confronted suddenly and for the first time successively with a white rat, a rabbit, a dog, a monkey, with masks, with and without hair, cotton wool, burning newspapers, etc. A permanent record of Albert's reactions to these objects and situations has been preserved in a motion picture study. Manipulation was the most usual reaction called out. *At no time did this infant ever show fear in any situation*. These experimental records were confirmed by the casual observations of the mother and hospital attendants. No one had ever seen him in a state of fear and rage. The infant practically never cried.

Up to approximately nine months of age we had not tested him with loud sounds. The test to determine whether a fear reaction could be called out by a loud sound was made when he was eight months, twenty-six days of age. The sound was that made by striking a hammer upon a suspended steel bar four feet in length and three-fourths of an inch in diameter. The laboratory notes are as follows:

> One of the two experimenters caused the child to turn its head and fixate her moving hand; the other, stationed back of the child, struck the steel bar a sharp blow. The child started violently, his breathing was checked and the arms were raised in a characteristic manner. On the second stimulation the same thing occurred, and in addition the lips began to pucker and tremble. On the third stimulation the child broke into a sudden crying fit. This is the first time an emotional situation in the laboratory has produced any fear or even crying in Albert.

We had expected just these results on account of our work with other infants brought up under similar conditions. It is worth while to call attention to the fact that removal of support (dropping and jerking the blanket upon which the infant was lying) was tried exhaustively upon this infant on the same occasion. It was not effective in producing the fear response. This stimulus is effective in younger children. At what age such stimuli lose their potency in producing fear is not known. Nor is it known whether less placid children ever lose their fear of them. This probably depends upon the training the child gets. It is well known that children eagerly run to be tossed into the air and caught. On the other hand it is equally well known that in the adult fear responses are called out quite clearly by the sudden removal of support, if the individual is walking across a bridge, walking out upon a beam, etc. There is a wide field of study here which is aside from our present point.

*Watson, J. B., & Rayner, R. (1917). Emotional reactions and psychological experimentation. *American Journal of Psychology, 28*, 163–174.

The sound stimulus, thus, at nine months of age, gives the means of testing several important factors. I. Can we condition fear of an animal, e.g., a white rat, by visually presenting it and simultaneously striking a steel bar? II. If such a conditioned emotional response can be established, will there be a transfer to other animals or other objects?

I.   The establishment of conditioned emotional responses. At first there was considerable hesitation upon our part in making the attempt to set up fear reactions experimentally. A certain responsibility attaches to such a procedure. We decided finally to make the attempt, comforting ourselves by the reflection that such attachments would arise anyway as soon as the child left the sheltered environment of the nursery for the rough and tumble of the home. We did not begin this work until Albert was eleven months, three days of age. Before attempting to set up a conditioned response we, as before, put him through all of the regular emotional tests. Not the slightest sign of a fear response was obtained in any situation.

The steps taken to condition emotional responses are shown in our laboratory notes.

11 MONTHS 3 DAYS

1. White rat suddenly taken from the basket and presented to Albert. He began to reach for the rat with left hand. Just as his hand touched the animal the bar was struck immediately behind his head. The infant jumped violently and fell forward, burying his face in the mattress. He did not cry, however.

2. Just as the right hand touched the rat the bar was again struck. Again the infant jumped violently, fell forward and began to whimper.

   In order not to disturb the child too seriously no further tests were given for one week.

11 MONTHS 10 DAYS

1. Rat presented suddenly without sound. There was steady fixation but no tendency at first to reach for it. The rat was then placed nearer, whereupon tentative reaching movements began with the right hand. When the rat nosed the infant's left hand, the hand was immediately withdrawn. He started to reach for the head of the animal with the forefinger of the left hand, but withdrew it suddenly before contact. It is thus seen that the two joint stimulations given the previous week were not without effect. He was tested with his blocks immediately afterwards to see if they shared in the process of conditioning. He began immediately to pick them up, dropping them, pounding them, etc. In the remainder of the tests the blocks were given frequently to quiet him and to test his general emotional state. They were always removed from sight when the process of conditioning was under way.

2. Joint stimulation with rat and sound. Startled, then fell over immediately to right side. No crying.

3. Joint stimulation. Fell to right side and rested upon hands, with head turned away from rat. No crying.

4. Joint stimulation. Same reaction.

5. Rat suddenly presented alone. Puckered face, whimpered and withdrew body sharply to the left.

6. Joint stimulation. Fell over immediately to right side and began to whimper.

7. Joint stimulation. Started violently and cried, but did not fall over.

8. Rat alone. The instant the rat was shown the baby began to cry. Almost instantly he turned sharply to the left, fell over on left side, raised himself on all fours and began to crawl away so rapidly that he was caught with difficulty before reaching the edge of the table.

This was as convincing a case of a completely conditioned fear response as could have been theoretically pictured. In all seven joint stimulations were given to bring about the complete reaction. It is not unlikely had the sound been of greater intensity or of a more complex clang character that the number of joint stimulations might have been materially reduced. Experiments designed to define the nature of the sounds that will serve best as emotional stimuli are under way.

II. When a conditioned emotional response has been established for one object, is there a transfer? Five days later Albert was again brought back into the laboratory and tested as follows:

11 MONTHS 15 DAYS

1. Tested first with blocks. He reached readily for them, playing with them as usual. This shows that there has been no general transfer to the room, table, blocks, etc.

2. Rat alone. Whimpered immediately, withdrew right hand and turned head and trunk away.

3. Blocks again offered. Played readily with them, smiling and gurgling.

4. Rat alone. Leaned over to the left side as far away from the rat as possible, then fell over, getting up on all fours and scurrying away as rapidly as possible.

5. Blocks again offered. Reached immediately for them, smiling and laughing as before.

    The above preliminary test shows that the conditioned response to the rat had carried over completely for the five days in which no tests were given. The question as to whether or not there is a transfer was next taken up.

6. Rabbit alone. The rabbit was suddenly placed on the mattress in front of him. The reaction was pronounced. Negative responses began at once. He leaned as far away from the animal as possible, whimpered, then burst into tears. When the rabbit was placed in contact with him he buried his face in the mattress, then got up on all fours and crawled away, crying as he went. This was a most convincing test.

7. The blocks were next given him, after an interval. He played with them as before. It was observed by four people that he played far more energetically with them than ever before. The blocks were raised high over his head and slammed down with a great deal of force.

8. Dog alone. The dog did not produce as violent a reaction as the rabbit. The moment fixation occurred the child shrank back and as the animal came nearer he attempted to get on all fours but did not cry at first. As soon as the dog passed out of his range of vision he became quiet. The dog was then made to approach the infant's head (he was lying down at the moment). Albert straightened up immediately, fell over to the opposite side and turned his head away. He then began to cry.

9. The blocks were again presented. He began immediately to play with them.

10. Fur coat (seal). Withdrew immediately to the left side and began to fret. Coat put close to him on the left side; he turned immediately, began to cry and tried to crawl away on all fours.

11. Cotton wool. The wool was presented in a paper package. At the end the cotton was not covered by the paper. It was placed first on his feet. He kicked it away but did not touch it with his hands. When his hand was laid on the wool he

immediately withdrew it but did not show the shock that the animals or fur coat produced in him. He then began to play with the paper, avoiding contact with the wool itself. He finally, under the impulse of the manipulative instinct, lost some of his negativism to the wool.

12. Just in play W. put his head down to see if Albert would play with his hair. Albert was completely negative. Two other observers did the same thing. He began immediately to play with their hair. W. then brought the Santa Claus mask and presented it to Albert. He was again pronouncedly negative. . . .

From the above results it would seem that emotional transfers do take place. Furthermore it would seem that the number of transfers resulting from an experimentally produced conditioned emotional reaction may be very large. In our observations we had no means of testing the complete number of transfers which may have resulted. . . .

INCIDENTAL OBSERVATIONS

a. Thumb sucking as a compensatory device for blocking fear and noxious stimuli. During the course of these experiments, especially in the final test, it was noticed that whenever Albert was on the verge of tears or emotionally upset generally he would continually thrust his thumb into his mouth. The moment the hand reached the mouth he became impervious to the stimuli producing fear. Again and again while the motion pictures were being made at the end of the thirty-day rest period, we had to remove the thumb from his mouth before the conditioned response could be obtained. This method of blocking noxious and emotional stimuli (fear and rage) through erogenous stimulation seems to persist from birth onward. . . .

b. Equal primacy of fear, love and possibly rage. While in general the results of our experiment offer no particular points of conflict with Freudian concepts, one fact out of harmony with them should be emphasized. According to proper Freudians sex (or in our terminology, love) is the principal emotion in which conditioned responses arise which later limit and distort personality. We wish to take sharp issue with this view on the basis of the experimental evidence we have gathered. Fear is as primal a factor as love in influencing personality. Fear does not gather its potency in any derived manner from love. It belongs to the original and inherited nature of man. Probably the same may be true of rage although at present we are not so sure of this. . . .

It is probable that many of the phobias in psychopathology are true conditioned emotional reactions either of the direct or the transferred type. One may possibly have to believe that such persistence of early conditioned responses will be found only in persons who are constitutionally inferior. Our argument is meant to be constructive. Emotional disturbances in adults cannot be traced back to sex alone. They must be retraced along at least three collateral lines—to conditioned and transferred responses set up in infancy and early youth in all three of the fundamental human emotions.

THE WATSON OF OZ*

Matthew R. Merrens and Charles R. Potkay

Editors' Note:

The well-known story of The Wizard of Oz is examined behaviorally by Matthew Merrens and Charles Potkay. The "cures" that are experienced by the Scarecrow, the Tin Woodman, and the Cowardly Lion are seen to be a result of assertive training, desensitization, and modeling.

In The Wizard of Oz we encounter Dorothy, a young girl, who has been separated from her family as a result of a cyclone. She finds herself in a totally unfamiliar environment inhabited by strange beings. Her problem is rather straight-forward—she is unhappy in the bizarre world of Oz and wants very much to return to her home in Kansas. Her feelings and the problems she encounters are similar to the kind of "culture shock" that frequently affects immigrants arriving in a new country. To a lesser degree her situation is reminiscent of being "homesick." The impact of the culture of Oz upon Dorothy's behavior can be observed in her frustration, helplessness, loneliness, and general unhappiness. The above constellation of behaviors combined with her behaviors of sadness and crying suggests mild depression. In behavioral terms this might be understood as a "loss of major sources of reinforcement or a severe change in role status." The above analysis seems to be exactly Dorothy's situation. Dorothy has lost the major reinforcements provided by her family, friends, and familiar environment; and her role status has certainly changed by being in the strange land of Oz. Instead of attempting to adapt totally to this alien world, Dorothy seeks help in returning to her aunt and uncle in Kansas. No one in the land of Oz seems to know how to assist her, and so she is referred to the Wizard-Therapist. When all else fails call the therapist.

On her trip to consult with the Wizard-Therapist (who predictably lives in the city—an "emerald" city) she meets three other troubled individuals, each with problems that also have caused them extreme hardship. Dorothy tells them of her situation and describes how the Wizard-Therapist also might be of help to them. These three potential "patients" are the Scarecrow who states that he is stupid, the Tin Woodman who states that he lacks emotion, and the Cowardly Lion who claims to lack courage. In each of the above cases the "problematic" behavior appears to be a self-defined behavioral deficit; i.e., the individual considers himself maladjusted by reason of the absence of capacities or skills normally expected. The difficulties of each member of this troubled trio might also be understood in terms of self-fulfilling prophecy since each has been behaving in ways consistent with a self-applied negative label. Through their encounters with Dorothy and facilitated by cultural conditioning and social pressure, they all become convinced that the only person who can help them with their difficulties is the Wizard-Therapist.

After considerable difficulty in arranging an appointment with [the] Wizard-Therapist (a not uncommon event in therapeutic practice), the foursome is granted a consultation. During this brief intake session the Wizard-Therapist listens to their difficulties and directively predicts that their problems will be resolved if they behave in a prescribed fashion. The foursome's role in this behavior contracting is to bring the Wizard-Therapist the broom of a Wicked Witch (possibly a competing therapist). Although the task assigned by the Wizard-Therapist is extremely difficult, and possibly designed to rid him of these unwanted patients, it ultimately has the effect of alleviating the presenting complaints brought by each of the foursome minus Dorothy. This provides a good illustration of the successful operation of behavioral principles irrespective of the theoretical framework in which they are used. It also illustrates an instance of the success of the therapy in spite of the therapist.

The success of the Wizard-Therapist's directives may be traced to three behavioral components, interacting simultaneously: *assertive training, desensitization, and modeling*. The assertive training follows the approach suggested by Wolpe where the therapist sets up a series of tasks in which the patient must perform the target behaviors that are in need of strengthening. High cultural-personal expectations are set up in this process. The process insures that the patients will attempt the new more adaptive responses, and eventually be successful in adopting them as components of their behavioral repertoire. Therefore, in capturing the Witch's broom, the Scarecrow must display intelligent behaviors (e.g., he devises a plan to enter the Witch's castle), the Tin Woodman must demonstrate emotion (e.g., he cries when Dorothy is captured), and the Cowardly Lion must behave in brave ways (e.g., he courageously fights the Witch's soldiers). In such a manner the difficult task is accomplished, and is successful, because each of the patients engaged in the very behaviors previously self-defined as deficient.

* Merrens, M. R., & Potkay, C. R. (1974). The Watson of Oz. *Voices, 10*, (2), 11–14.

The influence of desensitization may be recognized through application of Wolpe and Rachman's reinterpretation of Freud's analysis of Little Hans. Wolpe and Rachman suggest that it was not the therapist's traditional analysis that affected lessened phobic behavior in Little Hans, nor insight, but situational desensitization over many and varied situations and contexts "which may have inhibited the anxiety and in consequence diminished its habit strength." In parallel fashion, the trio underwent various desensitizing experiences—relating to Dorothy and each other, undertaking new challenges and risks, adapting to stresses, etc.

Up to now our analysis has focused on the Wizard as being the Watson of Oz, a behavior therapist. Perhaps we have over-credited the Wizard-Therapist (a frequent contemporary occurrence) and his therapeutic influence, to the exclusion of more natural and humble influences. The Wizard himself admits to his own shortcomings by stating, "I'm really a very good man, but I'm a very bad Wizard." And we cannot overlook the beneficial impact of Dorothy as a model for her trio of friends. Dorothy, in spite of having her own problems, demonstrates courage, intelligence, emotional expression and an adaptive resourcefulness in response to her new and potentially stressful environment. It is quite likely that observation of these adaptive behaviors was instrumental in the trio's acquisition and performance of similar behaviors. In addition, Dorothy never responds to the trio as if they were "sick" and therefore does not provide reinforcement for their negative self-labels. Instead, she strikes up a helpful, peer companionship type of relationship, very similar to the role of some paraprofessionals in crisis intervention centers. Upon completion of the task, Dorothy and her friends return to the Wizard-Therapist with the Witch's broom. Lacking "insight" they are still largely unaware that their behavioral "problems" have been remedied successfully. The Wizard-Therapist, like any effective behavior therapist, provides a functional analysis of how each has amply demonstrated an adaptive level of competence in the area initially viewed as problematic. Furthermore, to help maintain the newly acquired assertive behaviors, the Wizard as behavior therapist awards each of the trio a distinctive symbolic token reinforcer. In the film version, the Scarecrow is given a diploma for further recognition of his "intelligence"; the Tin Woodman is given a heart-shaped watch symbolizing his ability to show "emotion"; and the Cowardly Lion is given an impressive medal in recognition of his "bravery."

Since Dorothy's problem was of a different type from her friends', the Wizard-Therapist offers a different solution, essentially based on environmental management and a reinstatement of previously successful reinforcement contingencies. In short, he offers to take Dorothy back home where reinforcement from friends and family would alleviate her mildly "depressed" condition. However, at the start of the trip back to Kansas the Wizard-Therapist ascends in his balloon before Dorothy can climb aboard (possibly another instance of the therapist "moving" too quickly for the patient). However, in Dorothy's case all is not lost because she learns that despite the Wizard-Therapist's failure to help her, she always had the ability to effect changes in her life if she elected to assume responsibility by enacting the appropriate roles. This seems to be an example of therapy sought by people who ultimately have the capacity to successfully solve their "problems" without professional assistance.

SPOTLIGHT
BEHAVIORISM*

Our conclusion, then, is that we have no real evidence of inheritance of traits. I would feel perfectly confident in the ultimately favorable outcome of careful upbringing of a *healthy, well-formed baby* born of a long line of crooks, murderers and thieves, and prostitutes. Who has any evidence to the contrary? Many, many thousands of children yearly, born from moral households and steadfast parents become wayward, steal, become prostitutes, through one mishap or another of nurture. Many more thousands of sons and daughters of the wicked grow up to be wicked because they couldn't grow up any other way in such surroundings. But let one adopted child who has a bad ancestry go wrong and it is used as incontestable evidence for the inheritance of moral turpitude and criminal tendencies. As a matter of fact, there has not been a double handful of cases in the whole of our civilization of which records have been carefully enough kept for us to draw any such conclusions—mental testers, Lombroso, and all other students of criminality to the contrary notwithstanding. As a matter of fact adopted children are never brought up as one's own. One cannot use statistics gained from observations in charitable institutions and orphan asylums. All one needs to do to discount such statistics is to go there and work for a while, and I say this without trying to belittle the work of such organizations.

I should like to go one step further now and say, "Give me a dozen healthy infants, well-formed, and my own specified world to bring them up in and I'll guarantee to take any one at random and train him to become any type of specialist I might select—doctor, lawyer, artist, merchant-chief and, yes, even beggar-man and thief, regardless of his talents, penchants, tendencies, abilities, vocations, and race of his ancestors." I am going beyond my facts and I admit it, but so have the advocates of the contrary and they have been doing it for many thousands of years. Please note that when this experiment is made I am to be allowed to specify the way the children are to be brought up and the type of world they have to live in.

*Watson, J. B. (1958). *Behaviorism*, (pp. 103–104). New York: W.W. Norton.

READING

THE TOWN B. F. SKINNER BOXED*

Steve Fishman

Editors' Note:

Many of you may be familiar with B. F. Skinner's fictional utopian community, Walden Two. Steve Fishman takes us on an insider's tour of Los Horcones, an actual community built on the behavioral principles advocated by Skinner.

Lately Ivan, who is two years old, has been emitting some undesirable verbal behavior.

Where Ivan lives, the Code of Children's Behavior is quite explicit about what is desirable: Orderliness and cleanliness, for example; singing, laughing, dancing. And speaking positively.

"Great!" "I like it." "I'm happy"—these are the kinds of statements Ivan should be making. But Ivan has been negative. Linda, the leader of the committee on children's behavior, reports that he has been saying things like "The sky is not blue," or "You can't run," or "No, that is not yours, that is every- one's"—which could be considered desirable "sharing behavior," if it weren't for all the other negatives.

It's Thursday night and the committee is holding its weekly meeting in the children's house, where the community's four youngest children live. In these get-togethers, the adults discuss everything about the kids, from how they ought to behave to what medical care they should receive to how long their hair should be. The eleven adults listening to Linda's recitation of Ivan's negatives—two biological parents and nine "behavioral" parents—sit in the dining room clumped around the long, low children's table.

Linda explains that for the past week, the grownups who care for the youngest children have been wearing counters around their necks—little silvery devices like those that ticket takers use to click off the number of people entering a theater. Every time Ivan, who has brown bangs, brown eyes, and a voice that pene- trates like a foghorn, has emitted a negative verbal behavior, *click*. "I don't like the beans." *Click*. "It's too cold outside." *Click*.

Linda holds up a piece of peach-colored graph paper with penciled peaks: Ivan has averaged 18 negative verbal behaviors per day. She poses the crucial question: "Should we intervene now to correct Ivan's behavior?"

WELCOME TO LOS HORCONES, a tiny enclave in the barely hospitable stretches of Mexico's Sonora Desert, 175 miles south of the U.S. border. Here 26 adults and children are attempting to live according to the teachings of the late Harvard behaviorist Burrhus Frederic (B. F.) Skinner—one of the most widely rec- ognized and most often maligned of psychologists.

In the cultural lab they call home, this outpost community of Mexicans has been at it for 17 years, experimenting with Skinner's idea, working away on themselves and their children. So that no visitor will miss the point, there is this welcome sign at the edge of their land, written in both Spanish and English: "We apply the science of behavior to the design of a new society."

The idea, first Skinner's and now theirs, is as ambitious as it sounds: By the methodical application of the science of behav- iorism, the little band at Los Horcones believes it can transform selfish human beings into cooperative, sharing ones.

Until his death this past August, B. F. Skinner argued that his psychology was both potent and practical. His fundamental dis- coveries, made 55 years ago, rest on this idea: If any particular behavior is reinforced, it will continue. If not, it will cease.

For pigeons, Skinner found, reinforcement came in the form of dry, hard food pellets. What a hungry pigeon wouldn't do for the promise of a pellet! Climb stairs, peck a key 10,000 times, even guide a missile—which Skinner demonstrated to U.S. Army officials in World War II.

Give Skinner some lab time—he was one of psychology's first great experimenters—and he'd figure out which reinforcers, administered how often and for how long, would not only make people share but make them *like* to share. "We can *make* men adequate for group living," boasted the protagonist in Skinner's classic 1948 utopian novel, *Walden Two*.

Over the past two decades, Skinner's behaviorism and his ideas about what motivates people have largely been supplanted in the world of academic psychology. The trend now is toward cognitive psychology, which concentrates on the unconscious causes of human behavior, processes that cognitive psychologists say cannot or should not be subject to systems of reward and punishment.

But in this desert proving ground, behaviorism is as alive as the tarantulas that take up guard on the drainpipes, as hardy as the boa constrictors that swallow live rabbits whole. In the children's house and on the whitewashed bungalows of the community of Los Horcones, behaviorism still has a shot.

"It's true," says Juan Robinson, the community's coordinator of adult behavior. "A person can be made to enjoy what he did not at first enjoy."

Take Ivan.

Ivan's biological parents, Luciano Coronado Paredes, 26, and Maria Guadalupe Cosio de Coronado, 26, better known as Lucho and Lupita, sit in the tiny children's chairs with the other adults. They met elsewhere, but heard about Los Horcones and were married here. They vowed to put the community first. "If you ever decide to leave, just go, don't even tell me," said Lupita. Both Ivan and his brother Sebastian, aged four, were born at Los Horcones, and live together in the children's house.

Lucho and Lupita are tired after a long day's work, and remain quiet even when the subject is their younger son. Lucho, in fact, peruses a book on rabbits while Linda's discussion goes on. "Did you know," he asks a neighbor, "that rabbits eat their food twice?" No one is really worried about Ivan. It is just behavior, after all. Ivan used to cry when he wanted something, instead of asking for it. That took but a few weeks to correct.

An approach is suggested for Ivan's negative emissions—straightforward Skinnerian science. When Ivan says something positive, he'll be reinforced with attention—hugs and kisses, pats on the head, and M&Ms. His negative comments will be ignored (but still counted with the clickers). Punishment isn't shunned out of principle; it is just, as Skinner saw it, that the consequences can turn out to be troublesome.

Linda (the children all call her La Linda) asks if everyone agrees. In the community's open family, all decisions must be made unanimously. One by one, the adults, all of whom are considered parents, nod. "Adults are difficult to change," says a parent. "Pigeons and children are easy."

B. F. Skinner experimented on pigeons and also on rats. In his crucial experiments of the 1930s, he demonstrated that by offering a simple food pellet as a "reinforcer"—a term first used by the famed Russian physiologist Ivan Pavlov—he could condition laboratory rats to press a bar when a light came on, to hold it down for as long as 30 seconds, and to keep pressing harder.

To Skinner, humans were bigger and more complex but not fundamentally different from lab animals. For the right reinforcers, he claimed, they would do almost anything.

Critics denounced Skinner's science, when it came to humans, as simplistic, manipulative, and reductionist—as well as downright unflattering. They argued that people, unlike pigeons, have rich inner lives and complex, hidden motivations. What, for goodness' sake, of a person's free will? cried the critics. Skinner harrumphed. Free will, he said, was illusory. He preferred to talk about the predictability of people.

The late psychologist wasn't, however, a cold, impersonal manipulator. Rather, he seems to have been as cheery and optimistic as a handyman who says, Hey, I can fix that. After his wife complained that the first years of child-rearing were hell, he devised the "baby tender," a glass-enclosed, temperature-controlled crib that eliminated the need to change the baby's clothes so often. His own daughter tried it out and became the notorious baby in the "Skinner box." After noticing how dull his other daughter's grammar school was, Skinner built a "teaching machine," decades ahead of today's interactive learning systems.

In the same problem-solving spirit, the late behaviorist sat down in 1947 and in seven weeks wrote the book outlining his plan to ease society's woes through behaviorism. In Skinner's utopia, 1,000 citizens work four hours a day for no money, share their children, develop their artistic talents. As literature, *Walden Two* is a bore, freighted with long arguments between the proselytizing Frazier and his skeptical foil, a character named Castle. But the ideas have had a long life.

The book became a staple of college psychology classes as behaviorism flourished in the 1950s and 1960s. Two million copies are in print today. To a disposed mind, it can read like a do-it-yourself kit.

In the late 1960s, Juan Robinson, a handsome young middle-class Mexican (descended from a Scottish grandfather), was a university psychology student in Mexico City. Robinson read *Walden Two* and quickly became a convert.

In 1972, on the dusty edge of the Mexican town of Hermosillo, he and his wife, Mireya Bustamente Norberto, then 21, decided to give behaviorism a practical try. They founded a school for retarded children, many of them so unmanageable that their parents were prepared to ship them to an institution. Subjected to behavioral techniques, the 20 students fell into line.

Consider the case of Luis, an autistic teen who threw as many as three tantrums a day. Did Luis sit quietly? Very nice, the behaviorists said, and handed him a coin. Shake hands? Very good. Another coin. Do anything but throw a fit? One more coin. Merchant Luis began bartering half hours of appropriate behavior—he even did chores!—for coins redeemable for meals, and his tantrums virtually ceased. "We can modify antisocial behavior," Juan concluded, "in three months."

At the end of the school day, Juan and Mireya hosted gatherings. Linda (La Linda), just 19, a volunteer at the school attended; so did her husband, Ramon Armendariz, 21. Juan, old man of the group at 24, would break out his copy of *Walden Two* and read aloud. Juan's voice is high and breathy, like the sound produced by blowing air into a Coke bottle. Night after night, his audience listened to that eerie hoot go on about how, with the aid of Skinner's science, a new society could be formed.

Among the small following, the idea started to take. They would start a community called Los Horcones—or "the pillars"—of a new society, nothing less. It would be a living experiment, a "cultural lab." They would be the researchers, they and their children the pigeons. Together they'd take Skinner's behaviorism another step down the road.

They drafted a Code of Adult Behavior—41 pages in a green plastic binder, written in a style about as lively as a traffic ticket's—and in it they spelled out the details of the communitarian lifestyle. All adults would be parents to all children. Residents would be discouraged from saying "mine" and encouraged to say "ours"—as in "This is our daughter," even if one was not a blood relation. If an adult was working and a child asked a question, the adult would drop everything and explain what was going on. In addition, the older children would serve as teachers for the younger ones. Casual sex would not be considered a good example for "our" children.

In general, residents were to keep the community in mind at all times. They had to stop getting satisfaction from receiving more—whether pie or praise—and start getting excited about giving more. "Have approving thoughts about others" was a key dictum. The worst adjective that could be applied to someone at Los Horcones was "individualistic."

In all, six young urban friends gave up the career track in society—"the outside"—and moved to the countryside to build houses and to farm. They knew nothing about these endeavors, and Ramon recalls that for a few moments in 1973, the idea of building a new society with these ragtag city kids seemed like a very silly idea. It was dawn and the brand new behaviorists found themselves circling a fawn and white Guernsey cow, trying to figure out how to milk it.

In 1980, the citizens of Los Horcones departed that first desolate site for the current patch of desert: an even more remote 250 acres of brush, cactus, and mesquite, 4 miles from Hermosillo. The new land might as well have been a stretch of concrete. They dug a small reservoir and carved out irrigation ditches to compensate for the parching lack of rain, and they hauled in trees. With a mania for systems, they not only planted but numbered every one of them. "Orderliness," Mireya says with a chortle, "is reinforcing."

Today Los Horcones is an oasis. "Everywhere you look, there we have done something," says Lucho. Vegetables grow in flawless stripes on seven acres. Orchards produce grapefruits as big as melons and lemons the size of baseballs. There are pigs, rabbits, chickens, 13 cows, electric milking machines, and a cheese factory. The community is, in fact, 75 percent food self-sufficient, buying only such staples as rice and flour. They have a Caterpillar tractor, trucks, and a school bus converted into a touring vehicle—sleeps nine—for occasional group forays to the outside world.

There's a basketball court and a plaza where they hold pig roasts and dances for guests from Hermosillo. They've dug a swimming hole, called Walden Pond, and built wood and metal shops. There's a dormitory for the dozen or so mentally impaired children they care for, which earns them cash to buy supplies. Luis is still there, helping to milk the cows for coins. The huge main house has a living room, communal dining room, and an office featuring a couple of computers. A lab contains cages of cooing pigeons used in behavioral experiments.

This has taken considerable work, far more than the four hours a day Skinner projected in his book. "I did like to play sports, but for me, it's not so important now," says Lucho, who, as all the adults do, works six and a half days a week. What's important to him now? "Building a building, fixing a toilet," he says simply.

The only space an adult can call his or her own at Los Horcones is one of the 25 assigned white stucco residences, each no more than a bedroom. Meager quarters for a private life, but the idea, after all, was to build a place where people shared not only space but belongings and emotions. The bedrooms are starkly utilitarian, with perhaps a table, an overhead fan—and no closets.

That's because the clothes at Los Horcones belong to everybody and are stored in one building: rows of jeans, neatly pressed and arranged by size, rows of shirts on hangers. First come, first served; too bad what goes best with your eyes. "I have four or five shirts I like," says Ramon. "I don't care who uses them. How could you build a community on sharing and be worried about who uses shirts?"

At first, it's fair to say, newcomers couldn't believe they had to do this clothes-swap thing. Even those dedicated to the design of a new society found it strange to see someone else in the clothes they were wearing yesterday.

And yet, in the long run, sharing clothes has turned out to be one of the easier things to adjust to. Some of the less tangible behaviors have been tougher to master. The main hurdle for the individual and for the new society is this: How can someone who's been reared to believe that if you don't look out for yourself, no one else will, suddenly believe that other people's happiness is your happiness, too?

"It's like being born again," says Juan.

But how to be reborn?

Fortunately, a day at Los Horcones is chock-full of strategies. Every activity can, it seems, be a form of reinforcement. Not only do the residents pick beans side by side, and take turns cooking together, they hold meetings to air any thoughts about how everyone behaved during the picking and cooking.

If you don't show up where you are supposed to, or if your tone of voice is too authoritarian, someone will take note of it. Alcohol, and even coffee, are allowed only in moderation because they aren't good for you. The place is like a big self-improvement camp, with lots of monitors. Lucho wrote in his notebook how many times his coworker was late for his shift at the cheese factory. That way, he said, there would be no argument when they were both sitting down with the behavior coordinator, trying to improve the situation.

If the extended family's kindhearted badgering can't haul a newcomer into line, there are, of course, other weapons for promoting utopia in the desert. That's where Skinner's science comes in. "That's right," says Juan, "we have the technology to change behavior."

In theory, no behavior is beyond the technology's reach. One woman—who prefers to remain anonymous, so we'll call her Susan—was interested in improving her relationship with her husband, so she designed a self-management program. She translated relationship-with-husband into graphable entities—positive verbal contacts, or PVCs, and negative verbal contacts, NVCs. She collected the data on a notepad she hid in her pocket, and after nine days she checked her chart: on average, 3.5 PVCs and 1.8 NVCs per day. Secretly, she also tallied her husband's communications. His score: 2.5 PVCs and 1.5 NVCs.

For Susan, or anyone, to learn a new behavior, it's essential to figure out what reinforces that behavior. Busi, 15 years old, taught Sebastian, but four, how to read in an astonishingly quick 15 hours. As he sounded out words, syllable by syllable, she patted his head and pushed a few of his reinforcers, Fruit Loops, into his mouth. But pats and sweets don't work for everybody. There is also the "participative reinforcer." To reward someone for cooking a nice meal, you not only applaud—though they like applause here—you offer to help afterwards with the dishes.

The most reliable reinforcer, though, is what the behaviorists at Los Horcones call a "natural" one, in which the person practicing a new behavior is reinforced by the consequences of that behavior. When Linda, for instance, discovered that she didn't run to other people's babies when they cried, she made herself run. The babies smiled in her arms, which, she explained, reinforced her response, naturally.

Susan, too, chose a natural reinforcer: her husband's response. She set a goal for herself: She would emit seven PVCs a day, and drop her NVCs to zero. Her husband had no idea about this particular behavior management program—it's hard to always know who's managing whose behavior at Los Horcones—but Susan noted that his PVCs increased to almost eight a day and his NVCs fell to zero. Both their PVCs up, Susan felt a lot better about their relationship.

PVCs? NVCs? They make lovely points on a graph, but are they love? It's not a distinction that behaviorists are troubled by. They're interested in observable behavior, not hidden recesses of the psyche. "How can you see what is inside except by the outside product" explains Linda. "Anyone can imagine that if you, as a wife, have more pleasing interactions with your husband, you feel like he loves you more."

Despite the behaviorist lingo and the laboratory overtones, there is a bit of common sense to all this. A baby's smile can make someone feel good. And many people know that lending a hand, the essence of "participative reinforcement," or making tender comments, as Susan did to increase her PVCs, brings returns in good will. The difference is that at Los Horcones, these insights are applied in a deliberated system.

What's more, in a community that's also a behaviorism laboratory, reinforcers are the object of methodical study. Every morning, Linda experiments with the little ones. One current topic: Can children learn to consider future consequences? Linda doles out the investigative tool: M&M's. "You can eat it now," she tells the two- through seven-year-olds, "but if you wait until I say 'eat,' you get another." On a wall are the graphs she has charted; the lines reveal that the children will wait up to four minutes.

Los Horcones may, in fact, be one of the most self-studied communities in history. The results of the group's self-scrutiny, 20 papers, have been published in academic journals over the past 15 years—each signed communally, of course: "Los Horcones." The articles have examined the steps the community has taken to make its system of government by consensus more democratic, or revealed some of the reinforcers they've discovered to be most effective in motivating people to clean their rooms (candy and praise for a 14-year-old) or help harvest the crops (participation rather than sweets).

Still, when it comes to human overhaul, there are sticky areas. Even the technology, apparently, cannot always correct a history of individualistic living. Jealousy, for instance. That most individualistic of emotions, which says this is mine and not yours, seems to be stubborn as hell.

At Los Horcones possessiveness is discouraged. You aren't supposed to waltz into the dining room where the kids slide from one adult's lap to another's and check that your child or your husband has enough of Lupita's special rabbit-garlic stew on his or her plate. Spouses rarely sit together, often don't acknowledge each other, and a visitor doesn't at first know who the pairs are. One couple who became too much of a couple, walking hand in hand and generally behaving like honeymooners, was booted out. The community may be sexually monogamous, but it is emotionally polygamous. "You're married to everyone," Lupita explains.

"Yes, I had jealousy," says Ramon. "I went to Juan, the behavior manager. Here, your problem is everybody's. We had long meetings about it. It helped, though I think behaviors that you have when you are an adult you can't entirely get rid of."

Clearly, the brightest hopes for the redesigned society are the people without an individualistic past, those who have benefited from the technology starting at the earliest stages of their lives: the children. If anyone is to carry out the caring and cooperative ideal, it ought to be those who have grown up here. "I never wanted kids before this," says Ramon, who is the father of four. "I didn't think I had anything to offer them, not until Los Horcones."

The children receive an enormous amount of attention from lots of adults. They're bright and outgoing, and from all appearances, feel capable and loved and useful. Skinner himself, who met the youngsters on several visits they paid to the United States, approved. "They've done wonderful things with their children," he said.

The first wave of the community's children are teenagers now. They have spent weekends with friends from the outside, and have had their friends visit them at Los Horcones. They know their upbringing has been different, but they dismiss the issue with a big shrug.

Ask them, for instance: If you had a problem, would you go to your mother?

"Sometimes when I have a problem I go to La Linda because she is the coordinator of child behavior," says Esteban, 12, son of Juan and Mireya.

Or you could ask: Who won the game of Monopoly?

"I think we all did," one child says. "We were all rich."

Or, Wouldn't you like a little pocket money?

Another shrug, confused, like when you try to explain something to a cat. "I have the money I need," says a teenager named Javier. "Whenever I go to town, they give me some money to buy a soda or something."

Or, Wouldn't you like to live somewhere else?

"I can't stand to stay away more than a couple of days," says Busi, her hands filled with fruit from the orchard.

None of the kids can; but none have had to. That may all change. The teenagers may soon be sent to Tucson, Arizona, to a branch of the community to be opened there, so they can enroll at the University of Arizona—not for a diploma, just to attend classes and learn. The prospect of this exodus makes some nervous, and not just the kids.

Who knows how many of the five teenagers will return? Or will these behaviorally brought up young people make their lives elsewhere?

"I accept both possibilities," says Juan.

Walden Two was a community of a thousand people; Los Horcones hovers at 25 to 30, and can seem at times on the verge of depopulating. They would like to boost the population to 100 or 200; that would be much more reinforcing. Then at midday, children would greet workers with fresh lemonade and maybe a band would be playing.

"Then, even the people we lost would return," says Ramon. As it is now, members, even those who share the ideals, fall away, beyond the reach of the technology. Over the past 17 years, 60 people have come and gone—from South America, the United States, even as far away as Europe. Perhaps some were simply lonely, or seeking food and shelter, or curious because they'd heard about the community or seen an ad. (Yes, Los Horcones advertised in the local newspaper.) They stayed a few months or a couple of years, and drifted away. Leaving is the worst anticommunitarian behavior, and yet, it would seem, the toughest to change.

Last spring, just as the counter revealed that four in five of tiny, horned-voiced Ivan's commentaries were positive, Lupita and Lucho packed up their sons and left for Lupita's family home in Hermosillo. Lucho said he had wearied of trying, against his nature, to put the community first, whether by working more or organizing better. Lupita was torn, but followed her husband.

Lucho had succeeded through behavioral self-management in giving more approval to the kids, but he had never found a program that would make him think less often of his family and himself. "I just didn't want to change for what the community was offering me," he says. "It was simply that."

It was an awful failure of the technology—that was the shared analysis of the members who remained, though the discussions weren't so analytical. There were tears. The departure was like a divorce, an angry divorce.

With the exception of one founder who stayed 12 years before leaving, Lupita and Lucho had been there longer than any of the dozens who had passed through. But years spent at the community were evidently no guarantee of continued commitment.

Outside Los Horcones, Lucho said, things seemed easier. "Here it's not the same as starting a new society and defining everything. Here, the rules of the game are easy. I feel energized to do something. I think this energy I got—at Los Horcones, and I am thankful for that." He got other things, too, like knowledge of how to make cheese, which is the business he and Lupita have chosen to go into for themselves—competing, of all things, for Los Horcones's customers.

Maybe Lucho would have liked some other reinforcers: additional time for himself, more trips outside the community, perhaps a few more economic incentives?

"If there had been those, I would have felt much better," Lucho said after he left.

And now, into this 17-year-old utopia, new "experimental" reinforcers soon may be creeping: credits for work, and paid vacations. That's what Los Horcones is considering. "People won't try to live communitarianly if they are not earning something more individualistic," says Juan pragmatically.

Individual rewards for living together? It sounds against the grain. Could behaviorism have pecked up against its limits?

"With investigation, you rise above the limits," says Juan, faithful as Skinner's *Walden Two* hero, Frazier. "We must investigate in more detail the variables that control these problems."

As the late great experimenter himself might have said: Back to the lab.

NAME _____

DATE _____

ACTIVE LEARNING EXERCISE 6.1

OBSERVING AND RECORDING A PERSONAL BEHAVIOR

The best way to appreciate and understand the behavioral perspective is to engage actively in the process of recording and analyzing a segment of your own behavior. The initial step will be for you to choose a behavior that you engage in on a regular basis. The following is a list of some behaviors that students have selected in the past:

smoking	fears
eating	smiling
studying	exercise
arguing	using profanities
nail biting	socializing
hair twirling	telephoning
looking in mirrors	sleeping

This list is meant to give you an idea of some possibilities. Don't think of it as the definitive list for you to choose from. The list suggests some ideas to help you select a behavior that you want to observe and record. It is often interesting to record a behavior that you might want to modify (e.g., increase or decrease in frequency of occurrence). A project that is important to you will be more fun and ultimately yield more useful information. Remember to pick a behavior that occurs with sufficient frequency so that you have something to record. (Do not pick how many times a day you run a 1-minute mile [likely to be never] or how many times you move your thumb [likely to be too frequent].)

GUIDELINES

1. Make sure the behavior you are observing and recording is clearly specified so that you don't have to make decisions about whether it has occurred. Clear up all doubts about the characteristics of the response before you start recording.

2. While recording your behavior look out for the situations in which the behavior occurs and what happens once you initiate the behavior. Behaviors often do not occur in a random manner, and they often have consequences that are significant. For example, some people smoke while driving or studying but not while eating or watching TV. Some smokers experience coughing or nausea after smoking. Recognizing the contexts in which behaviors occur and the consequences of the behaviors gives us useful information for analysis and behavior change.

3. There are two basic ways of recording behavior: (a) counting the frequency of the occurrence of the behavior and (b) recording the time duration of the behavior. If you are interested in your smoking behavior, you could count the number of cigarettes you smoke per day (frequency) or the amount of time, in minutes and seconds, you engage in smoking. With some behaviors a frequency counting system is easier to employ (e.g., smoking), while with other behaviors, duration may be more desirable (e.g., running, swimming). Whatever system you use, be sure it adequately reflects the behavior you are interested in. A student who was interested in her telephone usage set up a system in which she recorded the number of phone calls she made each day. The results indicated that she made one or two phone calls a day, which

did not seem to be a problem. On closer inspection, the results revealed that she mostly talked to her boyfriend, who attended another college, and that each phone call lasted 1 to 2 hours. The student should have used a duration measure, recording the amount of time engaged in talking on the phone behavior. By doing so, the data would have better reflected her behavior. Her behavior should not have been the frequency of phone calling but rather the time spent on the phone.

4. It is important to record behavior as it occurs without delay. Don't attempt to remember the data and record them later. A good system is to carry a file card with you and keep records up to date by recording the frequency or time durations immediately. Be strict and count all occurrences, even if you are surprised, elated, or annoyed by the data. Don't use other people to help you recognize or record your behaviors. It is important for you to be alert and focus on the target behavior you have identified. It is important not to intervene or modify your behavior intentionally during this recording project. Sometimes people discover unexpectedly high or low rates of behavior in a study like this and immediately attempt to intervene. For example, if a student who believes he is studying 3 hours per night discovers by careful recording that he is actually studying only 40 minutes per night, he might want to make some behavioral changes. Indeed, recording one's behavior may serve not only as a method of analysis but also as a treatment. Once you have discovered the actual rates of certain behaviors, you may immediately want to intervene to increase or decrease their occurrence. For this project, try to restrain yourself from making personal changes and complete the recording period without modifying your actions.

5. At the end of each day, transfer your daily data to a permanent record that you keep at home. This lessens the danger of losing all the data if you misplace the daily record card. You should record your behavior for 10 consecutive days. This will allow you to observe the effect of days of the week, particularly the weekend, on your data. It is also a long enough period of time to allow you to get a sense of the typical rates of the behavior. The period of recording in behavioral interventions is referred to as the *baseline*. It is the period that reflects typical behaviors and the period against which behavioral interventions and treatments are compared.

6. It is also useful to graph the data so that you can get a visual picture of your recorded behavior. The following graph is a sample of what you might use for this exercise. Use the X and Y axes on the next page to display your data.

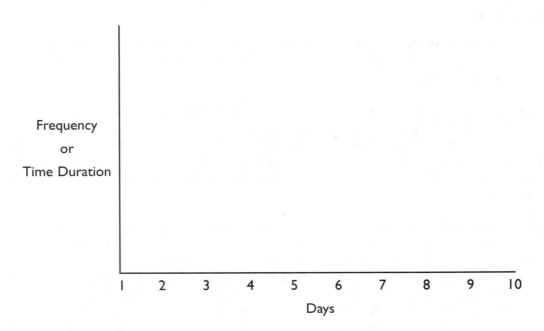

YOUR BEHAVIOR RECORDING

Target Behavior: _____

Specific Behavior Recorded: _____

Method of Recording: _____

Data:

    Day 1: _____

    Day 2: _____

    Day 3: _____

    Day 4: _____

    Day 5: _____

    Day 6: _____

    Day 7: _____

    Day 8: _____

    Day 9: _____

    Day 10: _____

Contexts/situations in which behavior occurs:

Consequences of behavior:

Your observations and conclusions:

What behavioral strategy would you use to modify the rate of your target behavior?

READING
IMITATION OF FILM-MEDIATED AGGRESSIVE MODELS*
Albert Bandura, Dorothea Ross, and Sheila A. Ross

Editors' Note:

In this classic study we find empirical support for the powerful effect that modeling can have on the development of aggressive patterns of behavior. The following Spotlight, "On Screen, In Life," in this chapter provides current examples of the influence of observational learning.

. . . **A** recent incident (*San Francisco Chronicle*, 1961) in which a boy was seriously knifed during a re-enactment of a switchblade knife fight the boys had seen the previous evening on a televised rerun of the James Dean movie, *Rebel Without a Cause*, is a dramatic illustration of the possible imitative influence of film stimulation. Indeed, anecdotal data suggest that portrayal of aggression through pictorial media may be more influential in shaping the form aggression will take when a person is instigated on later occasions, than in altering the level of instigation to aggression.

In an earlier experiment (Bandura & Huston, 1961) it was shown that children readily imitated aggressive behavior exhibited by a model in the presence of the model. A succeeding investigation (Bandura, Ross, & Ross, 1961) demonstrated that children exposed to aggressive models generalized aggressive responses to a new setting in which the model was absent. The present study sought to determine the extent to which film-mediated aggressive models may serve as an important source of imitative behavior.

Aggressive models can be ordered on a reality–fictional stimulus dimension with real-life models located at the reality end of the continuum, nonhuman cartoon characters at the fictional end, and films portraying human models occupying an intermediate position. It was predicted, on the basis of saliency and similarity of cues, that the more remote the model was from reality, the weaker would be the tendency for subjects to imitate the behavior of the model. . .

. . . To the extent that observation of adults displaying aggression conveys a certain degree of permissiveness for aggressive behavior, it may be assumed that such exposure not only facilitates the learning of new aggressive responses but also weakens competing inhibitory responses in subjects and thereby increases the probability of occurrence of previously learned patterns of aggression. It was predicted, therefore, that subjects who observed aggressive models would display significantly more aggression when subsequently frustrated than subjects who were equally frustrated but who had no prior exposure to models exhibiting aggression.

METHOD

SUBJECTS

The subjects were 48 boys and 48 girls enrolled in the Stanford University Nursery School. They ranged in age from 35 to 69 months, with a mean age of 52 months.

Two adults, a male and a female, served in the role of models both in the real-life and the human film-aggression condition, and one female experimenter conducted the study for all 96 children.

GENERAL PROCEDURE

Subjects were divided into three experimental groups and one control group of 24 subjects each. One group of experimental subjects observed real-life aggressive models, a second group observed these same models portraying aggression on film, while a third group viewed a film depicting an aggressive cartoon character. The experimental groups were further subdivided into male and female subjects so that half the subjects in the two conditions involving human models were exposed to same-sex models, while the remaining subjects viewed models of the opposite sex.

Following the exposure experience, subjects were tested for the amount of imitative and nonimitative aggression in a different experimental setting in the absence of the models. . .

. . . Subjects in the experimental and control groups were matched individually on the basis of ratings of their aggressive behavior in social interactions in the nursery school. The experimenter and a nursery school teacher rated the subjects on four five-point rating scales which measured the extent to which subjects displayed physical aggression, verbal aggression, aggres-

*Bandura A., Ross, D., & Ross, S. A. (1963). "Imitation of film-mediated aggressive models." *Journal of Abnormal and Social Psychology*, 66, 3–11. Copyright © 1963 by The American Psychological Association. Reprinted with permission.

sion toward inanimate objects, and aggression inhibition. The latter scale, which dealt with the subjects' tendency to inhibit aggressive reactions in the face of high instigation, provided the measure of aggression anxiety. Seventy-one percent of the subjects were rated independently by both judges so as to permit an assessment of interrater agreement. The reliability of the composite aggression score, estimated by means of the Pearson product-moment correlation, was .80. . .

...EXPERIMENTAL CONDITIONS

Subjects in the Real-Life Aggressive condition were brought individually by the experimenter to the experimental room and the model, who was in the hallway outside the room, was invited by the experimenter to come and join in the game. The subject was then escorted to one corner of the room and seated at a small table which contained potato prints, multicolor picture stickers, and colored paper. After demonstrating how the subject could design pictures with the material provided, the experimenter escorted the model to the opposite corner of the room which contained a small table and chair, a tinker toy set, a mallet, and a 5-foot chair, a tinker toy set, a mallet, and a 5-foot inflated Bobo doll. The experimenter explained that this was the model's play area and after the model was seated, the experimenter left the experimental room.

The model began the session by assembling the tinker toys but after approximately a minute had elapsed, the model turned to the Bobo doll and spent the remainder of the period aggressing toward it with highly novel responses which are unlikely to be performed by children independently of the observation of the model's behavior. Thus, in addition to punching the Bobo doll, the model exhibited the following distinctive aggressive acts which were to be scored as imitative responses:

> The model sat on the Bobo doll and punched it repeatedly in the nose.

> The model then raised the Bobo doll and pommeled it on the head with a mallet.

Following the mallet aggression, the model tossed the doll up in the air aggressively and kicked it about the room. This sequence of physically aggressive acts was repeated approximately three times, interspersed with verbally aggressive responses such as "Sock him in the nose . . .," "Hit him down . . .," "Throw him in the air . . .," "Kick him . . .," and "Pow."

Subjects in the Human Film-Aggression condition were brought by the experimenter to the semi-darkened experimental room, introduced to the picture materials, and informed that while the subjects worked on potato prints, a movie would be shown on a screen, positioned approximately 6 feet from the subject's table. The movie projector was located in a distant corner of the room and was screened from the subject's view by large wooden panels.

The color movie and a tape recording of the sound track were begun by a male projectionist as soon as the experimenter left the experimental room and was shown for a duration of 10 minutes. The models in the film presentations were the same adult males and females who participated in the Real-Life condition of the experiment. Similarly, the aggressive behavior they portrayed in the film was identical with their real-life performances.

For subjects in the Cartoon Film-Aggression condition, after seating the subject at the table with the picture construction material, the experimenter walked over to a television console approximately 3 feet in front of the subject's table, remarked, 'I guess I'll turn on the color TV," and ostensibly tuned in a cartoon program. The experimenter then left the experimental room. . .

. . . In both film conditions, at the conclusion of the movie the experimenter entered the room and then escorted the subject to the test room. . .

...AGGRESSION INSTIGATION

In order to differentiate clearly the exposure and test situations subjects were tested for the amount of imitative learning in a different experimental room which was set off from the main nursery school building.

The degree to which a child has learned aggressive patterns of behavior through imitation becomes most evident when the child is instigated to aggression on later occasions. Thus, for example, the effects of viewing the movie, *Rebel Without a Cause*, were not evident until the boys were instigated to aggression the following day, at which time they re-enacted the televised switchblade knife fight in considerable detail. For this reason, the children in the experiment, both those in the control group and those who were exposed to the aggressive models, were mildly frustrated before they were brought to the test room.

Following the exposure experience, the experimenter brought the subject to an anteroom which contained a varied array of highly attractive toys. The experimenter explained that the toys were for the subject to play with, but, as soon as the subject became sufficiently involved with the play material, the experimenter remarked that these were her very best toys, that she did not let just anyone play with them, and that she had decided to reserve these toys for some other children. However, the subject could play with any of the toys in the next room. The experimenter and the subject then entered the adjoining experimental room. . .

...TEST FOR DELAYED IMITATION

The experimental room contained a variety of toys, some of which could be used in imitative or nonimitative aggression, and others which tended to elicit predominantly nonaggressive forms of behavior. The aggressive toys included a 3-foot Bobo doll, a mallet and peg board, two dart guns, and a tether ball with a face painted on it which hung from the ceiling. The nonaggressive toys, on the other hand, included a tea set, crayons and coloring paper, a ball, two dolls, three bears, cars and trucks, and plastic farm animals. . .

. . . The subject spent 20 minutes in the experimental room during which time his [or her] behavior was rated in terms of predetermined response categories by judges who observed the session through a one-way mirror in an adjoining observation room. The 20-minute session was divided in 5-second intervals by means of an electric interval timer, thus yielding a total number of 240 response units for each subject.

. . . RESULTS

TOTAL AGGRESSION

. . . The results of the analysis of variance performed on these scores reveal that the main effect of treatment conditions is significant, confirming the prediction that exposure of subjects to aggressive models increases the probability that subjects will respond aggressively when instigated on later occasions. . .

. . . IMITATIVE AGGRESSIVE RESPONSES

The prediction that imitation is positively related to the reality cues of the model was only partially supported. While subjects who observed the real-life aggressive models exhibited significantly more imitative aggression than subjects who viewed the cartoon model, no significant differences were found between the live and film, and the film and carton conditions, nor did the three experimental groups differ significantly in total aggression or in the performances of partially imitative behavior. Indeed, the available data suggest that, of the three experimental conditions, exposure to humans on film portraying aggression was the most influential in eliciting and shaping aggressive behavior. Subjects in this condition, in relation to the control subjects, exhibited more total aggression, more imitative aggression, more partially imitative behavior, such as sitting on the Bobo doll and mallet aggression, and they engaged in significantly more aggressive gun play. In addition, they performed significantly more aggressive gun play than did subjects who were exposed to the real-life aggressive models. . .

. . . INFLUENCE OF SEX OF MODEL AND SEX OF CHILD

Sex of subjects had a highly significant effect on both the learning and the performance of aggression. Boys, in relation to girls, exhibited significantly more total aggression, more imitative aggression, more aggressive gun play, and more nonimitative aggressive behavior. Girls, on the other hand, were more inclined than boys to sit on the Bobo doll but refrained from punching it.

The analyses also disclosed some influences of the sex of the model. Subjects exposed to the male model, as compared to the female model, expressed significantly more aggressive gun play. The most marked differences in aggressive gun play, however, were found between girls exposed to the female model and males who observed the male model. . .

. . . DISCUSSION

The results of the present study provide strong evidence that exposure to filmed aggression heightens aggressive reactions in children. Subjects who viewed the aggressive human and cartoon models on film exhibited nearly twice as much aggression [as] did subjects in the control group who were not exposed to the aggressive film content. . .

. . . Filmed aggression not only facilitated the expression of aggression, but also effectively shaped the form of the subjects' aggressive behavior. The finding that children modeled their behavior to some extent after the film characters suggests that pictorial mass media, particularly television, may serve as an important source of social behavior. In fact, a possible generalization of responses originally learned in the television situation to the experimental film may account for the significantly greater amount of aggressive gun play displayed by subjects in the film condition as compared to subjects in the real-life and control groups. It is unfortunate that the qualitative features of the gun behavior were not scored since subjects in the film condition, unlike those in the other two groups, developed interesting elaborations in gun play (for example, stalking the imaginary opponent, quick drawing, and rapid firing), characteristic of the Western gunfighter. . .

. . . In assessing the possible influence of televised stimulation on viewers' behavior, however, it is important to distinguish between learning and overt performance. Although the results of the present experiment demonstrate that the vast majority of children learn patterns of social behavior through pictorial stimulation, nevertheless, informal observation suggests that children do not, as a rule, perform indiscriminately the behavior of televised characters, even those they regard as highly attractive models. The replies of parents whose children participated in the present study to an open-end questionnaire item concerning their handling of imitative behavior suggest that this may be in part a function of negative reinforcement, as most parents were quick to discourage their children's overt imitation of television characters by prohibiting certain programs or by labeling the imitative behavior in a disapproving manner. From our knowledge of the effects of punishment on behavior, the responses in question would be expected to retain their original strength and could reappear on later occasions in the presence of appropriate eliciting stimuli, particularly if instigation is high, the instruments for aggression are available, and the threat of noxious consequences is reduced.

REFERENCES

BANDURA, A., & HUSTON, A. C. Identification as a process of incidental learning. *J. Abnorm. Soc. Psychol.*, 1961, *63*, 311–318.

BANDURA, A., ROSS, D., & ROSS, S. A. Transmission of aggression through imitation of aggressive models. *J. Abnorm. Soc. Psychol.*, 1961, *63*, 575–582.

San Francisco Chronicle. "James Dean" knifing in South City. *San Francisco Chron.*, March 1, 1961, 6.

SPOTLIGHT
ON SCREEN, IN LIFE*

New Jack City: Mario Van Peebles's visceral 1991 drama about two former police officers hired to bring down a drug lord was blamed for an outbreak of violence outside shopping-mall theaters.

The Program: A 1993 film about the abuses of college sports led to the death of one youth and the injury of two others, who were run over while imitating a scene in which a football player demonstrates his toughness by lying down on the center line of a highway at night. The scene was subsequently deleted from the film.

Natural Born Killers: Oliver Stone's 1994 film about a murderous young couple, was cited by the Utah police as prompting a teen-ager to kill his step-mother and half sister.

Beavis and Butt-Head: After television's dimwitted duo demonstrated the use of aerosol spray to ignite a fire, three Ohio girls set a bedroom ablaze in 1993. Two weeks later, a 5-year-old Ohio boy, who began to play with matches after watching the fire-is-fun episode, killed his younger sister by setting his mobile home afire.

Under attack as the supposed inspiration for the igniting of a New York City subway token booth, "Money Train" joins a long list of films and television shows blamed for prompting acts of violence. Among them:

Taxi Driver: Martin Scorsese's 1976 film about a New York City taxi driver stalking a political candidate was cited by prosecutors as the inspiration for John W. Hinckley Jr.'s attack on President Reagan in 1981.

The Burning Bed: The 1984 television movie, starring Farrah Fawcett as a battered wife who sets her former husband afire, was said to have prompted a Milwaukee viewer to splash gasoline on his wife and burn her to death.

Boulevard Nights: On opening night of the 1979 drama about street gangs in Los Angeles, five people were shot and three others stabbed in California theaters. As a result, Universal Pictures canceled the opening of a film about Mexican-American gangs, Robert Collins's "Walk Proud," in Hispanic areas of Los Angeles, San Francisco, Dallas and Denver.

Colors: Dennis Hopper's 1988 film about street gangs in Los Angeles touched off a wave of violence. One gang member was shot to death outside a Stockton, California, theater where the film was being shown. Violence occurred at other movie houses, and the police arrested nearly 150 people as the film opened in Los Angeles.

*Reprinted with permission from *The New York Times*, November 30, 1995.

NAME _____

DATE _____

ASSERTIVENESS*

Assertive behavior has been investigated by behaviorists for many years. A significant number of people find it difficult to act in an assertive manner and often resort to passive behaviors. For example, it is appropriate to state complaints when you feel they are justified rather than to accept poor service or a mediocre product. Although assertiveness is not passivity, it is also not aggressive behavior. Behavior therapists have been successful in treating nonassertive behavior through a variety of strategies. This exercise will assess your level of assertiveness and give you a chance to compare your score to established norms.

Directions: Indicate how well each item describes you by using this code:

3 = very much like me	-1 = slightly unlike me
2 = rather like me	-2 = rather unlike me
1 = slightly like me	-3 = very much unlike me

_____ 1. Most people seem to be more aggressive and assertive than I am.*

_____ 2. I have hesitated to make or accept dates because of "shyness."*

_____ 3. When the food served at a restaurant is not done to my satisfaction, I complain about it to the waiter or waitress.

_____ 4. I am careful to avoid hurting other people's feelings, even when I feel that I have been injured.*

_____ 5. If a salesperson has gone to considerable trouble to show me merchandise that is not quite suitable, I have a difficult time saying "No."*

_____ 6. When I am asked to do something, I insist upon knowing why.

_____ 7. There are times when I look for a good, vigorous argument.

_____ 8. I strive to get ahead as well as most people in my position.

_____ 9. To be honest, people often take advantage of me.*

_____ 10. I enjoy starting conversations with new acquaintances and strangers.

_____ 11. I often don't know what to say to attractive persons of the opposite sex.*

_____ 12. I will hesitate to make phone calls to business establishments and institutions.*

_____ 13. I would rather apply for a job or for admission to a college by writing letters than by going through with personal interviews.*

_____ 14. I find it embarrassing to return merchandise.*

_____ **15.** If a close and respected relative were annoying me, I would smother my feelings rather than express my annoyance.*

_____ **16.** I have avoided asking questions for fear of sounding stupid.*

_____ **17.** During an argument I am sometimes afraid that I will get so upset that I will shake all over.*

_____ **18.** If a famed and respected lecturer makes a comment which I think is incorrect, I will have the audience hear my point of view as well.

_____ **19.** I avoid arguing over prices with clerks and salespeople.*

_____ **20.** When I have done something important or worthwhile, I manage to let others know about it.

_____ **21.** I am open and frank about my feelings.

_____ **22.** If someone has been spreading false and bad stories about me, I see him or her as soon as possible and "have a talk" about it.

_____ **23.** I often have a hard time saying "No."*

_____ **24.** I tend to bottle up my emotions rather than make a scene.*

_____ **25.** I complain about poor service in a restaurant and elsewhere.

_____ **26.** When I am given a compliment, I sometimes just don't know what to say.*

_____ **27.** If a couple near me in a theater or at a lecture were conversing rather loudly, I would ask them to be quiet or to take their conversation elsewhere.

_____ **28.** Anyone attempting to push ahead of me in a line is in for a good battle.

_____ **29.** I am quick to express an opinion.

_____ **30.** There are times when I just can't say anything.*

*Rathus, S. D. (1973). A 30-item schedule for assessing assertive behavior. _Behavior Therapy, 4_, 399–400.
Copyright © 1973 by the Association for the Advancement of Behavior Therapy. Reprinted by permission of the publisher and the author.

SCORING

Tabulate your score as follows: For those items followed by an asterisk (*), change the signs (plus to minus; minus to plus). For example, if the response to an asterisked item was 2, place a minus sign (-) before the two. If the response to an asterisked item was -3, change the minus sign to a plus sign (+) by adding a vertical stroke. Then add up the scores of the 30 items. Scores on the assertiveness schedule can vary from +90 to -90.

Score =

INTERPRETATION

The following table will show you how your score compares to those of 764 college women and 637 men from 35 campuses across the United States. For example, if you are a woman and your score was 26, it exceeds that of 80 percent of the women in the sample. A score of 15 for a male exceeds that of 55–60 percent of the men in the sample.

WOMEN'S SCORES	PERCENTILE	MEN'S SCORES
55	99	65
48	97	54
45	95	48
37	90	40
31	85	33
26	80	30
23	75	26
19	70	24
17	65	19
14	60	17
11	55	15
8	50	11
6	45	8
2	40	6
- 1	35	3
- 4	30	1
- 8	25	- 3
-13	20	- 7
-17	15	-11
-24	10	-15
-34	5	-24
-39	3	-30
-48	1	-41

Nevid, J. S., & Rathus, S. D. (1978). Multivariate and normative data pertaining to the RAS with a college population. *Behavior Therapy, 9,* 675. Copyright © 1978 by the Association for the Advancement of Behavior Therapy. Reprinted by permission of the publisher and the authors.

CHAPTER
7

Humanistic Perspective

Introduction

The humanistic perspective is sometimes referred to as the third force in psychology because it developed in reaction to the behavioral and psychoanalytic approaches. It differs from the first two forces in many respects, but mostly in its emphasis on human potential. Humanistic psychology offers a positive view of people exercising their free will to actualize their potential.

The readings and exercises in this chapter focus on the two central figures in the humanistic movement, Carl Rogers and Abraham Maslow. In addition to reading about the philosophical and psychological underpinnings of humanistic psychology, you will have an opportunity to assess your current level of actualization, analyze a personal "peak experience," and examine your self-ideal perceptions utilizing the Q-sort technique.

HUMANISTIC THEORY: THE THIRD REVOLUTION IN PSYCHOLOGY*

Floyd W. Matson

Editors' Note:

During the twentieth century, three forces or movements have had a tremendous impact on psychological thinking. In this article, Floyd Matson contrasts the humanistic movement with the other dominant forces in psychology: behaviorism and psychoanalysis. In his depictions of the three forces, he highlights such issues as autonomy, responsibility, wholeness, and authenticity.

Humanistic psychology tries to tell it not like it is, but like it ought to be. It seeks to bring psychology back to its source, to the *psyche*, where it all began and where it finally culminates. But there is more to it than that. Humanistic psychology is not just the study of "human being"; it is a commitment to human becoming.

It was a humanistic philosopher, Kurt Riezler, who said that "science begins with respect for the subject matter." Unfortunately that is not the view of all scientists, whether in the hard sciences of nature or in the softer sciences of man and mind. It is almost, as it seems to me, a defining characteristic of behaviorist psychology that it begins with *dis*respect for the subject matter, and therefore leads straight-away to what Norbert Wiener (a pretty hard scientist himself) called the "inhuman use of human beings." At any rate, I know of no greater disrespect for the human subject than to treat him as an object—unless it is to demean that object further by fragmenting it into drives, traits, reflexes, and other mechanical hardware. But that is the procedure of behaviorism, if not of all experimental psychology; it is a procedure openly admitted, indeed triumphantly proclaimed, in the name of Science and Truth, of Objectivity and Rigor, and of all else that is holy in these precincts. And it leads in a straight line out of the ivory tower into the brave new world of Walden Two.

Everyone remembers, I am sure, that curious utopian novel, *Walden Two*, written more than 20 years ago by the preeminent behaviorist of our generation, B. F. Skinner. His book presented such a stark scenario of behavioral engineering and mind manipulation, such a "conditional" surrender of autonomy and freedom on the part of its docile characters, that many readers at the time mistakenly supposed it to be a clever put-on, a satirical prophecy of the nightmare shape of things to come if ever a free society should relax its vigilant defense of the values of liberty and responsibility—especially the liberty and responsibility of choice.

But that was what Skinner's novel openly defied and disparaged; the Elysian community it projected was a sort of crystal palace (or womb with a view) within which perfect peace and security might abide forever—tranquillity without trauma, pleasure without pain, attainment without struggle—and all at the trivial price of the freedom to make choices, the right (as it were) to blunder. The key to the kingdom of Walden Two was operant conditioning; by this magical technique, applied to all residents from birth, the "Hamlet syndrome" (the anxiety of choice) was efficiently removed. Like that wonderful Mrs. Prothro in Dylan Thomas's Christmas story, who "said the right thing always," so the creatures of Skinner's novel were conditioned to make the right choices automatically. It was instant certitude, at the price of all volition. Like Pavlov's dogs, Skinner's people make only conditioned responses to the stimulus of their master's voice.

Let us recognize that such a homeostatic paradise, like the classless society and the heavenly city, has great seductive appeal for many, especially in an age of anxiety and a time of troubles. It appeals particularly to those with a low tolerance for ambiguity and a high rage for order. I believe it was Thomas Huxley who was so fearful of chance and choice as to declare that if he were offered a world of absolute security and certainty, at the price of surrendering his personal freedom, he would close instantly with the bargain. Unlike his grandson, Aldous, whose own futuristic novel made just the opposite point, the elder Huxley would surely have enjoyed the still life on Skinner's Walden Pond.

Let me recall now a different disposition, both existential and humanistic. It is Dostoevsky's underground man, struggling to be heard by the Establishment above. "After all," he says,

> I do not really insist on suffering or on prosperity either. I insist on my caprice, and its being guaranteed to me when necessary.

*From Humanistic theory: The third revolution in psychology, by Floyd W. Matson, *The Humanist*, Vol. 31, No. 2, pp. 7–11. (Mar./Apr. 1971). Reprinted with the permission of the publisher, The American Humanist Association, Copyright © 1971.

Suffering would be out of place in vaudevilles, for instance; I know that. In the crystal palace it is even unthinkable; suffering means doubt, means negation, and what would be the good of a crystal palace if there could be any doubt about it? . . . You believe in a crystal edifice that can never be destroyed; that is, an edifice at which one would neither be able to stick out one's tongue nor thumb one's nose on the sly. And perhaps I am afraid of this edifice just because it is of crystal and can never be destroyed and that one could not even put one's tongue out at it even on the sly. (*The Short Novels of Dostoevsky*, Dial Press, New York, 1945, p. 152).

Now there, as Sartre might say, is an existentialism that is a humanism.

There have been, as I believe, three distinct conceptual revolutions in psychology during the course of the present century. The first, that of behaviorism, struck with the force of a revelation around 1913 and shook the foundations of academic psychology for a generation. Behaviorism arose in reaction to the excessive preoccupation of 19th-century psychology with consciousness, and with introspection as a way of getting at the data of conscious mental activity. The behaviorists reacted with a vengeance. They threw out not only consciousness, but all the resources of the mind. The mind, to them, was the ghost in the machine, and they did not believe in ghosts. The founding father of the movement, John B. Watson, declared in an early proclamation, a kind of behaviorist manifesto, that the behaviorist began "by sweeping aside all medieval conceptions. He dropped from his scientific vocabulary all subjective terms such as sensation, perception, image, desire, purpose, and even thinking and emotion as they were subjectively defined" (*Behaviorism* [1924]. University of Chicago Press, Chicago, 1958, pp. 5–6).

Overt behavior, that which could be seen and measured, was all that counted. And all that was needed to explain it was the simple and classical formula of stimulus–response—with one added refinement, that of the conditioned reflex. It was this concept of conditioning, borrowed from the Russian laboratories of Pavlov and Bechterev, that gave the real revolutionary impetus to Watson's behaviorist movement. Conditioning was power; it was control. This was not merely objective psychology, for all its scientific claims; it was an applied psychology—and what it was applied to, or rather against, was man. "The interest of the behaviorist," said Watson, "is more than the interest of a spectator; he wants to control man's reactions as physical scientists want to control and manipulate other natural phenomena" (Ibid., p. 11). Just as man was simply "an assembled organic machine ready to run," so the behaviorist was no pure scientist but an engineer unable to keep from tinkering with the machinery. Pointing out that such sciences as chemistry and biology

were gaining control over their subject matter, Watson inquired, "Can psychology ever get control? Can I make someone who is not afraid of snakes, afraid of them, and how?" The answer was clear: And how!

"In short," said Watson, "the cry of the behaviorist is, 'Give me the baby and my world to bring it up in and I'll make it crawl and walk; I'll make it climb and use its hands in constructing buildings of stone or wood; I'll make it a thief, a gunman, or a dope fiend.' The possibility of shaping in any direction is almost endless" (*The Ways of Behaviorism*, Harper, New York, 1926, p. 35).

That should be enough to suggest the general character (and authoritarian personality) of behaviorist psychology, the first of the three psychological revolutions that have taken place in our century. The second revolution was, of course, that of Freud. It is noteworthy that psychoanalysis and behaviorism made their appearance at roughly the same time, give or take a decade, and that both of them emerged in reaction against the accent on consciousness in traditional psychology. Apart from these coincidences, however, there was little in common between these two movements, and there was a great deal that put them at opposite poles.

Whereas behaviorism placed all its stress upon the external environment (that is, upon stimuli from the outer world) as the controlling factor in behavior, psychoanalysis placed its emphasis upon the internal environment (upon stimuli from within, in the form of drives and instincts). For Freud, man was very much a creature of instinct—and in particular of two primary instincts, those of life and death (*Eros* and *Thanatos*). These two instincts were in conflict not only with each other but with the world, with culture. Society was based, said Freud, on renunciation of the instincts via the mechanism of repression. But the instincts did not give up without a struggle. In fact, they never gave up; they could not be vanquished, only temporarily blocked. Life, then, was a constant alteration between frustration and aggression. Neither for the individual person nor for the culture was there a permanent solution or "happy ending"; there were only compromises, expedients, working adjustments. The price of civilization, indeed, was mass neurosis—the result of the necessary suppression of the natural instincts of man. But if that seems bad, the alternative was worse: whenever the repressive forces are for a moment relaxed, declared Freud, "we see man as a savage beast to whom the thought of sparing his own kind is alien" (*Civilization and Its Discontents*, Hogarth, London, 1930, p. 86).

Perhaps the most interesting, not to say frightening, concept advanced by Freud was that of *Thanatos*, the aggression or death instinct, which he regarded as an innate and irresistible drive toward the destruction of oneself and others. What is especially significant about this bleak conception of man's aggressive nature is the "comeback" it has been making in recent years after a long period of almost total eclipse. The current revival of the shadow side of Freud, the pessimistic musings of his later years, does not tell us so much about Freud as it does about the temper of our own time. I shall return to this point.

The main point I want to make immediately about the psychoanalytic movement, in its Freudian form, is that it presents a picture of man as very much the "victim-spectator," as Gordon Allport has put it, of blind forces working through him. For all its differences with behaviorism, Freudian theory agrees in the fundamental image of man as a stimulus–response machine, although the stimuli that work their will upon the human being come from within rather than from without. Freud's determinism was not environmental, like Watson's, but psychogenetic; nevertheless, it was a determinism, and it left little room for spontaneity, creativity, rationality, or responsibility. The declared faith in conscious reason that underlay Freudian therapy (rather more than Freudian theory) did not prevent his insistently minimizing the role of reason as an actual or potential determinant of personality and conduct—nor, on the other hand, from maximizing the thrust of irrational forces that press their claims both from "below" (the id) and from "above" (the superego). In Freud's topographical map of the mind, the ego, itself only partially conscious, never achieves full autonomy but functions as a kind of buffer state between the rival powers of instinct and introjected culture, between animal nature and social nurture.

I have been deliberately hard on Freud in these remarks in order to emphasize those aspects of his theory and therapy that, by virtue of their pessimism and determinism, have called out over the years the critical and creative response that (for want of a better term) we may call "humanistic psychology." This new psychology, the third revolution, represents a reaction against both behaviorism and orthodox psychoanalysis; it is for that reason that humanistic psychology has been called the "third force." But perhaps the first thing to say about it is that, unlike the two movements of thought that precede and oppose it, humanistic psychology is not a single body of theory but a collection or convergence of a number of lines and schools of thought. If it owes nothing to behaviorism, it does owe much to psychoanalysis, although less perhaps to Freud himself than to the considerable number of Freudian heretics and deviationists, beginning with his own associates of the original Vienna Circle and culminating in the so-called neo-Freudians (anti-Freudians, really) of the second generation.

For despite the many differences among them, those who broke away one by one from the side of Freud shared a number of crucial insights and commitments. Adler, Jung, Rank, Stekel, Ferenczi—all these early associates found themselves unable to accept Freud's theory of instinctual determinism (specifically, his libido theory) and his tendency to find the source of all difficulty and motivation in the remote past. These deviationists began to place equal or greater emphasis upon the present (that is, upon the here-and-now, the "presence" of the patient) and also upon the future (that is, upon the pull of aspiration and purpose, the goal or life-plan of the individual). What this implied was a greater reliance upon the consciousness of the person in analysis or therapy: a new respect for his powers of will and of reason, his capacity to choose and to understand.

In Adler's work, this emphasis took the form of virtually converting the psychoanalytic therapy session into a dialogue or conversation on the conscious level—which of course enraged Freud, who thought that Adler had betrayed the basic postulate of unconscious motivation. In Jung's work, the new approach took the form of emphasizing what he called the "prospective factor," the pull of purpose as opposed to the push of instinct (and in particular the push of erotic instinct); it also took the form, in Jung's later years, of increasing stress upon understanding the other, whether neurotic patient or normal individual, in his unique identity. This involved a kind of intuitive and sympathetic understanding, which Jung distinguished from scientific knowledge and which led him finally to advocate abandoning the textbooks altogether in any venture into helping or healing. In the case of Otto Rank, another of the heretics of the original Freudian circle, the deviation took the form of an emphasis upon the existential will of the person, that is, upon his capacity for self-direction and self-control.

The common denominator in these various lines of theory and therapy was, I believe, *respect for the person*, recognition of the other not as a case, or an object, or a field of forces, or a bundle of instincts, but as himself. In terms of theory, it meant respect for his powers of creativity and responsibility: in terms of therapy, it meant respect for his values, his intentions, and, above all, his peculiar identity.

This recognition of *man-in-person*, as opposed to *man-in-general*, goes to the heart of the difference between humanistic psychology, in any of its forms or schools, and scientific psychologies such as behaviorism. Not only in psychoanalysis, but in other fields as well, increasing numbers of students have found themselves drawn to the unsettling conclusion that the definitive features of a human being cannot be made out at all from a "psychological distance," but can be brought into focus only by understanding (literally, by "standing under") the unique perspective of the individual himself.

This emphasis upon the human person, upon the individual in his wholeness and uniqueness, is a central feature of the "psychology of humanism." But there is an important corollary without which this personalistic emphasis would be inadequate and distorted. That corollary is the recognition, to use a phrase of Rank, that "the self needs the other." This recognition is variously expressed: For the neo-Freudians, it points to the importance of relationship in the growth of personality; for the existentialists, it leads to emphasis on the themes of dialogue, encounter, meeting, intersubjectivity, and so on.

. . .

In Paul Tillich's "therapeutic theology," this general appreciation of the enlightening role of engagement or meeting is applied directly to psychotherapy, which is regarded as the "community of healing." In common with other existentialists, Tillich believes that the personal troubles represented by neurosis stem fundamentally from failures in relationships with others, thereby resulting in self-alienation from any genuine contact with the world. The central therapeutic problem thus becomes one of "acceptance" or, more precisely, of successive stages of acceptance culminating in acceptance of oneself and of the world of others.

In this new kind of therapeutic encounter—and here is another humanistic tenet—there are no silent partners. The existential therapist (which is to say, the humanistic therapist) is no longer the blank screen or "mute catalyzer" that he was in Freud's day, but rather is a participant with the whole of his being. He participates not only for the purpose of helping, but even more basically for the purpose of knowing or understanding. "You must participate in a self," according to Tillich, "in order to know what it is. By participation you change it" (*The Courage to Be*, Yale University Press, New Haven, 1959, p. 124). The inference is that the kind of knowledge essential to psychology and psychotherapy is to be gained not by detached observation but by participant-observation (to use Harry Stack Sullivan's phrase). It may be possible, through detachment, to gain knowledge that is "useful"; but only through participation is it possible to gain the knowledge that is *helpful*.

In any adequate account of the sources and forces that have nourished the movement of humanistic psychology (which this brief sketch does not pretend to be), much more would have to be said in acknowledgment of the contributions of individual theorists and therapists. Fortunately, there are a number of comprehensive surveys available: among them James Bugental's *Challenges of Humanistic Psychology*, Anthony Sutich and Miles Vich's *Readings in Humanistic Psychology*, and my own *The Broken Image* (especially Chapters 6 and 7). But even the present essay cannot avoid mention of at least a few of the movers and shakers behind the third revolution, notably: Abraham Maslow, who more than any other deserves to be recognized as the "spiritual father" of the humanistic movement in psychology; Gordon Allport, the great American personalist and heir to the mantle of William James; Rollo May, who introduced the existential approach to American psychology and has developed it creatively; Carl Rogers, whose therapeutic mandate of "unconditional regard" for the client resembles Tillich's philosophy of ultimate concern; Erich Fromm, the most influential of the neo-Freudians, who has long since moved from psychoanalysis to the higher ground of social philosophy and cultural criticism; Henry A. Murray, inspired teacher and exemplar of humanism; Charlotte Buhler, who has made us all aware of how important personal goal-values and the whole course of human life are to psychological understanding.

In conclusion—if I may be excused the puff of vanity—I wish to suggest something of the activist potential of humanistic psychology by repeating a few paragraphs from a talk I gave before the annual conference of the Association for Humanistic Psychology:

I'd like to propose one line of commitment, and of protest, that we might well undertake as humanistic psychologists. That course is, following Jefferson, to swear undying opposition to all forms of tyranny over the mind of man. I propose that we commit ourselves to the defense of psychological liberty. For I believe that quite possibly the greatest threat to freedom in the world today (and tomorrow) is the threat to freedom of the mind—which is, at bottom, the power to choose.

That freedom is threatened now on all sides. It is threatened by what Herbert Marcuse has called the "one-dimensional society," which seeks to reduce the categories of thought and discourse to a kind of consensual endorsement of the directives of an aggressive and acquisitive culture. It is threatened by the technology of mass society, mass culture and mass communication, which manufactures (*pace* Marshall McLuhan) a marshmallow world of plastic pleasures in which the bland lead the bland endlessly into the sea of tranquillity.

Freedom of the mind is also threatened by the biological revolution and its psychological corollaries—not only by the familiar cuckoo's nest of lobotomies and shock treatments, over which no one can fly, but by the imminent breakthroughs in "genetic surgery" and kindred interventions that promise to make feasible the rewiring and reprogramming of the brain mechanism.

Perhaps most critically of all, our psychological liberty is threatened by failure of nerve: by our inability to live up to and live out the democratic dogma, which rests upon faith in the capacity of the ordinary human being to lead his own life, to go his own way and to grow his own way, to be himself and to know himself and to become more himself. This failure of nerve is rampant in the field of education; it is a kind of occupational disease of social work, where the aided person becomes a client who is treated as a patient who is diagnosed as incurable. And it is a pervasive feature of the landscape of academic psychology and behavioral science in so many saddening ways that it would take a book (which I have already written) to enumerate them all.

But let me mention just one of the ways in which this failure of nerve manifests itself in the study of man. The old reactionary doctrine of Original Sin, of innate depravity, has lately been enjoying a very popular and large-scale revival. It takes the form of the hypothesis of aggression as a fixed instinctual endowment of man—a genetic taint in the blood, as it were, a dark stain in the double helix of each of us. The alleged discovery or rediscovery of this killer instinct is being hailed in the book clubs and popular journals as if it were the ultimate benediction, the final good news of man's redemption. How are we to account for the popularity of this darkly pessimistic thesis? How [do we] account for the best-seller status of Lorenz's *On Aggression*, Ardrey's *Territorial Imperative* and *African Genesis*, and Desmond Morris's *Naked Ape*?

I believe the answer is clear: mass failure of nerve. Nothing could be better calculated to get us off the uncomfortable hook of personal responsibility, of self-control and self-determination, than this doctrine of our innate aggressive propensities. That's why we fight; that's why we hate; that's why we cannot love one another or ourselves. People are no damn good—and there's an end of it.

Well, I do not believe that humanistic psychologists will accept that cop-out. I propose therefore that we place the full weight of our movement, the whole third force of it, against this and all other threats to the freedom of the mind and the autonomy of the person. Let us become the active conscience of the psychological fraternity, searching out and exposing—and condemning—each and every dehumanizing, depersonalizing and demoralizing force that would move us further down the road to the Brave New World and the technocratic society—that social laboratory of the behaviorist's dreams and the humanist's nightmares.

For down that road lies not just the end of psychological freedom, but the death of humanity.

NAME _____

DATE _____

Q-SORT

This exercise is designed to give you experience with the Q-Sort technique—a major assessment device used by humanistic psychologists. While the actual procedure is more comprehensive, this modified version will give you an opportunity to experience the Q-Sort. In this exercise, you will first sort the 25 statement cards according to your perception of your "actual" self. You will then re-sort the statement cards according to your perception of your "ideal" self. After each sort, you will record the rank-order placement of each statement card so that you will be able to make a comparison in the form of a correlation. The correlation will yield information about the relationship between your actual and ideal self-perceptions.

PROCEDURE

1. Cut out the 25 statement cards and the nine category cards on the following pages.

2. Arrange the nine category cards in a line ranging from #1 to #9 on a table. In each of the two "sorts" that you will be doing, you are required to place a specific number of statements in each of the nine categories. The following distribution will tell you how many of the 25 statement cards must be placed in each of the nine categories:

Category	No. of Statements	Rank No.
I Most Characteristic	I	I
2 Very Characteristic	2	2.5
3 Moderately Characteristic	3	5
4 Mildly Characteristic	4	8.5
5 Neutral	5	13
6 Mildly Uncharacteristic	4	17.5
7 Moderately Uncharacteristic	3	21
8 Very Uncharacteristic	2	23.5
9 Most Uncharacteristic	I	25

3. First sort (Actual Self)—sort the 25 statement cards into the nine categories according to how you feel these statements characterize your Actual Self. After you complete the sorting, transfer the rank number associated with each category to the Data Sheet. For example, if you put "Independent" in Category 4, you would enter "8.5" on the Data Sheet in the Actual Self Rank column next to "Independent."

4. Second Sort (Ideal Self)—sort the 25 statement cards into the nine categories according to how you feel these statements characterize your Ideal Self. After you complete the sorting, transfer the rank number associated with each category to the Data Sheet. For example, if you put "Assertive" in Category 8, you would enter "23.5" on the Data Sheet in the Ideal Self Rank column next to "Assertive."

5. Actual–Ideal Correlation—steps (a) to (f) will guide you through the calculation of a rank-order correlation (rho) that will compare your ratings of actual and ideal self. The actual formula that the calculation is based on is :

$$rho = 1 - \frac{6\sum D^2}{N(N^2 - 1)}$$

D = absolute difference between actual and ideal self ratings.

N = number of ranked pairs, in this case, 25.

a. Obtain the absolute difference between actual and ideal ranking for each self characteristic by subtracting the smaller rank from the larger rank. This is the Absolute Rank Difference score. Do this for all 25 self characteristics.

b. Square each Absolute Rank Difference Score and sum up all 25 squared differences.

c. Multiply the sum of the differences by 6.

d. Take the outcome of step c and divide it by 15,600.

e. Subtract the outcome of step d from +1.00

f. The number you obtained in step e will be the rho between your actual and ideal self. The number must lie between -1.00 and +1.00. If it doesn't, you made an arithmetic error.

Correlation =

INTERPRETATION OF CORRELATION

A positive correlation indicates a similarity between actual and ideal self, whereas a negative correlation indicates a dissimilarity. The closer the correlational number is to -1.00 or +1.00, the greater the dissimilarity or similarity, respectively. The following graphic display illustrates this interpretation.

-1.00..0...+1.00

| High Dissimilarity | Moderate Dissimilarity | Mild Dissimilarity | Mild Similarity | Moderate Similarity | High Similarity |

Another approach to interpretation is to review the particular shifts in placement of statement cards between actual and ideal self ratings. Shifts of specific statement card ratings tell you a great deal about how individual self characteristics are viewed. For example, what characteristics would you ideally like to have as part of your self that are currently not characteristic?

Q-SORT DATA SHEET

Self Characteristic	Actual Self Rank	Ideal Self Rank	Absolute Rank Difference	Difference Squared
Independent				
Assertive				
Sociable				
Studious				
Confident				
Helpful				
Open-minded				
Careful about appearance				
Insightful				
High personal standards				
Goal-oriented				
Adventurous				
Energetic				
Happy				
Responsible				
Tolerant of others				
Exercise regularly				
Wide interests				
Eat right				
Even-tempered				
Creative				
Competent				
Organized				
A Leader				
Enjoy leisure time				

SUM OF DIFFERENCES SQUARED = _____

Category 1

**MOST
CHARACTERISTIC**

_____

1 statement

Category 2

**VERY
CHARACTERISTIC**

_____

2 statements

Category 3

**MODERATELY
CHARACTERISTIC**

_____

3 statements

Category 4

**MILDLY
CHARACTERISTIC**

_____

4 statements

Category 5

NEUTRAL

_____

5 statements

Category 6

**MILDLY
UNCHARACTERISTIC**

_____

4 statements

Category 7

**MODERATELY
UNCHARACTERISTIC**

_____

3 statements

Category 8

**VERY
UNCHARACTERISTIC**

_____

2 statements

Category 9

**MOST
UNCHARACTERISTIC**

_____

1 statement

A Leader	Enjoy leisure time	Helpful	Confident
Studious	Organized	Competent	Insightful
Open-minded	Assertive	Creative	Independent
Careful about appearance	Even-tempered	Sociable	High personal standards
Tolerant of others	Adventurous	Eat right	Wide interests
Responsible	Exercise regularly	Happy	Energetic
Goal-oriented			

SPOTLIGHT
SELF-IDEAL CONGRUENCE*

What actually happens during psychotherapy? John Butler examined this question by evaluating clients' *self-ideal congruence* before and after therapy. The self and ideal descriptions were drawn from two Q-Sorts involving 100 cards with statements based on personality traits. Each individual's actual and ideal descriptions of self were correlated.

The intercorrelations of the descriptions before therapy were low (near zero), indicating that the descriptions were quite dissimilar. However, the post-therapy measures were well above zero (ranging from .26 to .44). Further, increases in congruence were noted for different therapeutic approaches (i.e., client-centered and Adlerian) and for time-limited as well as unlimited therapy.

More important, there were significant differences between clients who were rated as "definitely improved" as opposed to "not definitely improved" (based on projective testing and therapists' ratings). The mean correlation was .52 for the definitely improved group and .05 for the not definitely improved group.

One view of psychotherapy highlights constructive personality change that is reflected in greater congruence between one's actual and ideal selves.

*Based on material in Butler, J. M. (1968). Self-ideal congruence in psychotherapy. *Psychotherapy: Theory, Research and Practice, 5,* 13–17.

NAME _____

DATE _____

ACTIVE LEARNING EXERCISE 7.2

SELF-ACTUALIZATION*

Self-actualization is a central theme in humanistic psychology. It generally refers to the life long process of realizing our potentialities and becoming fully functioning persons.

The following questionnaire is one attempt to measure this elusive concept. To determine how you stand in your progress toward this goal, follow the instructions below.

Please indicate to what extent you agree or disagree with each of the following statements by placing an X on the appropriate line.

	Strongly Agree	Agree	Somewhat Agree	Somewhat Disagree	Disagree	Strongly Disagree
1. I do not feel ashamed of any of my emotions.	_____	_____	_____	_____	_____	_____
2. I feel I must do what others expect of me.	_____	_____	_____	_____	_____	_____
3. I believe that people are essentially good and can be trusted.	_____	_____	_____	_____	_____	_____
4. I feel free to be angry at those I love.	_____	_____	_____	_____	_____	_____
5. It is always necessary that others approve what I do.	_____	_____	_____	_____	_____	_____
6. I don't accept my own weaknesses.	_____	_____	_____	_____	_____	_____
7. I can like people without having to approve of them.	_____	_____	_____	_____	_____	_____
8. I fear failure.	_____	_____	_____	_____	_____	_____
9. I avoid attempts to analyze and simplify complex domains.	_____	_____	_____	_____	_____	_____
10. It is better to be yourself than to be popular.	_____	_____	_____	_____	_____	_____
11. I have no mission in life to which I feel especially dedicated.	_____	_____	_____	_____	_____	_____
12. I can express my feelings even when they may result in undesirable consequences.	_____	_____	_____	_____	_____	_____
13. I do not feel responsible to help anybody.	_____	_____	_____	_____	_____	_____
14. I am bothered by fears of being inadequate.	_____	_____	_____	_____	_____	_____
15. I am loved because I give love.	_____	_____	_____	_____	_____	_____

INTERPRETATION

Each response receives a score of 1 through 6. Items 1, 3, 4, 7, 10, 12, and 15 are scored as follows: strongly disagree = 1, disagree = 2, somewhat disagree = 3, somewhat agree = 4, agree = 5, and strongly agree = 6. Items 2, 5, 6, 8, 9, 11, 13, and 14 are scored in the reverse direction (e.g., strongly disagree = 6, strongly agree = 1).

Total your scores across the 15 items. The higher the score, the more self-actualized you are at this time.

The following table will show you how your score compares to those of other college students.

Score =

SCORE	PERCENTILE
77	99
76	95
75	90
73	80
71	70
69	60
67	50
65	40
60	30
55	20
53	10
52	5
51	1

SPOTLIGHT
SELF-DISCLOSURE*

According to humanistic psychologists, self-disclosure plays an important role in personal growth. By expressing our deepest thoughts and feelings we gain greater self-knowledge and become more fully functioning individuals. Further, recent research shows that there may be health benefits as well.

James Pennebaker, Michelle Colder, and Lisa Sharp divided a sample of college freshmen into experimental and control groups. Members of each group were seen individually on 3 consecutive days (20 minutes per session).

Subjects in the experimental group were told "to let go and write about your very deepest thoughts and feelings about coming to college" (p. 531). Issues they might focus on included leaving friends or parents, adjusting to college, and their future.

Subjects in the control group were told to write about specific topics (e.g., what they had done since waking that morning). They were instructed to provide detailed descriptions and to be as objective as possible, but not to mention emotions, feelings, or opinions.

Since the experimenters were interested in the physical and psychological effects of self-disclosure in writing, data from the health center (i.e., the number of visits for illnesses) were gathered for each participant. They found that subjects in the experimental group visited the health center for illnesses significantly less often than those in the control group.

The experimenters stressed the implications of self-disclosure for individuals who are trying to cope with trauma. Based on this and previous research, it appears that writing about stressors had physical and psychological benefits.

*Based on material in Pennebaker, J. W., Colder, M., & Sharp, L. K. (1990). Accelerating the coping process. *Journal of Personality and Social Psychology, 58*, 528–537.

NAME _____

DATE _____

ACTIVE LEARNING EXERCISE 7.3
PEAK EXPERIENCE*

By describing and analyzing a meaningful personal event in your life, this exercise will help you to understand Maslow's concept of the peak experience.

In the space below, describe a peak experience you have had. To quote from Maslow's book *Toward a Psychology of Being*, "think of the most wonderful experiences of your life: the happiest moments, ecstatic moments, moments of rapture" (1962, p. 67).

*Adapted from Polyson, J. (1985). Students' peak experiences: A written exercise. *Teaching of Psychology*, 12(4), 211–213.

After completing your essay, respond to the following questions:

1. Where were you at the time of this peak experience?

2. What were you doing?

3. How did you feel during this experience?

4. How did you feel after the experience?

5. What did the experience mean to you then?

6. What does the experience mean to you now?

REFERENCE

MASLOW, A. H. (1962). *Toward a psychology of being*. New York: Van Nostrand.

SPOTLIGHT
WHATEVER TURNS YOU ON*

Carolyn Keutzer conducted an interesting study of the transcendent experiences of 146 upper division college students. After responding to the question "With what frequency have you had the experience that you felt as though you were very close to a powerful, spiritual force that seemed to lift you out of yourself?" those who reported such experiences (65% of the sample) were asked to identify the triggers or specific events that set this off. In typical Letterman style, the top 10 triggers for transcendent (peak) experiences are:

10   Looking at a painting

9   Sexual lovemaking

8   Prayer

7   (tie) Reading a poem or novel/Your own creative work

6   Watching little children

5   Physical exercise

4   Drugs

3   Music

2   Quiet reflection

1   Beauties of nature

*Based on material in Keutzer, C. S. (1978). Whatever turns you on: Triggers to transcendental experiences, *Journal of Humanistic Psychology, 18*, 77–80.

READING
THE MEANING OF PERSONAL GROWTH*
Abe Arkoff

Editors' Note:

Throughout our lives, we ponder questions about who we are and where we are headed. In this article, Abe
Arkoff provides a detailed account of the topic of personal growth. He addresses such issues as our innate
drive toward growth and our potential for growth, as well as the obstacles to growth, the burden of growth, and
the pathways to growth.

Imagine yourself in this situation: You are an illegitimate, six-year-old child. Your mother is a deaf-mute. You have spent most of your life with your mother in a dark room separated from the rest of your mother's family. What kind of person would you be and become?

Isabelle (a pseudonym) actually spent the first part of her life in the condition just noted. When she was discovered at the age of six, she appeared to be half infant and half wild animal. The professionals who examined her concluded she was feeble-minded and uneducable. Fortunately, they decided to try. A year and a half later Isabelle had blossomed into a "very bright, cheerful, and energetic little girl." At the time of the last report, she was fourteen, doing well, and had just passed the sixth grade (Davis, 1940, 1947).

There appears to be a strong impulse to grow in every person (as indeed there was in Isabelle). We desire to be more than we are. Each of us will have our own idea of what we wish to become. Perhaps more informed and knowledgeable, or more understanding and loving, or more capable and creative, or more joyful and serene.

On the path of growth, sometimes we trudge and sometimes we leap ahead. We occasionally have a growth spurt when we make rapid progress and we have an exhilarating sense of being more than we were. It may be a particular summer or year when everything seems to be going just right or it may involve a particular relationship in which we find an enlarged sense of ourselves.

Just as there is a strong impulse to grow, there are strong impediments to growth. Rarely are they as complete and obvious as in the case of Isabelle. But there are growth blocks or impasses in which we are frustrated and seem unable to progress at all. There are even growth reversals—times when we appear to regress and give up hard-earned gains.

Personal growth, as it is defined here, is simply change in a desired or valued direction. Values, of course, vary from person to person. I may feel I have grown when I have freed myself from dependence on my parents. You may experience personal growth when you change your conception of yourself and begin to respond to the world in a new and freer way. My parents, however, may not agree that my new-found autonomy is growth, and your spouse may be threatened by your new self-definition and put pressure on you to revert to the person you were.

Potentiality refers to inherent capacity for growth. What's possible for us? What can we become? What can keep us from becoming all we wish to become? How can we find a path of growth that's right for us? These are some of the questions we will consider in the material that follows.

THE POTENTIAL FOR GROWTH

A Russian scientist has estimated that with our brain working at only half capacity, we could learn 40 languages with no difficulty (Otto, 1972). Many of us, however, find it something of a struggle to learn more than 1. From this perspective, we certainly seem to be less than we could be.

What has come to be called the "human potential movement" began during the 1960s and was dedicated to helping people make the most of their capacities. An underlying assumption—sometimes called "the human potential hypothesis"—was that most people function at only a small fraction of their potential. A further assumption was that by proceeding in certain ways much more of this potential could be realized.

Nearly a century ago William James, one of the earliest American psychologists, estimated that humans, on the average, functioned at about 10% of their capacity. Later, anthropologist Margaret Mead put this figure at 6%. Human potentialist Herbert Otto's original estimate of average fulfillment was a modest 5%, which he later reduced to 4%. He writes that the estimated percentage has been decreasing because "we are discovering that every human being has more powers, resources, and abilities than we suspected ten years ago, five years ago" (1972, p. 14).

*Arkoff, A. (1992). The meaning of personal growth. In A. Arkoff & S. Jurick (Eds.), *Psychology and personal growth* (4th ed., pp. 278–292), Boston: Allyn & Bacon. Copyright © 1992 by Allyn & Bacon. Reprinted by permission.

A trio of psychologists—Arthur Combs, Donald Avila, and William Purkey (1978)—maintain that human beings are "over-built." They write, "One of the most exciting discoveries of this generation is the idea that human capacity is far greater than anything ever thought possible. The fascinating thing about human beings is not their limitations, but their immense capabilities. . . . From everything we can observe, it seems clear that few of us ever remotely approach the potentialities for effective behavior that lie within us. Most of us use but a small fraction of our capabilities" (pp. 69–70, 71).

Norman Cousins administered his own recovery from a supposedly incurable illness. In looking back on this experience, he wrote that what he had learned was to "never underestimate the capacity of the human mind and body to regenerate—even when the prospects seem most wretched" (1977, p. 5). Later, in looking back on his entire life, he wrote,

> What, then, have I learned? The most important thing I think I have learned is that human capacity is infinite, that no challenge is beyond comprehension and useful response. I have learned that the uniqueness of human beings is represented by the absence of any ceiling over intellectual or moral development. In this sense, the greatest gains achieved by the species are not connected to the discovery of nuclear fission or the means by which humans can be liberated from earth gravity. The greatest gains are related to expanding knowledge about the human brain itself. (1980, p. 10)

One of the most optimistic of the human potentialists is Will Schutz (1979). "As human beings," he writes, "we are without limit" (p. 25). In his opinion, the limits we experience are "limits of belief" but not "limits of the human organism." He points out that there are pragmatic advantages to assuming that one is limitless: "If indeed I am truly limitless, and I assume I am, then I may discover that limitlessness. On the other hand, every limit I assume I have prevents me from discovering whether that limit is in fact real" (p. 26). Claim a limit, Richard Bach says, and it's yours.

Despite these enthusiastic voices, optimism about human potentiality is not widespread. Psychiatrist Cornelis Bakker (1975) has observed a deep sense of pessimism in some quarters concerning basic personality change. Bakker calls this "the myth of unchangeability." It is a myth to which some persons in mental health subscribe when they see dramatic improvements that somehow do not last. It is a myth held by parents who look at their adult child and see what appears to be almost the same personality that was present at age seven or eight. It is a myth

any one of us might tend to embrace as we see ourselves wrestling with seemingly the same basic problems year after year or decade after decade.

Bakker has found "a good deal of evidence" to support the thesis that "people are extremely changeable" (p. 164). He feels there are two reasons why the myth of unchangeability persists. One reason is the long-standing hypothesis in Western culture that each person has a basic essence or soul or personality or character which biases the observer against perceiving change. The second reason is [that] there are a number of stabilizing factors that can keep people the same if they allow this to happen. Some of these stabilizing factors are considered later in the section concerning obstacles to growth.

Support for Bakker's thesis is provided by George Vaillant's study (1977) of a group of Harvard students. Vaillant followed this group from college age to about age 50 and found their lives were "full of surprises" and even "startling change and evolutions" (p. 372). Quite notable was a subset of men in the study who had very serious psychological problems, which they dealt with by themselves to arrive at quite satisfactory patterns of adjustment.

Not all students of human nature are convinced that the myth of unchangeability is fully a myth. One of the most eloquent of these is psychologist Bernie Zilbergeld (1983). From his examination of the evidence, he arrives at conclusions far different from [those of] Bakker. Summing up, he writes that "people are very difficult to change" and "there are limits to how much each of us can change." In his opinion, "the limits of human malleability are much closer to the ground than they are to the sky" (p. 247). He adds that we may have to question utopian notions and give up our ideas about what is possible for humans.

However, there is a silver lining to Zilbergeld's dark cloud. Although he believes that human beings are difficult to change, he also concludes that there is not as much need for change as is commonly thought. He makes a strong case that many of the most creative and productive persons—Charles Darwin, Abraham Lincoln, Goethe, William James, August Strindberg, Virginia Woolf, Van Gogh, Einstein, etc.—were laden with personal problems and far from "normal." Zilbergeld believes that people don't need fixing as much as they need to change their unrealistic notions of what life can be. He writes, "Much of what we think of as problems—things that ought to be altered and for which there are solutions—are not so much problems as inescapable limits and predicaments of life" (p. 251).

THE IMPULSE TO GROW

A point emphasized by the human potentialists is that we have not only a considerable potential for growth but also a powerful impulse to make the most of this potential. Albert Szent-Gyoergyi, a research biologist who twice was awarded the Nobel Prize, has written that it would be impossible to approach the data he had observed without supposing that there is an "innate drive in living matter to perfect itself" (1974, p. 14). A number of personality theorists have similarly hypothesized an "actualizing tendency" in humans, that is, a drive toward growth, enhancement, and perfection.

Carl Rogers (1975) wrote that each living organism is born with "an inherent tendency to develop all his/her capacities in ways that serve to maintain or enhance the organism." And, he added, each has an inherent wisdom that allows differentiation between experiences that do or do not further the actualization process.

Abraham Maslow (1970) put it succinctly when he wrote, what we *can* be, we *must* be. We must be true to ourselves—to our basic nature. Our capabilities are a promise that begs to be kept. Even if all our basic needs are met, we develop a restlessness, a discontent unless we are keeping that promise. As Maslow wrote, "A musician must make music, an artist must paint, a poet must write, if he is to be ultimately at peace with himself" (p. 46).

THE BURDEN OF GROWTH

Is the impulse to grow a blessing or a burden? Little Linus in a Peanuts comic strip once lamented his own situation, saying "there is no heavier burden than a great potential." Maslow (1972) cautioned his own students: "If you deliberately plan to be less than you are capable of being, then I warn you that you'll be deeply unhappy the rest of your life" (p. 36).

In one of her books, Eda LeShan (1976) eloquently describes her own feelings of guilt for not having made more of her own childhood opportunities for growth:

> Many years ago my husband [psychologist Lawrence LeShan] explained to me the meaning of "ontological guilt." He told me it was the very worst kind. It means feeling guilty because one is not living one's own life, fulfilling one's own potentials. As the years have passed I have come to understand this more deeply, and it accounts for my awful sensitivity about examining my own adolescence; I have too much ontological guilt.
>
> The problem is that no matter how much one learns about human fallibility, compassion and acceptance are still hard to come by. When I became deeply depressed at the prospect of having to write this chapter, I said to Larry, "I can't forgive myself for the fact that I was a coward; that I didn't have the guts to fight harder to

become free, when that's what I should have been doing." His answer was "You have nothing to forgive yourself for. You were a nice person—decent and brave— and you couldn't bear to hurt your parents when you know how much they loved you. You made a sacrifice which you later discovered had cost you too much—but it was done out of tenderness, and you have had the courage to fight for your own growth ever since." (p. 128).

In her notebook, Jungian analyst Florida Scott-Maxwell (1968) writes of our need to "live our strengths." She recalls that a client once told her: "I don't mind your telling me my faults, they're stale, but don't tell me my virtues. When you tell me what I could be, it terrifies me" (p. 22).

In her book *Smart Girls, Gifted Women*, Barbara Kerr (1986) takes gifted women to task for not achieving their full potentiality. She maintains that women "are too well adjusted for their own good. They are great at adjusting resourcefully and congenially to whatever situation is handed to them" (p. 5). Kerr herself was criticized for not accepting the women's own choices, but she stuck to her guns, suggesting that self-actualization is more than a right—it is a responsibility.

The human potentialists and, indeed, the entire field of psychotherapy have been criticized for tending to make people dissatisfied with themselves. Like some other industries that sell their products by convincing people they are not all they should be or can be—that they don't look right or smell right or are not always free of aches and anxieties—potentialists may create or exacerbate the very conditions or dissatisfactions they seek to correct.

Schutz (1979) takes a view contrary to those who see potential as a burden. He understands his own assumption of "human limitlessness" is frequently resisted since there is an implied demand that one live up to one's potential. He maintains there is no obligation to be everything of which one is capable. "If I wish," he writes, "I can choose to feel inadequate because I have not realized myself fully. But it is not inherent in the assumption of limitlessness that failure to achieve all that is possible must lead to feelings of guilt and depression" (p. 26).

Those who have been stuck on life's path—at impasses, up blind alleys, forever marking time, caught up in maintenance, low-level enterprises, getting by perhaps but not getting anywhere—will know the burden that the potentialists write about. Those who have gotten themselves "unstuck" and suddenly able to make more, maybe much more of their lives will know the exhilaration that comes when one is becoming more and more who one can be.

SUCCESS AND FAILURE IN GROWTH

Not long ago, one of my friends was telling me about an old acquaintance who was going to visit him soon. It was someone with whom he had gone to college but who afterward never seemed to make very much of his life. This acquaintance had never married and had moved from job to job in the same industry but none very much different or better from the other. From the outside, at least, it looked like not very much of a life.

A character in Anne Tyler's novel *Breathing Lessons* is rather taken aback when her daughter asks her, "Mom? Was there a certain conscious point in your life when you decided to settle for being ordinary?" Do any of us prepare ourselves for an "ordinary" life? What would you have answered if someone at your high-school graduation asked if you would be willing "to settle for being ordinary?"

Thinking it over, I wonder how my friend's acquaintance regarded his life. Did he see it as disappointingly ordinary, comfortably ordinary, or not ordinary at all—which is the way Tyler's character responded as she recalled the incident with a friend: "It got to me," she said. . . . "I mean, to *me* I'm not ordinary."

. . .

OBSTACLES TO GROWTH

Why don't we make more of ourselves and our lives? Why don't we realize more of our potential? These are important questions, and ones many philosophers and psychologists, and stuck, bewildered souls have pondered.

A Diminished Conception of Ourselves. One reason we don't make more of ourselves is that we may have a diminished view of who we are and what we can become. To some extent, we are who we *think* we are, and some of us may not think we're much. Although research suggests we are more likely to overestimate than underestimate ourselves, two psychologists, Ellen Langer and Carol Dweck (1973), write, "We maintain that there are few, if any, of us who have truly satisfying self-concepts. People occasionally put on a good show and seem to others to be on top of it all, but these very same people often think: 'if they only knew the real me'" (p. 29).

The basic goal of many personal growth programs and psychotherapies is to get the individuals concerned to enhance their self-concept and to accept, love, and prize themselves more. A basic goal of some transpersonal approaches is to inspire persons with awe or reverence for themselves and their place in the universe. As such individuals come to see more in themselves, they attempt and accomplish more, and accomplishing more they further enhance their conception of themselves.

The following true story (recalled by a woman psychologist from her prepsychology days) indicates how important an obstacle a negative self-concept can be, and how a positive self-concept can both instigate and stem from growth:

I was living out in San Francisco at the time. While coming home from work one day I got involved in an accident and required the attention of a doctor. A friend of mine mentioned the accident to his friend, an eager, but not yet established, young lawyer. The lawyer contacted me, and then proceeded to persuade me that I had a case and that he was the one to handle it.

That was the way I met Hank. The impression I got of him after talking over the phone for the next week or so was that he was enthusiastic, good humored, and sort of charming. When he came over to my house to discuss the case further, I had to add unattractive to the list of adjectives.

After we concluded our discussion of business matters, we got involved in a friendly and rather personal conversation. Hank had recently come to San Francisco from New York. He was divorced and was eager to tell me about the marvelous changes in his life. It seemed that his ex-wife had constantly told him how ugly he was. I thought that that was both cruel and accurate—but kept the latter thought to myself. Hank explained how inhibited this made him with other people. "I had little confidence in myself and was enormously shy." I said I couldn't believe that he was very shy. He recounted some experiences he had had at parties and with clients to convince me. He was successful in gaining my sympathy.

Then he told me how different he was now. He had traveled across the country with the thought that he just might not be as homely looking as she said—so he took some risks. He gradually improved his opinion of himself. He put this a little differently though: "I slowly started to recognize how wrong she was. Now I know I'm good looking. When I walk into a room people take notice of me and believe it or not (I didn't) the girls are all over me at parties." We talked some more, and then a horn started honking outside. He said it was his new girlfriend picking him up. We went over to the terrace to see if it were she—it was, and she was simply beautiful. For a moment I couldn't believe the whole episode. What was even more bewildering was that I started finding him attractive.

Although Hank's somewhat dramatic tale is not unique, most people with negative self-concepts never bother to test out other hypotheses about themselves, as he did. While at first he accepted his wife's opinion as indisputable truth, he later formulated an alternative positive view, "I am *not* ugly," and set out to confirm it. Now Hank tells people how to respond to him. His new manner has an air of confidence, and the subtle and not so subtle cues are effective. It is not surprising that most people listen. (Langer and Dweck, 1973, pp. 40–42)

A Fixed Conception of Ourselves. A second reason we don't grow as much as we might is that we fix our conception of ourself. We begin to think, "Well, I've always been this way." We each begin to think of ourself as a person who can do this but can't do that. In this situation, growth concedes to "destiny."

To find out where our "I've always been this way" originated, Bloomfield and Kory (1980) recommend that we quiz the significant others of our childhood days. How did they see us? What labels did they apply to us? We may hear from their lips the same labels we have come to apply to ourselves. If we announce we're going to change, how do they respond? Does their response seem to say: "Lots of luck and you'll need it because 'you've always been this way.'" For illustration, here is a case presented by Bloomfield and Kory:

> John, a college student, complains, "I can count the number of dates I've had on one hand and not run out of fingers." He's obviously got a sense of humor, but he is afraid to be himself around women. "I'm shy," he says. "That's my nature." John recalls his mother telling people that he was "the shy one." He never realized that his mother had an emotional investment in keeping him tied to her apron strings. John spent his childhood and adolescence living up to the family label of "the shy one." No doubt he had a tendency to be shy as a little boy, but with their labeling, his parents helped him develop that ten-

dency into a full-blown personality characteristic. The question is whether John is going to continue justifying his fears of women with the rationale: "Shyness is my nature." (p. 167).

A fixed notion of who we are can easily result when we continue to move around in the same old sub-environments that call forth the same old response. We can develop a kind of comfort in leading our familiar life and in being our familiar self. To change and grow might bring welcome hope and pleasurable excitement, but it might also bring unwelcome anxiety. More about this in the material that follows.

The Need for Safety. A third obstacle to growth concerns an unwillingness to leave safe places. Maslow (1968) hypothesized that in addition to growth forces, each person also has safety forces and these two sets work in opposition to each other. Maslow noted that the conflict between these forces could block the individual. He diagrammed this process as follows:

Safety <——————-< PERSON >——————-> Growth

Elaborating on these opposing forces, Maslow wrote,

> Every human being has *both* sets of forces within him. One set clings to safety and defensiveness out of fear, tending to regress backward, hanging on to the past, *afraid* to grow away from the primitive communication with the mother's uterus and breast, *afraid* to take chances, *afraid* to jeopardize what he already has, *afraid* of independence, freedom and separateness. The other set of forces impels him forward toward wholeness of Self and uniqueness of Self, toward full functioning of all his capacities, toward confidence in the face of the external world at the same time that he can accept his deepest, real, unconscious Self. (p. 46).

Maslow noted that both safety and growth have drawbacks and attractions for the individual. The person grows when the drawbacks of safety and the attractions of growth are greater than the attractions of safety and the drawbacks of growth. Parents, teachers, and therapists sometimes are able to step in to change the weight of safety and growth vectors. As our conception of ourselves is enhanced, safety becomes less attractive and necessary and growth becomes more attractive and even irresistible.

When I consider the lives of my mother and father, it is easier for me to think of my mother's life as a success. Both my parents were immigrants, my mother from Latvia, my father from Russia.

Both were looking for better lives in a new land, and both made their way to a small Midwestern city where they found each other, married, and raised five children.

Success in life, according to Freud's barebones set of criteria, requires success in loving and working, but I never felt my father found his true work or calling. He was a brilliant and spiritual man who would have been fulfilled as a rabbi or teacher. Instead, for almost all of his adult life, he spent six-and-one-half long days a week in a little store, an occupation for which he exhibited little zest or talent. In his late-middle years, he became for awhile quite depressed—his response, I believe, to his inability to move his life along.

Some years ago, I went back to my home town just to wander again around old boyhood places. My parents were long since dead, and no relatives or close friends remained, but I found a man who had known my father quite well. We had coffee together and talked about the old days. He remembered how my father had been a force in the usually rabbi-less Jewish community and one who took it upon himself to round up 10 mostly reluctant men so that a Friday night Sabbath prayer meeting could be held. "But," he added, "one thing about your father, he wasn't willing to take a chance."

I wondered about that: my father, a man who went AWOL from the Czar's army and came to a far-away land whose language and culture was completely strange to him, who fell in love, married, started a business, had five children, became a pillar of his religious community. He had taken chances, made commitments, achieved. What had happened to him along the way? How had he gotten so mired, so struck?

In her book *Pathfinders*, Gail Sheehy describes a group of "people of high well being"—those who successfully negotiate the crises of life. She concludes that the "master quality" possessed by pathfinders is their willingness to take risks. In her study of lives she found that a continuing sense of well-being generally required a continual willingness to risk change. Similar findings came out of a longitudinal study of men and women by social scientists at the University of California at San Francisco (Lowenthal, 1980). Although the researcher expected [that] those adults who showed a strong sense of continuity in values and goals would show the greatest sense of well-being, instead it was those who demonstrated change.

The Fear of Growth. A fourth obstacle to growth concerns fear of what growth may bring. A number of students of human nature have noted an absolute fear of growth in some individuals. Why should some of us fear to grow? One reason may be that we fear the unknown. Even if we do not like or are not comfortable with who we are, at least we are accustomed to ourselves. We hesitate to risk what we have (even though it's not all we want) to get something that may be less or worse.

A second reason we fear growth is that we may see growth as bringing responsibilities we doubt we will be able to meet. If we

succeed, more will be expected of us and we may doubt our ability to continually meet these expectations. "The higher you climb, the harder you fall," we tell ourselves, "so maybe it's better not to reach too high."

There is a third fear of growth that Maslow (1971) called "the Jonah Complex." This complex (named after Jonah, who wound up in the whale when he ran from a mission he had been given from on high) refers to our fear of our own greatness. Maslow hypothesized that in the presence of very special individuals (saintly persons, geniuses, beauties, etc.) we may tend to feel uneasy, envious, or inferior and therefore countervalue (or depreciate) them or their qualities. Maslow suggests that if we could bring ourselves "to love more purely the highest values in others," we would become better able to discover and love and make the most of these qualities in ourselves.

PERSONAL GROWTH IN THERAPY

I have been a therapist many years, and I have been in therapy myself three times during my life. The first time was in graduate school when each of us students entered counseling as a didactic or educational exercise. The second occasion was in my thirties when I seemed to be stuck and unable to move my personal life along. The third involved my whole family and came at a time when my wife and I were at our wit's end and ready to put our adolescent children out for adoption. Thinking back on this experience, I see how I grew quite a bit in the first, very little in the third (except in humbleness), but greatly in the second—when that particular experience was complete I was in some ways a crucially different human being.

There are so many different kinds of therapy and therapists and so many different reasons for entering therapy that it is difficult to generalize about the amount and kind of growth that occurs. It has been estimated that two out of every three people who undergo therapy benefit from it (Garfield, 1983). (That is somewhat in accord with my story since I entered therapy three times and benefited twice.) For many the gains are modest, but for some it can be the doorway to a fuller, richer life.

Carl Rogers (1961), one of the most eminent of all psychologists and therapists, has described how his clients have grown in therapy. His description seems relevant to the growth many of us experience, whether or not it is within a formal therapeutic relationship. Like Rogers' clients, we seem to be asking these two questions: "Who am I?" "How can I become myself?"

The first change Rogers noted in the persons he helped toward growth was that they became more open to their experience. They became less defensive and more able to put aside their masks. They became more aware of their own feelings and attitudes and could respond to the world around them without distortion or preconception.

A second change that Rogers observed in his clients was a growth of trust in themselves, which relates to and stems from the increased openness:

. . . When a client is open to his experience, he comes to find his organism more trustworthy. He feels less fear of the emotional reactions which he has. There is gradual growth of trust in, and even affections for, the complex, rich, varied assortment of feelings and tendencies which exist in him at the organic level. Consciousness, instead of being the watchman over a dangerous and unpredictable lot of impulses, of which few can be permitted to see the light of day, becomes the comfortable inhabitant of a society of impulses and feelings and thoughts, which are discovered to be very satisfactorily self-governing when not fearfully guarded. (p. 119)

A third change was that individuals in therapy increasingly accepted responsibility for making judgments about what was happening in their lives and for determining the directions their lives were to take. They depended less and less on others for approval or disapproval or for standards to live by or for choices and decisions. To see that one is responsible for one's own life, Rogers wrote, is both frightening and an invigorating realization.

The final change concerned the willingness to be a process rather than a finished, perfected product. Rogers noted that when persons entered therapy, they were likely to want to arrive at some fixed state of being or a place where their problems were fixed once and for all. In therapy, they came to accept [that] they were fluid—not static entities—and capable of dealing with whatever arose in their lives. Rogers' clients replaced their need for fixity with the realization that they were and always would be in a "process of becoming."

PATHWAYS TO GROWTH

All of life is concerned with growth, as is all of this book. It would be impossible and unnecessary here to review every pathway to growth that has been proposed or pursued. But it may be helpful to distinguish between two main paths that have aroused some controversy.

One path to growth is an individual way. Its emphasis is on oneself and involves developing one's own potentiality and making the most of one's life and spirit. It is an essentially inner path, although it may move out like a widening spiral to encompass more than oneself.

A second path is an outer and collective path—one of social activism and change. It involves finding ways to change the institutions of society—for example, the home and school and marriage—to enhance the lives of all people. It involves taking responsibility for the betterment of everyone everywhere and especially those less fortunate than oneself.

Some advocates of the second path have called the first a "narcissistic" one because they view it as a selfish pursuit. To them, it is a kind of self-absorption when the times call for social change and the reconstruction of social agencies. They fear that in frustration, people are "searching within" when they should be "reaching out."

Proponents of the first path vigorously disagree. They feel that personal growth or enhancement is a necessary first step—that one cannot reach out if one's center is hollow. If one wants a better world, the way to begin is to make oneself a better or fuller person. They ask how those who do not and cannot respect and love and help themselves hope to relate to and help others.

Robert Samples (1977) calls the first path "selfness." This is "the state in which self is celebrated in a nonexploitative mode." It is distinct from *selfish*, the exploitation of others for the benefit of oneself, and also distinct from *selfless*, the exploitation of oneself for the benefit of others. He writes,

> The search for self, alone and in the
> quiet of one's own skills of introspection,
> is never done at the expense of the whole.
> A person who looks inward is no more a
> deviant from the whole than is a cloud
> from rivers and seas when one contemplates the water cycle. When one looks
> inward, it is difficult to avoid coming back
> more whole, more intact. Of course, here
> I exclude that small fringe group who look
> inward and stay there. When those who
> come back choose to enter a relationship,
> a community or a culture, they seldom
> bring a more despotic, more deficient
> human back into the action. Such people,
> with a fuller knowledge of their own
> strengths and limitations, are richer and
> closer to being psychically balanced and
> complete.
>
> It is these balanced humans who can be
> counted on to exercise the most basic
> kind of morality. I call it *selfness*. From
> this point, growth and being become a celebration of one's own person and the

purity of all that is called humanness is then extended outward to the whole community of humankind. The extension of this process one day will hopefully eliminate the social and cultural inequities that currently exist—inequities nourished by leaders and followers whose psychic selves are empty. (p. 2)

There is, it seems, nothing essentially incompatible in the two paths. Service to others is a time-honored avenue to transcendence and so is the deep inner pursuit of oneself. One can grow from the inside out or from the outside in or both ways at once. There are many kinds of growth and many routes—each of us can find our own way.

REFERENCES

BAKKER, C. B. (1975). Why people don't change. *Psychotherapy: Theory, Research and Practice, 12*(2), 164–172.

BLOOMFIELD, H., & KORY, R. B. (1980). *Inner joy.* New York: Wyden.

COMBS, A. W., AVILA, D. L., & PURKEY, W. W. (1978). *Helping relationships: Basic concepts for the helping professions* (2nd ed.). Boston: Allyn and Bacon.

COUSINS, N. (1977, May 28). Anatomy of an illness (as perceived by the patient). *Saturday Review,* pp. 4–6, 48–51.

COUSINS, N. (1980, September). Capacity and control. *Saturday Review,* p. 10.

DAVIS, K. (1940). Extreme social isolation of a child. *American Journal of Sociology, 45,* 554–565.

DAVIS, K. (1947). Final note on a case of extreme isolation. *American Journal of Sociology, 52,* 432–437.

GARFIELD, S. L. (1983). *Clinical psychology: The study of personality and behavior* (2nd ed.). New York: Aldine.

KERR, B. (1986). *Smart girls, gifted women.* Columbus: Ohio Psychology Publishing.

LANGER, E. J., & DWECK, C. S. (1973). *Personal politics: The psychology of making it.* Englewood Cliffs, NJ: Prentice-Hall.

LeSHAN, E. J. (1976). *In search of myself and other children.* New York: M. Evans.

MASLOW, A. H. (1968). *Toward a psychology of being* (2nd ed.). New York: Van Nostrand   Reinhold.

MASLOW, A. H. (1970). *Motivation and personality* (2nd ed.). New York: Harper & Row.

MASLOW, A. H. (1972). *The farther reaches of human nature.* New York: Viking.

OTTO, H. A. (1972). New light on human potential. In College of Home Economics, Iowa State University (Ed.), *Families of the future* (pp. 14–25). Ames: Iowa State University Press.

ROGERS, C. R. (1961). *On becoming a person* (pp. 107–124). Boston: Houghton Mifflin.

ROGERS, C. R. (1975). Client-centered psychotherapy. In A. M. Freedman, H. I. Kaplan, & B. J. Sadock (Eds.), *Comprehensive textbook of psychiatry* (Vol. 2, pp. 1831–1843). Baltimore: Williams & Wilkins.

SAMPLES, B. (1977, May). Selfness: Seeds of a transformation. *AHP Newsletter,* pp. 1–2.

SCHUTZ, W. (1979). *Profound simplicity.* New York: Bantam.

SCOTT-MAXWELL, F. (1968). *The measure of my days.* New York: Knopf.

SZENT-GYOERGYI, A. (1974). Drive in living matter to perfect itself. *Synthesis, 1,* 14–26.

VAILLANT, G. E. (1977). *Adaptation to life.* Boston: Little, Brown.

ZILBERGELD, B. (1983). *The shrinking of America: Myths of psychological change,* Boston: Little, Brown.

CHAPTER
8

Cognitive Perspectives

Introduction

Cognitive views, once preeminent across psychology, diminished with the advent of radical behavioral views in the 1960s. However, in recent years there has been a strong return of cognitive perspectives in psychology, particularly in the study of personality. Cognitive perspectives in personality emphasize the role of attitudes, values, and beliefs, as well as the power of a person's thinking to influence behavior. Cognitive perspectives make important contributions in the area of overall adjustment, including general health and emotional adaptation. You will have the chance to read about some of these contributions, particularly in the areas of optimism, internal-external locus of control, and cognitive approaches to psychotherapy. The Active Learning Exercises will give you the opportunity to assess your own cognitive styles and modes of thinking.

NAME _____

DATE _____

ACTIVE LEARNING EXERCISE 8.1

LIFE ORIENTATION TEST*

Indicate the extent to which you agree with each of the following statements using the following response scale:

0 = strongly disagree

1 = disagree

2 = neutral

3 = agree

4 = strongly agree

Place the appropriate number in the blank before each item.

_____ **1.** In uncertain times, I usually expect the best.

_____ **2.** It's easy for me to relax.

_____ **3.** If something can go wrong for me, it will.

_____ **4.** I always look on the bright side of things.

_____ **5.** I'm always optimistic about my future.

_____ **6.** I enjoy my friends a lot.

_____ **7.** It's important for me to keep busy.

_____ **8.** I hardly ever expect things to go my way.

_____ **9.** Things never work out the way I want them to.

_____ **10.** I don't get upset too easily.

_____ **11.** I'm a believer in the idea that "every cloud has a silver lining."

_____ **12.** I rarely count on good things happening to me.

*Scheier, M., & Carver, C. (1985). Optimism, coping, and health: Assessment and implications of generalized outcome expectancies. *Health Psychology, 4*, 219–247. Reprinted with permission.

The Life Orientation Test, which you just completed, was developed by Scheier and Carver (1985) to measure how favorably or unfavorably one sees the future. In essence, it is an assessment of optimism/pessimism. To obtain your score on this measure, follow these steps:

1. For questions 3, 8, 9, and 12, reverse the ratings you assigned (a score of 0 becomes 4, a score of 1 becomes 3, a score of 2 remains the same, a score of 3 becomes 1, and a score of 4 becomes 0).

2. Questions 2, 6, 7, and 10 do not count. They are referred to as filler questions and are used to disguise the true nature of the test.

3. Sum up your scores on questions 1, 3, 4, 5, 8, 9, 11, and 12.

   Score =

4. Because there are eight scorable items with ratings from 0 to 4, it is possible to obtain a final score of 0 to 32. Research has indicated that the mean score is close to 21.

Scheier and Carver's (1993) article, which follows, describes the research on optimism and strongly suggests the benefits of this orientation in a number of areas of adaptation. Optimists tend to cope more effectively in stressful situations, they are more focused in attempting to deal with problems, they tend to learn from negative experiences, and they plan to deal with bad times through direct action. In terms of health and physical adjustment, optimists do better in surgery and in postoperative recovery. Furthermore, optimism is negatively correlated with postpartum depression. In terms of adjustment, students who are optimistic make better adjustments to college life than their pessimistic peers.

REFERENCE

SCHEIER, M., & CARVER, C. (1993). On the power of positive thinking: The benefits of being optimistic. *Current Directions in Psychological Science, 2*, 26–30.

NAME _____

DATE _____

ACTIVE LEARNING EXERCISE E.2

SELF-RATINGS*

Now that you have completed a course on personality, complete the following scale.

Instructions: Compared with other college students of the same class level and sex as yourself, how would you rate yourself on the following characteristics? Use the following scale in marking your responses.

1 = considerably well below average
2 = well below average
3 = below average
4 = slightly below average
5 = average
6 = slightly above average
7 = above average
8 = well above average
9 = considerably well above average

_____ **1.** leadership ability

_____ **2.** athletic ability

_____ **3.** ability to get along with others

_____ **4.** tolerance

_____ **5.** energy level

_____ **6.** helpfulness

_____ **7.** responsibility

_____ **8.** creativeness

_____ **9.** patience

_____ **10.** trustworthiness

_____ **11.** sincerity

_____ **12.** thoughtfulness

_____ **13.** cooperativeness

_____ **14.** reasonableness

_____ **15.** intelligence

SEE NEXT PAGE FOR INTERPRETATION

After completing the Self-Rating questionnaire, calculate your mean score by adding up all 15 items and dividing by 15.

Score =

1. Compare your ratings to those in Active Learning Exercise 1.5.

2. How do your current ratings compare with your earlier ratings? How have your ratings changed? What do you attribute this change to?